Leadership and Change Management

T0358985

A leader's role in the management of change is a critical issue for successful outcomes of strategic initiatives. Globalization and economic instability have prompted an increase in organizational changes related to downsizing and restructuring in order to improve financial performance and organizational competitiveness.

Researchers agree that a leader's inability to fully understand what is needed in order to guide their organization through successful change can be a reason for failure. Proper planning and management of change can reduce the likelihood of failure, promote change effectiveness, and increase employee engagement. Yet, change in organizations must be viewed as a continuous activity that affects both organizational and individual outcomes. If change management can be considered as an event induced by socio-cultural factors, the cultural variable gains greater significance when applied to the quality of the relationship between a leader and their team. Many organizations today are on the verge of internationalization. It is here that the cultural context can affect behaviors and, in the same way, leadership style.

The research presented in this book by an eminent group of scholars explores the influence of culture – ethnic, regional, religious – on how leaders manage change within organizations.

Daphne Halkias, PhD is a distinguished academic, researcher, published author, and consultant in the areas of international marketing, family business, coaching and mentoring family businesses, organizational psychology, education, and sustainable entrepreneurship. She is Professor of Management Research at International School of Management, Paris, France; a Founding Fellow at the Institute of Coaching at McLean Hospital, a Harvard Medical School Affiliate, USA; a Research Affiliate at the Institute for Social Sciences, Cornell University, USA; and Senior Research Fellow at The Center for Youth and Family Enterprise, University of Bergamo, Italy. Dr. Halkias is CEO of Executive Coaching Consultants, and Editor of *International Journal of Technology-Enhanced Learning*, *International Journal of Teaching and Case Studies*, and *International Journal of Social Entrepreneurship and Innovation*. She is a Member of the Family Firm Institute, American Psychological Association, Society for Industrial and Organizational Psychology and Business Fights Poverty.

Joseph C. Santora, EdD is Distinguished Visiting Professor of Management and Director of Research and Executive Doctorate of Business Administration (E-DBA) doctoral program at Ecole des Ponts Business School, France. He was a Dean and Director of doctoral studies, and has taught in several doctoral, MBA, and IEMBA programs at business schools in Australia, the Balkans, Europe, Georgia, Russia, Taiwan, the UK and the US. Professor Santora was also an Adjunct Senior Research Fellow at Monash University, Australia. He has written two books, and published more than four dozen refereed articles and teaching cases in ranked journals and

150+ academic and practitioner papers, blogs, cases, book chapters and reviews, along with numerous publishing and presentation awards. His research focuses on coaching, leadership, executive succession and leadership transition in non-profit organizations, family businesses, managing and leading change, and teams. Professor Santora is the founding and current Editor of the *International Leadership Journal*, an online refereed academic journal devoted to exploring multidisciplinary organizational leadership issues. He has done postdoctoral work at Harvard, Princeton, and New York University, and serves on nine international academic editorial boards. He founded and served as Managing Director of two for-profit companies, and has consulted to more than two dozen non-profit organizations and major corporations in Europe and the US. Professor Santora has also done corporate training for several large multinational companies in Italy and Spain.

Nicholas Harkiolakis, PhD is Vice President for Europe and Middle East and Director of Research for Executive Coaching Consultants. He is Editor of *International Journal of Teaching and Case Studies* and Associate Editor of *International Journal of Social Entrepreneurship and Innovation*. He is the author of 'e-Negotiations: Networking and Cross-Cultural Business Transactions', 'Multipreneurship: Diversification in Times of Crisis', and 'Leadership Explained: Leading Teams in the 21st Century'. He teaches graduate courses and supervises dissertations at various universities in France, the UK, and the US.

Paul W. Thurman, DrPH is Professor of Management and Analytics at Columbia University's School of International and Public Affairs and at its Joseph L. Mailman School of Public Health in New York, USA. His consulting and management experience spans strategic visioning, operations and change management, technology strategy and implementation, and executive coaching. Dr. Thurman has been a Visiting Professor and Research Fellow at leading graduate schools including the London Business School and the Haas School of Business at the University of California, Berkeley, and is CEO of Thurman and Associates, a consultancy he founded in 2000.

Leadership and Change Management

A Cross-Cultural Perspective

**Edited by Daphne Halkias,
Joseph C. Santora, Nicholas Harkiolakis
and Paul W. Thurman**

Routledge
Taylor & Francis Group

LONDON AND NEW YORK

First published 2017
by Routledge

2 Park Square, Milton Park, Abingdon, Oxfordshire OX14 4RN

52 Vanderbilt Avenue, New York, NY 10017

Routledge is an imprint of the Taylor & Francis Group, an informa business

First issued in paperback 2020

British Library Cataloguing in Publication Data
A catalogue record for this book is available from the British Library

Library of Congress Cataloging in Publication Data
Names: Halkias, Daphne, editor.
Title: Leadership and change management : a cross-cultural perspective / edited by Daphne Halkias, Joseph C. Santora, Nicholas Harkiolakis and Paul Thurman.
Description: New York : Routledge, 2017.
Identifiers: LCCN 2016041407 | ISBN 978-1-472-47166-6 (hardback) | ISBN 978-1-315-59176-6 (ebook)
Subjects: LCSH: Leadership. | Organizational change. | Industrial management.
Classification: LCC HD57.7 .L431354 2017 | DDC 658.4/092—dc23LC record available at https://lccn.loc.gov/2016041407

ISBN: 978-1-4724-7166-6 (hbk)
ISBN: 978-0-367-59536-4 (pbk)

Typeset in Bembo
by Fish Books Ltd.

Contents

Contributors

Dr. Mary Barrett is Professor of Management at the School of Management, Operations and Marketing, University of Wollongong, Australia.

Dr. Cecilia Bjursell is Director of Encell at the School of Education and Communication, Jönköping University, Sweden.

Dr. Vyacheslav Boltrukevich is MBA-Production Systems Program Director and Associate Professor of Operations Management at Lomonosov Moscow State University Business School, Russia.

Dr. Dimitris Bourantas is Professor of Organisational Behaviour at the Department of Management Science and Technology, Athens University of Economics and Business, Greece.

Dr. Steve Elers (Ngāti Kauwhata) is Lecturer at School of Communication, Journalism and Marketing, Massey University, New Zealand.

Dr. Joseph E. Hamlett is Affiliate Faculty Member at Southwestern College, Winfield, Kansas, USA.

Dr. Gazi Islam is Associate Professor at Department of People, Organizations and Society, Grenoble Ecole de Management, Grenoble, France.

Dr. Simon Jones is Pro-Vice-Chancellor at Cranfield University, UK.

Ms. Marina Karli is PhD Candidate at Athens University of Economics and Business, Greece.

Dr. Marcos Komodromos is Assistant Professor at the Department of Communications, School of Humanities, Social Sciences & Law, University of Nicosia, Cyprus.

Dr. Mari Kooskora is Associate Professor and Head of Centre for Business Ethics, Estonian Business School, Tallinn, Estonia.

Dr. Melquicedec Lozano is Professor-Researcher at Center for Entrepreneurship Development, Icesi University, Cali, Colombia.

Dr. Emmanouela Mandalaki is Affiliate Professor/Researcher of Organizational Behavior and Ethics at Grenoble Ecole de Management, Grenoble, France.

Dr. Shefali Nandan is Assistant Professor at Department of Commerce and Business Administration, University of Allahabad, Allahabad, India.

Dr. Alexander Naumov is Associate Professor at Lomonosov Moscow State University Business School, Russia.

Ms. Marina Niforos is a Fellow at Centre Européen de Droit et d'Economie (CEDE), ESSEC Business School, Paris, France.

Dr. Kathy Overbeke is a Research Fellow and Executive Coach at Weather School of Management, Case Western Reserve University, Cleveland, Ohio.

Ms. Marta Piigli is CEO at Paulig Professional Business in Baltics, Paulig Coffee Estonia Ltd., Tallinn, Estonia.

Dr. Grant Jewell Rich is a Consulting Psychologist in Juneau, Alaska, USA.

Dr. Renee Sabbagh Ghattas is Assistant Professor at the Department of Accounting/Management, Lebanese American University, Lebanon.

Dr. Andrea Santiago is Full Professor at Asian Institute of Management, Makati, Philippines.

Dr. Claire Seaman is Reader in Enterprise and Family Business at Queen Margaret University, Edinburgh, United Kingdom.

Dr. Filipe Sobral is Associate Professor at Brazilian School of Public and Business Administration, Getulio Vargas Foundation, Rio de Janeiro, Brazil.

Dr. Franco Vaccarino is Senior Lecturer at School of Communication, Journalism and Marketing, Massey University, New Zealand.

Dr. Maria Vakola is Associate Professor at School of Business, Athens University of Economics and Business, Greece.

Dr. Natalia Vinokurova is Assistant Professor at the Business School of Lomonosov Moscow State University, Russia.

Ms. Janine Saba Zakka is Lecturer at the Department of Finance and Accounting, Adnan Kassar School of Business, Lebanese American University, Lebanon.

1 Change leadership in a cross-cultural context

A case study of Italy and Australia

Mary Barrett

Overview

Successful leaders of change are wary of simple, mechanistic, step-by-step views of achieving change. Rather, they recognize that organizations are always in motion and that change emerges from many pressures and directions, even though management may be able to steer the change to some degree (Clegg, Kornberger and Pitsis, 2005; Pettigrew, 1985; Van de Ven and Poole, 1995). In the case that follows, the different cultural profiles of Italy and Australia and the family nature of the business made change both easier and more difficult. Further, the fact that a husband and wife team, Catherine and David, managed the business together – albeit in different roles and with different management styles – is important to understanding why change was difficult and how it was managed successfully.

Background to the case

Harris Farm Markets is an Australian grocery chain that specializes in fruit, vegetables, delicatessen, and other grocery items. Established in 1971, with a single shop in Villawood, New South Wales, Australia, it was the first Australian fruit and vegetable company to open a supermarket-style operation. It currently enjoys the highest customer rating on product review.com.au for major supermarket chains in Australia (ProductReview, 2015).

Method

Catherine Harris was interviewed at the Harris Farm Markets' main premises in Sydney. At the time of the interview, her husband, David Harris, the founder of the business, was still the CEO. He has since passed on the leadership of the business to three of his five sons. Other family members in the business include Angus Harris (co-CEO), Luke Harris (co-CEO), Tristan Harris (co-CEO) and Catherine Harris (chairperson).

Ms. Harris talked at length about her life in the business and outside it, but the case focuses on a time when Ms. Harris was charged with making major changes to the business after a goods and services tax (GST) was introduced in Australia on 1 July 2000. The new legislation required many businesses, especially small ones, to operate more formally and transparently than they had done previously. The case primarily reflects Ms. Harris's viewpoint, but the author's observations during site visits also contributed to the case.

Analyzing Catherine's story

Catherine recalled the way the business got started:

> When I look back on it, [I see that] it was a good thing that we [David and I] both came
> from family business backgrounds. We met when we were both studying business at
> university. Seeing how it's such a big part of my life now, it's odd to think that, for the
> first 27 years or so, I had very little direct role in it. Not even David originally expected
> to go into the fruit and vegetable business. His dad had run a successful chicken process-
> ing firm, but he sold it to a multinational. David had expected to take it over, but the sale
> put an end to that idea! So David had to find his own path. He learned the practical side
> of fruit and vegetable wholesaling and distribution in another firm, before buying a
> business of his own.

Looking back on her experience, Catherine said that her contribution to the family firm's
knowledge base was to gain corporate skills in a retailing environment:

> David was off learning the [fruit and vegetable] business so I had to go and work. What
> we decided was I'd go to [M., a large, established Australian retail business] and learn the
> corporate side. What ended up happening was I never got out of that. David's business
> went like this [gesture indicating rapid growth] on the entrepreneurial side and I stayed
> at M., and then had babies. In those days, the minute you had babies you were out of the
> workforce. As soon as M. found out I was pregnant there was a huge celebration, but the
> clear assumption was that I would be leaving. So I left. I then had five children very
> rapidly, but worked the whole time doing various things. I worked in Mum's business.

As well as working in her mother's business, she started one of her own, in communications
and public relations. Both David's and Catherine's firms went very well for a while, but then
both hit problems around the same time. David's business faltered in the currency collapse of
the late 1980s and a major client of Catherine's firm went bankrupt. Catherine recalled it as a
very stressful time, and decided to make sure she could be the family breadwinner if necessary:

> I realized that I might be the income earner. My business was terrific and very glamorous,
> but my main client was going down, and I suddenly thought that it might be me in charge
> of the five children and the husband, so I'd better get a real job. I applied for a job at [an
> Australian university] as head of their alumni section and I was offered that job. So I then
> had a real job with real money and I felt secure. At least I knew we had enough to feed
> the kids.

While her husband's business struggles continued, Catherine was headhunted for a high-
profile government job. Her expertise in managing large corporate organizations, especially
guiding them through large-scale change, was becoming increasingly recognized. As she said
about her increasing public profile: "I became a bit of a change management guru person."

Catherine finally entered the family business at her husband's invitation to solve a specific
business problem in the firm. When the Australian tax system was overhauled in 2000, the
informal, cash basis for running her husband's business was no longer appropriate. Many
changes imposed on firms from the outside, such as new legislation, require adaptive rather
than large-scale change. However, David was worried that the extent of the overhaul needed

could threaten the viability of the firm, which had already experienced – and recovered from – major problems in the past. As Catherine put it: "David said to me that he didn't want to make the mistakes he made last time and he needed me in to corporatize [the family firm]."

The way the firm was being run was virtually incomprehensible to Catherine who was used to the formal governance approaches of public sector entities and large corporates in Australia:

> It [David's firm] was weird. It was a closed book – it had next to no formal systems. And yet it worked – it had for years. And, frankly, it intrigued me how it could have operated like this for so long. But it had to change – the new tax rules meant we couldn't go on the way we had before.

A major problem was that running a business on more transparent lines ran counter to the cultural traditions of the employees, many of whom who had emigrated to Australia from Italy. According to the current Index of Economic Freedom (2015), Italy is only the 80th freest economy in the world. The Italian economy remains burdened by political interference, bureaucracy, corruption, high levels of taxation, a rigid labor market, an ineffective judicial system, a complex regulatory framework, and the high cost of conducting business (Capuano, undated). Some aspects of the Italian way of doing business were reflected in the way David's business was managed, including the fact that it was run largely on a cash basis. As Catherine explained:

> One big problem was that the business ran on a cash basis. We had accounting systems, but it wasn't just a case of adding your GST on. I think that was part of the reason why there was so much secrecy, because everybody dealt in cash.
>
> …One of the things that we have spent the last five years doing is getting rid of every bit of cash in the business. … In a way it makes us non-competitive, because every other fruit market out there pays everybody $250 a week on the books and $500 in their hand. That is absolutely standard. It's the black economy. … It was just how you got staff. You didn't get staff by employing people on the books. They were all migrants, mostly from Italy, and nobody trusted the government.

Catherine's approach was to incorporate some 'Italian' aspects of the firm into her management style as a way of changing the way it ran. Italy has a very large percentage of family-owned small and medium-sized enterprises (SMEs), and even some of the largest corporations such as Fiat, Ferrero, Benetton, Mediaset, and so on are still controlled by single families (Capuano, undated). Because of the strong influence of family in Italian society and business, management structures are often weak. Most, if not all, of the decisions are made by the owner of the business, by the family, or by the very few key decision makers in a company. Italians respect and admire decision makers and leaders and accept their position in authority more than Australians do. This is reflected in the fact that Italy scores higher (50) on 'power distance' than Australia (36) (Hofstede Centre, undated). However, often a manager's power is determined by the strength of the relationships that a person has with the senior management or the owner of the business. Even though David was not Italian, his management style had adapted to the approach his workers were familiar with. As Catherine described it:

> He [David] has a real caring for the people who work for the firm. It's not even really paternalistic. He genuinely sees them as his colleagues and workers, and there is a

tremendous lack of hierarchy. My husband is not a very outgoing person. He's the strong silent type, and he loves the way his staff come and speak to him and share with him. He's a confidante. That's probably why it worked, having 500 employees and no systems – they felt part of the family. And in this business, of course, you really do rely on trust, because people still pay cash for their fruit and vegetables and it's a huge cash business. We don't touch it [cash] at all now because it just goes into the till and we have people to come and collect it and take it away. But in the [retail] shops it's there every day.

Catherine, rather than her husband, had the detailed, technical knowledge of how to add the architecture of structure and formal systems to a family firm. An early move was to implement a computerized accounting system. However, to do this, she had to deal with a deeply rooted 'family values' culture that opposed the changes she wanted. 'Familiness' – or the special bonds between firm members that are part of operating as a family firm – create many positive aspects, such as an ability for the firm to make and act on decisions quickly, a bias towards long-term rather than the short-term goals, and connectedness with the local community (Habbershon and Williams, 1999; Habbershon, Williams and MacMillan, 2003). Nevertheless, familiness can have a downside (Miller and Le Breton-Miller, 2005). Habbershon *et al.* (2003) refer to the 'distinctive' (positive) and 'constrictive' (negative) aspects of familiness. Because of the informal, even secretive way of making transactions both inside and outside the firm that was part of this family firm's traditions, staff resented Catherine's efforts to put in systems that accounted for transactions in a transparent way. They particularly disliked the fact that she had a formal title: executive director. As Catherine noted:

> People absolutely hated it [the title]. In fact, people even said that it used to be a family company before I came in, because I was getting rid of all the cash and making people do things, and sign dockets and so on.

Later, Catherine downplayed the title and made the most of the family firm's family culture. One of her tactics was to work through her husband, the firm's respected 'front person', its operational face, to persuade others to make changes. But this meant changing her husband's way of doing things as much as the way the firm did things. While this corresponds to the Italian approach – working through a close personal relationship with the CEO – it was still a difficult task:

> He [David] felt threatened. He didn't personally feel threatened, he just felt that it would all fall apart, that it wouldn't work. He was terrified that things would fall apart again. I started getting David to have managers' meetings and at the meetings I'd bring up occupational health and safety and everybody would roll their eyes. It wasn't until David really started hammering people that it changed. I didn't have an influence on changing the firm – I just changed the CEO … I don't think anybody else could have done what I did, not because I have the skills, but because I have David's trust.

Other aspects of David's management style were also a target for change. According to Catherine, her husband is "a definite person, and a bit of a dictator, and he doesn't like change." This manifested itself in his reluctance to consult staff before making changes in the business. David, unlike Catherine, had not worked in a range of other organizations before starting his own firm. So he lacked some of the conventional corporate disciplines. In Catherine's words:

Men like David, and other men who haven't been through that external experience, have missed out on consultation … I keep my ties strongly with the university, and there you wouldn't do anything without consultation. Also, in big business you consult on every-thing, even more so than universities. It's the same in the public sector … So you learn this word 'consultation'. These chaps that have gone out and started their own business, that word 'consultation' never enters their heads.

Catherine brought skills from the domestic sphere into the business arena. Despite acknow-ledging that her skills had pointed to the type of change needed in the business, Catherine consistently dismissed my suggestions that she was in fact a leader in the firm. On the contrary, she regarded her capacity to get things done in an indirect way as a 'female' skill:

> I'm sure wives bring that to family companies. Because as a mother, you don't get anything with power, you only get the kids to do things by cajoling – that's how you operate. Whereas David just says something and he expects it to be done. I think that somehow women bring that into the workforce so I sort of hold David's hand through these things and at least he appears to be consulting.

Catherine worked on the business as invisibly as possible, given the demands created by the scale of change she implemented. She never sought operational roles and insisted that firm strategy was her husband's territory: "He's the main strategist. Without him, there wouldn't be a business."

Measures of success and lessons for others

Part of the cultural success of the business, in Catherine's view, is that it still has the "look and feel" of a family business, but without the downsides that had made it a poor fit with the demands in Australian society for clarity and transparency. In view of her reluctance to des-cribe herself as a leader and to draw lessons for others from her experience, we can conclude that Catherine recognized how to work subtly with – rather than against – the cultural norms of the business, respecting its family nature and the spirit, if not the detail, of the Italian modes of business operations that its employees were familiar with. Catherine's influence manifested itself in the way she maintained the 'front stage' and 'back stage' division of labor between her and her husband, which made them more effective in combination than either would have been alone. Undoubtedly, however, without Catherine, there would not be a business run on professional lines.

References

Capuano, M. (undated). Challenges of doing business in Italy. *La Gazzetta Italiana*. Retrieved from www.lagazzettaitaliana.com/italy-business.aspx (last accessed 12 December 2016).

Clegg, S., Kornberger, M. and Pitsis, T. (2005). *Managing and organizations: An introduction to theory and practice*. London: Sage.

Habbershon, T. G. and Williams, M. L. (1999). A resource-based framework for assessing the strategic advantages of family firms. *Family Business Review, 12*, 1–25.

Habbershon, T. G., Williams, M. L. and MacMillan, I. C. (2003). A unified systems perspective of family firm performance. *Journal of Business Venturing, 8*(4), 451–465.

Hofstede Centre. (undated). Comparing countries. Retrieved from http://geert-hofstede.com/countries.html (last accessed 12 December 2016).

Index of Economic Freedom. (2015). Country rankings. Retrieved from www.heritage.org/index/ranking (last accessed 12 December 2016).

Miller, D. and Le Breton-Miller, I. (2005). *Managing for the long run: Lessons in competitive advantage from great family businesses*. Boston, MA: Harvard Business School Press.

Pettigrew, A. (1985). *Awakening giant: Continuity and change in ICI*. Oxford: Blackwell.

ProductReview. (2015). Supermarkets. Retrieved from www.productreview.com.au/c/supermarkets.html (last accessed 12 December 2016).

Van de Ven, A. and Poole, M. (1995). Explaining development and change in organizations. *Academy of Management Review, 20*(3), 510–540.

2 Leading organizational change in a Brazilian multinational

Crisis and restructuring in Globo organizations

Emmanouela Mandalaki, Gazi Islam and Filipe Sobral

Change is like death and taxes – it should be postponed as long as possible and no change would be vastly preferable. But in a period of upheaval, such as the one we are living in, change is the norm.

(Peter Drucker, 1999)

Introduction

A vast body of literature has studied the impacts of leadership on organizational change (e.g., Armenakis, Harris and Mossholder, 1993; Drucker, 1999; Kotter, 1996; Wilson, 2014). Studies of organizational change management have explored the management of different types of changes based on focus, scope, and time needed to be implemented, among others (e.g., Kotter, 1996; Michalak, 2010; Wilson, 2014). Namely, organizational changes can range from incremental improvements in organizational operations to radical, major, or even trans-formational changes. Examples of organizational changes involve mergers and acquisitions, introduction of new technologies in the organizational routine, geographical expansions, restructuring, downsizing, and cultural changes (e.g., Michalak, 2010; Smith, 2002). In this context, the existence of competent leaders who take into consideration the culture of the organization is a crucial factor driving the successful implementation of these changes.

A major reaction triggered by organizational change is individuals' coping abilities, involving the strategies people enlist to deal with changes. Research shows that problem-related coping strategies are more effective than those driven by emotions (Callan, 1993; Folkman, Lazarus, Dunkel-Schetter, DeLongis and Gruen, 1986). However, all coping strategies are informed by individuals' cognitive schemata and change attributes as well as the connection among different change events (Lau and Woodman, 1995). The same body of literature has established the importance of personality in shaping the change-coping mechanisms of leaders, managers, and individuals affected by organizational changes (e.g., Callan, Terry and Schweitzer, 1994; Holahan and Moos, 1987; Judge, Thoresen, Pucik and Welbourne, 1999).

Business literature has also discussed factors triggering organizational change as well as the challenges leaders are faced with when they try to drive successful organizational changes (Armenakis *et al.*, 1993; Smith, 2002; Thompson, 1967) of diverse scopes. The current chapter discusses organizational change and leadership, and stresses the importance of considering organizational culture before initiating change. Our discussion also stresses the importance of successfully communicating the change before initiating it and of developing a change strategy that is in line with the organizational culture of the organization in question. The chapter concludes with a case study illustrating the complexity of driving successful organizational changes as well as the importance of understanding organizational culture beyond mere economistic objectives before designing successful changes.

We suggest that there is no 'passe-partout' change strategy to be implemented independently of organizational context. On the contrary, leaders need to familiarize themselves with the particular organizational culture within which change is implemented and accordingly develop change strategies aligned with the business objectives of the organization and the concerned stakeholders.

Leadership in the context of organizational change

Literature on organizational change has widely discussed strategies that leaders should adopt to effectively guide organizations through change, as well as factors favoring or impeding change (Armenakis *et al.*, 1993; Wilson, 2014). Particularly, literature has stressed rigid organizational culture, employee resistance, lack of resilience to change, and inertia as well as unwillingness/difficulty to adapt to new routines as barriers to the implementation of successful changes (e.g., Carnall, 1990; Coulson-Thomas, 1992; Kotter, 1996). Similarly, leaders' inability to understand organizational cultures, successfully communicate the need for change, lack of top management commitment, and stagnant organizational culture are among the main reasons that change initiatives often fail (Burnes, 1992; Carnall, 1990; Ringer, 1998). Notably, research cites high failure rates, with over 30 percent failed implementation, although variations exist across change type and industry sectors (Coulson-Thomas, 1992; Kotter, 1996; Smith, 2002).

Employees may see changes as threatening, carriers of an unstable organizational future that may affect them negatively (Wilson, 2014). The reticence to embrace change highlights the necessity for leaders to successfully communicate the need for change, to reduce feelings of employee uncertainty and resistance to change. Leaders failing to understand the importance of communication in change implementation may see changes as necessary aspects of business strategy to be implemented irrespective of employee involvement (Aiken and Keller, 2009; Wilson, 2014). To the extent that leaders don't find the right way to communicate the need for change, they may demotivate employees and other interested stakeholders to embrace it.

Research suggests a misalignment between what motivates managers – for instance, increasing profits and outperforming competitors – and what motivates employees. It is argued that managerial 'stories' are often not appealing to their audience nor do they enable them to get their message across (Aiken and Keller, 2009). Thus, a large number of organizational change efforts fail as a result of leader inability to successfully communicate the value derived from the necessary changes – not only for the organization overall, but also for each employee separately.

Successfully managing change requires not only that leaders conceive the need for change, but that they also design, execute, and communicate the change in a convincing way in order to gain as many followers as possible (Kotter, 1996; Wilson, 2014). Literature suggests that leaders must communicate the desired behaviors and steps that the individuals concerned should adopt for the change to be successfully implemented (Kotter and Schlesinger, 2008; Wilson, 2014). The same body of literature argues that effective leaders should communicate to interested shareholders the new routines that the change is expected to bring and explain the expected benefits.

Similarly, Wilson (2014) argues that it is crucial that leaders reward those who make an effort to change and encourage all employees to contribute to the change. More than just motivating those who lag behind, smart leaders should try to understand the reasons behind resistance. The latter is especially true because resistance to change could potentially signal weaknesses in the change strategy, which if corrected could boost change success. Showing empathy can ultimately inspire more followers to embrace change and in turn lead to a more successful change. Overall, it is crucial that leaders realize the significant role that each employee can have in the change process and delegate responsibilities accordingly so as to encourage employees to personally identify with the need for change.

In light of the above, it is thus crucial that leaders acknowledge the major benefits that can be derived out of successfully managing highly heterogeneous teams of employees. Since such teams are formed by individuals with diverse competences, assigning to them diverse responsibilities according to their skills can allow leaders to successfully drive the change. Namely, literature suggests that diverse top management teams can manage changes more successfully than homogeneous teams because they can effectively deal with change-related conflicting demands (Naranjo-Gil, 2015). With the same rationale, leaders should not only leverage the heterogeneity of the management team, but also smartly leverage the heterogeneity of the teams they are managing by delegating tasks to the interested stakeholder groups. In this way, leaders can help stakeholders to find meaning in different aspects of the change process and embrace it. The latter would likely allow leaders to develop a committed pool of followers who would meaningfully contribute to the implementation of the organizational change in question. Similarly, another crucial element of change planning is a leader's ability to frequently assess the effectiveness of the change implementation strategy and make the necessary changes for the change to be successfully implemented.

To put in place such a frequent evaluation mechanism, leaders can start by testing planned changes in a pilot group of employees, before applying it to the entirety of the concerned stakeholders. This way, leaders can take corrective action in any aspects of their strategy needing improvement; a method that can allow them to lead the change more successfully overall. Another policy that can help leaders to successfully design changes and avoid running into serious fallacies that could potentially be prevented are the lessons learned from other organizations or their own past experience on how to lead certain changes (Kotter, 1996; Wilson, 2014). Last but not least, to eliminate feelings of insecurity on the part of the employees and increase the likelihood of change embracement and success, it is also important that leaders stress the aspects of the organizational routine that will not be affected by the change.

Besides the general change strategies suggested in the literature for successfully managing changes, a growing body of literature has also investigated the relation between different leadership styles enacted in different leadership behaviors and change success (Avolio, Walumbwa and Weber, 2009; Bass and Bass, 2009; Battilana, Gilmartin, Sengul, Pache and Alexander, 2010; Gilley, McMillan and Gilley, 2009; Herold, Fedor, Caldwell and Liu, 2008). Particularly, it has been suggested that task-oriented leadership styles are negatively related to change success whereas relation-oriented leadership styles are positively related to change success. The latter suggests the importance for leaders to consider human relations when designing change strategies, beyond mere economistic objectives. For instance, in the case that a leader's style is not informed by and does not match the culture of the organization in question, an efficient task-oriented leadership style is not likely to allow the leader to successfully drive the organization through the change. In other words, a change strategy that might be useful in one organizational context might prove to be useless in a different context if it is not enacted by a leader familiar with the organization's culture.

The latter evidence shows the importance of considering the soft elements of organizational structure, like the culture and the values of the organization, in an effort to implement successful changes. For instance, as will be discussed in the following case study, failing to consider the cultural values of the organization and assign to the human factor the value it merits can lead even successful strategies to failure. Thus, it is obvious that purely task-oriented leadership styles that might prove to be successful in one context (because they are in line with the focal organizational culture) might prove to be unsuccessful in different contexts, where organizational culture is centered on human relations. In the latter case, relation-oriented leadership styles are largely preferred to task-oriented ones for the successful implementation of changes.

Literature also argues that leadership styles comprised of both task and change-orientation tendencies, characteristics usually found in transformational leaders (Yukl, 1999; Yukl, Gordon and Taber, 2002), exhibit positive relation to change success (Herold *et al.*, 2008). Similarly, change-oriented leadership styles are found to have consistently positive relations with change success (Joffe and Glyn, 2002). These findings suggest that leaders who are resilient to and deeply aware of the need for change are more able to successfully design and communicate the need for change to their followers and thus successfully drive changes. The below case study clearly illustrates the role of leader awareness of change necessity and organizational culture in the successful implementation of changes as well as the way in which different leadership styles can bring very different results depending on whether they are informed by organizational culture or not.

Having said the above, it is also important to not disregard the extent to which the scale of a change affects the styles of leadership as well as the impact of those styles on change success. For example, when the change is small (e.g., Higgs and Rowland, 2005), change-oriented leadership is thought to be the most answered leadership style and has a positive impact on change outcomes. However, as the change scale increases, leaders tend to adopt a more distributive leadership style, whereby tasks are allocated among different groups for effective change management (Kotter, 1996).

The latter is clearly demonstrated in the below case study, where the need to drive a large-scale organizational change led organizational leaders to recruit external leaders, thus distributing leadership tasks across internal and external competent managers. However, the case study suggests that this strategy is not always successful, but it also depends on the extent to which externally recruited leaders are sensitized to the organizational culture in question and are able to adapt their leadership style to the needs of the organization for the change to be successfully implemented.

As is demonstrated by the above, not only is it important that leaders develop well-designed change strategies, they must also understand cultural and other value-based organizational specificities. Since change management is triggered by socio-cultural factors (Shapero and Sokol, 1982), the culture is a factor of high significance since it also shapes the relationship between leaders and the team they are managing. Thus, regardless of the extent of charisma and competence a leader possesses, it is crucial that he/she understands the particular elements of the organizational culture within which he/she operates in order to drive successful changes.

Organizational culture and change

As deduced by the above, understanding change initiatives involves taking into account organizational cultures. Organizational culture comprises both formal (i.e., mission statement, code of ethics, decision making style, etc.) and informal elements (i.e., behavioral norms, rituals, etc.) (Cohen, 1993; Schein, 1990), which interweave to shape employee attitudes and expectations. These attitudes and expectations guide employees' interpretations of the environment and are thus critical to change attempts. If leaders fail to consider such elements in their change strategies and align their planning with the organizational culture, then change is likely to fail (Kotter, 1996; Wilson, 2014). Organizational culture is an important element to consider not only when the subject of change is the culture itself, but in change more generally. For instance, in restructuring or mergers and acquisitions, culture shapes how employees react to new routines and their attitudes towards change.

Factors like national culture and industry sector can crucially inform how organizational cultures develop, and how routines emerge that often go beyond mere economic benefits. It is likely that charismatic and effective leaders in one industry might fail to implement successful changes in another industry if their approaches fail to align with the culture of the new organization. Thus, leaders' failures to familiarize themselves with particular organizational cultures may lead to unsuccessful organizational changes.

Literature on organizational culture stresses the importance of considering core values over and above economic benefits (Kotter, 1996). Particularly in the case of externally appointed leaders, it is important to become familiar with the culture of the organization that they are in charge of leading through the change. In cases where leaders develop policies intended to achieve mere economistic business objectives with no consideration of the cultural values of the organization, change efforts often fail. Thus, if leaders fail to adapt their change strategy to the culture of the organization, the change is likely to generate employee resistance and lack of commitment (Kotter, 1996; Pless and Maak, 2004; Wilson, 2014). So far, we have argued that top management team diversity is a crucial factor for successfully managing complex changes. However, as illustrated in the below case study, diversity by itself (e.g., achieved through externally appointed leaders) is not enough to guarantee change success if the leaders don't realize the need to familiarize themselves with the culture of the organization in question before initiating any kind of change.

At the same time, literature argues that leaders' abilities to drive successful organizational changes require nurturing a culture of diversity and inclusion in the organization (Pless and Maak, 2004). The latter includes promoting a multidimensional and inclusive culture whereby heterogeneity is encouraged. Such inclusive cultures are not rigid and thus easy to change (Emmott and Worman, 2008; Pless and Maak, 2004) and constitute favorable conditions for successful organizational changes.

Having drawn links between organizational culture, leadership, and change success, we now describe a case study drawn from the Brazilian business context. The below case study discusses the challenges faced by the Globo organization, the biggest media and communications group in Brazil. The case study describes how Globo's top management team attempted to manage change, and ultimately acknowledges the importance of understanding organizational culture before enacting any kind of change strategy.

Crisis and restructuring in Globo organizations in Brazil

A glimpse into the Brazilian organizational culture

Brazil is among the most dynamic and fast developing economies globally. As a result of its rapid growth, the country has faced several challenges to which it needed to adapt to secure a steady growth rate. The latter has cultivated a culture of resilience to change in Brazilian companies as a condition for success *vis-à-vis* international competitors (Ardichvili, Jondle, Kowske, Cornachione, Li and Thakadipuram, 2011).

Brazilian managerial culture is traditionally built on a paternalistic pattern referring to dyadic relationships between managers and their subordinates. In this context, leaders are in charge of protecting their subordinates, whereas subordinates extend loyalty and commitment in exchange (Kjellin and Nilstun, 1993). Beyond paternalism, Brazilian business culture is also characterized by strong personal relationships, power concentration, loyalty and preference to the in-group and the leader as well as flexibility (Tanure and Duarte, 2005). All those characteristics have built an organizational culture whereby human relationships and cultural values constitute a deeply engrained element of organizational culture.

However, given the strength of the aforementioned attributes, the latter can constitute both advantages and disadvantages for business change. On the one hand, the existence of strong personal relationships between managers and subordinates allows for rapid development of commitment to change (as well as any other initiatives taken by the admired leader) and identification with the change vision, thus upholding successful organizational changes. However, on the other hand, this commitment can potentially lead to failure in the case that the change is not implemented correctly or with no consideration for the particular nature of the organizational culture in question.

The below case study illustrates a Brazilian organization that underwent a major organizational change in view of financial hardships and shows the importance for leaders to consider the specific organizational culture of the firm in question before restructuring.

Introduction to the Globo industries

Globo Organization is a conglomerate serving a multiplicity of sectors, but primarily focused on media and entertainment. The business grew and developed under the leadership of Roberto Marinho, who inherited the journals *A Noite* and *O Globo* from his father, Irineu Marinho, in 1925. Under the management of Roberto Marinho, the group diversified its activities. First, it expanded its business beyond the press to include other media forms, and eventually moved into other sectors. The major accomplishment of the organization was the inauguration, in 1964, of TV Globo, whose launch led to the eventual domination of the television sector in Brazil. Currently, Globo is the largest media group in Latin America, and one of the largest in the world, exercising a powerful influence on the Brazilian society.

Crisis in Globo industries

In the second half of the 1990s, Brazilian communication groups had wagered on the continuing growth and stability of the national economy. With the objective of achieving greater growth, they invested massively in new distribution platforms, such as cable and satellite, and in new business forms like subscription-only television channels. As a result, many of these organizations became heavily indebted, often in foreign currency. Despite these grand investments, the expected growth did not turn out as planned. The projected growth in subscription television was far above actual growth. Interest rates in Brazil began to rise, and the US dollar increased in value *vis-à-vis* the Brazilian real (BRL), increasing debt levels. Further, the development of new forms of information access, and particularly the diffusion of the Internet, incited a deep crisis in the Brazilian communication sector. In 2002, analysts predicted that Globo Organization had reached the "bottom of the well." The company's debt had reached BRL 6 billion (around USD 2 billion), and by 2002 the company was unable to pay its debt levels (Bethlem, 2011).

The same year, the top management of Globo Organization, including Roberto Irineu Marinho, the son of Roberto Marinho, put into action a restructuring plan for the group. The management did not see any other solution to its serious problems other than the renegotiation of its debt and a radical corporate restructuring. According to this restructuring, the majority of companies within the group, including Globo Cable, Globo Publishing, and Globo Television, would undergo fundamental changes.

Immediately, two decisions were taken; decisions that were fundamental for the preservation of the business during the crisis. The first was to separate the restructuring team and the team responsible for the management of business units. "Keeping the teams separate ensured that people would remain focused in improving efficiency of the units, without losing time focusing on the restructuring," affirmed Roberto Irineu Marinho, president of Globo Organization. The second decision was to make it clear that the business was not for sale, and that creditor interference in the management of the business would not be tolerated. "Creditors do not know how to run media companies. This would put under risk the very businesses that pay our bills," affirmed Jorge Nobrega, corporate management director at Globo (Época Negócios, 2009).

Preserving the group and its business culture at that moment of financial vulnerability was the topic of heated conversations at the core of the Marinho family, who controlled Globo Organization. "In the first place, the businesses should continue to act within the scope of our values," explained Roberto Irineu. These values ranged from workplace diversity and a positive work environment to commitment to quality and innovation. "Beyond this, we decided to struggle to not cede the capital of our business to creditors."

The restructuration of Globo Cable and Globo Publishing

To lead the restructuring effort, Globo brought on board Henri Phillippe Reichstul, the ex-president of Petrobras and former banker, as the director-general of the group. Reichstul, with experience in the area of finance, would have wide authority to modify archaic structures within the organization and to initiate changes in the business that exhibited the most serious problems. His mission was to resolve the financial and corporate problems within the group, and for this purpose, to change the organizational model as necessary.

His first strategic decision was to focus on the core businesses of Globo and to divest from non-core businesses. Toward this end, Reichstul, with the approval of the top administration, decided to focus attention on Globo Cable, which brought together subscription television services (cable and satellite) and high-bandwidth Internet, via the businesses Net and Sky. Reichstul met with creditors to negotiate to lengthen the deadlines for debt payment. Further, he spurred a reorganization of the organizational structure. He implemented a plan of cost reductions with the objective of cutting unnecessary expenditures by the organization, and prepared it to confront market realities of the time (Sobral and Peci, 2013).

In the attempt to invigorate the financial and market position of the business, in 2004, Globo initiated a merger process, linking Sky with its principal competitor, DirecTV. The company also sold part of the capital of Net to the group America Movil, headed by the Mexican media giant Carlos Slim. Between 2009 and 2012, consolidating a strategy of abandoning the sector of subscription television distribution and high bandwidth Internet, Globo sold the rest of its shares in Sky and Net to the groups DirecTV and America Movil, keeping only a small, symbolic participation in both businesses. In this way, Globo not only distanced itself from the units producing the largest losses, but also acquired a large amount of revenue from the major sales. Further, it strengthened its activities in its core businesses, the production and sale of media content via Globosat, which is currently the largest source of paid television in Brazil. As noted by one of its top managers, "We are producers and programmers of content. That is what we know how to do."

The resistance of Globo Networks

The all-powerful Globo Television Network, which was the principal business of the group and largest television station in Brazil, also faced similar problems. Above and beyond high debt, the business also exhibited an inflated personnel pool, overly powerful managers, excessive manager salaries, and several bloated and unnecessary departments. All of these areas needed immediate attention.

However, an unexpected problem confronted Reichstul, given that the top managers of Globo Networks were resisting the changes, believing that these changes went against the culture of the business. Further, it appeared that they had some support from the president of the group. Differently than in the other units, Reichstul was unable to garner the support necessary to put in place the structural changes he had imagined, and which had worked across the other units. His banker mentality was not compatible with a business whose largest cultural value was human talent.

For Globo Television, journalists and actors should not be seen as cost centers, but rather as the principal assets of the company. For instance, one of the main cost-cutting projects envisioned by Reichstul was to cut expenditures on the world-famous *telenovelas* or soap-opera style television series, one of Globo Networks' main products. The network fundamentally disagreed with the executive's strategy, and the struggle between the two sides weakened the authority of the executive. The relationship between Reichstul and Globo Organization began to deteriorate, and he was finally removed from the presidency. Roberto Irineu Marinho, the son of Roberto Marinho, assumed the post of executive director of the company.

A second wind for Globo

In the period where Roberto Irineu Marinho took control of the executive leadership of the group, costs were cut and reforms and managerial changes were carried out regarding the corporate structure and business divisions. However, Marinho always attempted to preserve the culture and identity of the organization. He rejected solutions based on a purely economistic perspective, and emphasized an organizational culture where human talent was the principal asset rather than a cost.

This period was the beginning of a process of alterations that attempted, first, to reduce losses so as to, afterward, generate profits for the company. To a large extent, both of these objectives were met. For instance, after finishing the 2002 year with a loss of BRL 5 billion, the business returned to profitability in 2003 with revenue of BRL 47.5 billion. In the following years, the group was able to consolidate cash profits superior to BRL 500 million per year. By 2009, profits had hit BRL 2 billion per year. Further, the company was able to reduce its total debt, which amounted to more than BRL 8 billion in 2002, to approximately BRL 1 billion by the end of 2011 (Magalhães, 2012).

The reorganization provoked drastic alterations in the structural model of the organization of Globo. These alterations improved the organization's financial health and gave it new energy to confront future challenges, but also involved strong resistance to larger changes that would have eroded the organizational culture of the firm. In the end, change was possible only by holding true to core elements of the almost 100-year-old culture of Brazil's largest media and communications firm.

Discussion and conclusion

The above case study discusses the changes that were implemented in the Globo conglomerate, the biggest media and communications organization in Brazil. As described above, a number of factors in the extended market and economic and institutional environments, within which the Globo group was operating, created the need for change. When the top management team realized that a change should be implemented, they recruited Reichstul, an external leader with long experience in the banking sector to lead the organization through the change. However, although the newly appointed leader managed to successfully garner employee and other stakeholders' support and implement the necessary changes in some of the group's companies, the same was not the case for Globo Networks, one of the most financially significant members of the group with a very strong organizational culture.

When the owner of the organization realized that the newly appointed leader was mainly driven by primarily financial objectives, he decided to remove him from his position and take over the change implementation process, staying faithful to the strong organizational culture of the Globo group. The creation of a giant organization, which was steadily the first among competitors in the Brazilian media and communications sector, was mainly attributed to the strong organizational culture that the group had cultivated for the employees and the rest of the stakeholders. Thus, realizing the importance of maintaining those cultural values throughout a change implementation process and keeping the employee central to the process was crucial for a successful change. The latter attitude as well as detachment from purely financial objectives allowed Roberto, the owner of the group, and the Globo top management team to garner the necessary support from employees and other concerned stakeholders and guide the organization successfully through the change.

The above case study illustrates the significance of considering organizational culture before initiating major changes and that leader success and experience in one industry sector does not guarantee successful implementation of changes in another sector. The latter suggests that leadership styles have to be modeled upon organizational culture since a style that is effective in one organization might prove to be unsuccessful in another if it is not informed by organizational culture. Thus, top management team heterogeneity (here through an externally recruited leader) is effective only when managers make an effort to familiarize themselves with organizational culture, since if the latter is not the case, heterogeneity might lead to failure.

The case study points to the idea that there are no 'perfect strategies' in managing organizational changes, but that it is crucial that leaders model their change strategy upon the organizational culture of the organization in question in order to be able to garner the necessary stakeholder support to implement successful changes.

References

Aiken, C. and Keller, S. (2009). The irrational side of change management. *McKinsey Quarterly, 2*, 00475394.

Ardichvili, A., Jondle, D., Kowske, B., Cornachione, E., Li, J. and Thakadipuram, T. (2011). Ethical cultures in large business organizations in Brazil, Russia, India, and China. *Journal of Business Ethics, 105*(4), 415–428. doi:10.1007/s10551-011-0976-9

Armenakis, A. A., Harris, S. G. and Mossholder, K. W. (1993). Creating readiness for organizational change. *Human Relations, 46*(6), 681–703.

Avolio, B. J., Walumbwa, F. O. and Weber, T. J. (2009). Leadership: Current theories, research, and future directions. *Annual Review of Psychology, 60*, 421–449.

Bass, B. M. and Bass, R. (2009). *The Bass handbook of leadership: Theory, research and managerial applications* (4th ed.). New York: Simon & Schuster.

Battilana, J., Gilmartin, M., Sengul, M., Pache, A. C. and Alexander, J. A. (2010). Leadership competencies for implementing planned organizational change. *The Leadership Quarterly, 21*(3), 422–438.

Bethlem, A. (2011). *Caso Organizações Globo.* Rio de Janeiro: Instituto COPPEAD de Administração, Universidade Federal do Rio de Janeiro.

Burnes, B. (1992). *Managing change: A strategic approach to organisational development and renewal.* London: Pitman.

Callan, V. J. (1993). Individual and organizational strategies for coping with organizational change. *Work & Stress, 7*(1), 63–75.

Callan, V. J., Terry, D. J. and Schweitzer, R. (1994). Coping resources, coping strategies and adjustment to organizational change: Direct or buffering effects? *Work & Stress, 8*(4), 372–383.

Carnall, C. A. (1990). *Managing change in organisations.* London: Prentice Hall.

Cohen, D. (1993). Creating and maintaining ethical work climates: Anomie in the workplace and implications for managing change. *Business Ethics Quarterly, 3*(4), 343–358.

Coulson-Thomas, C. (1992). *Transforming the company: Bridging the gap between management myth and corporate reality.* London: Kogan Page.

Drucker, P. F. (1999). *Management challenges for the 21st century.* London: Routledge.

Emmott, M. and Worman, D. (2008). The steady rise of CSR and diversity in the workplace. *Strategic HR Review, 7*(5), 28–33. doi:10.1108/14754390810893071

Época Negócios (2009). *Rumo das estrelas* (January 20). Retrieved from http://epocanegocios.globo. com/Revista/Common/0,,EMI23302-16642,00-RUMO+DAS+ESTRELAS.html (last accessed 12 December 2016).

Folkman, S., Lazarus, R. S., Dunkel-Schetter, C., DeLongis, A. and Gruen, R. J. (1986). Dynamics of a stressful encounter: Cognitive appraisal, coping, and encounter outcomes. *Journal of Personality and Social Psychology, 50*(5), 992.

Gilley, A., McMillan, H. S. and Gilley, J. W. (2009). Organizational change and characteristics of leadership effectiveness. *Journal of Leadership & Organizational Studies, 16*(1), 38–47.

Herold, D. M., Fedor, D. B., Caldwell, S. and Liu, Y. (2008). The effects of transformational and change leadership on employees' commitment to a change: A multilevel study. *Journal of Applied Psychology, 93*(2), 346.

Higgs, M. and Rowland, D. (2005). All changes great and small: Exploring approaches to change and its leadership. *Journal of Change Management, 5*(2), 121–151.

Holahan, C. J. and Moos, R. H. (1987). Personal and contextual determinants of coping strategies. *Journal of Personality and Social Psychology, 52*(5), 946.

Joffe, M. and Glynn, S. (2002). Facilitating change and empowering employees. *Journal of Change Management, 2*(4), 369–379.

Judge, T. A., Thoresen, C. J., Pucik, V. and Welbourne, T. M. (1999). Managerial coping with organizational change: A dispositional perspective. *Journal of Applied Psychology, 84*(1), 107–122.

Kjellin, L. and Nilstun, T. (1993). Medical and social paternalism: Regulation of and attitudes towards compulsory psychiatric care. *Acta-Psychiatrica-Scandinavica, 88*(6), 415–419.

Kotter, J. P. (1996). *Leading change.* Boston, MA: Harvard Business School Press.

Kotter, J. P. and Schlesinger, L. A. (2008). Choosing strategies for change. *Harvard Business Review, 86*(7/8), 130–139.

Lau, C. M. and Woodman, R. W. (1995). Understanding organizational change: A schematic perspective. *Academy of Management Journal, 38*(2), 537–554.

Magalhães, H. (2012). Organizações Globo obtêm aumento de 12% na receita. *Valor Econômico* (April 3), 879.

Michalak, J. M. (2010). Cultural catalysts and barriers of organizational change management: A preliminary overview. *Journal of Intercultural Management, 2*(2), 26–36.

Naranjo-Gil, D. (2015). The role of top management teams in hospitals facing strategic change: Effects on performance. *International Journal of Healthcare Management, 8*(1), 34–41. doi:10.1179/2047971914 Y.0000000078

Pless, N. M. and Maak, T. (2004). Building an inclusive diversity culture: Principles, processes and practice. *Journal of Business Ethics*, *54*, 129–147.

Ringer, R. C. (1998). Managerial perceptions of change at a national laboratory. *Leadership and Organization Development Journal*, *19*(1), 14–21.

Schein, E. H. (1990). Organization culture. *American Psychologist*, *45*(2), 109–119.

Shapero, A. and Sokol, L. (1982). The social dimensions of entrepreneurship. In C. Kent, D. Sexton and K. Vesper (eds), *Encyclopedia of Entrepreneurship* (pp. 72–90). Englewood Cliffs, NJ : Prentice-Hall.

Smith, M. E. (2002). Success rates for different types of organizational change. *Performance Improvement*, *41*(1), 26–33.

Sobral, F. and Peci, A. (2013). *Administração: Teoria e Prática no Contexto Brasileiro* (2nd ed.). São Paulo, Brazil: Pearson.

Tanure, B. and Duarte, R. G. (2005). Leveraging competitiveness upon national cultural traits: The management of people in Brazilian companies. *International Journal of Human Resource Management*, *16*(12), 2201–2217.

Thompson, J. D. (1967). *Organizations in Action*. New York: McGraw-Hill.

Wilson, J. (2014). Managing change successfully: Overcome resistance through strategy, communications, and patience. *Journal of Accountancy* (April 1). Retrieved from www.journalofaccountancy.com/issues/2014/apr/change-management-20139196.html (last accessed 12 December 2016).

Yukl, G. (1999). An evaluative essay on current conceptions of effective leadership. *European Journal of Work and Organizational Psychology*, *8*(1), 33–48.

Yukl, G., Gordon, A. and Taber, T. (2002). A hierarchical taxonomy of leadership behavior: Integrating a half century of behavior research. *Journal of Leadership and Organizational Studies*, *9*(1), 15–32.

3 A leader with open mind and heart

A case study on leadership and change management from Colombia

Melquicedec Lozano and Kathy Overbeke

Introduction

This chapter explores strategic business change processes contextualized in the family experience. By including the family experience of the corporate leader, we are able to discover the influence of culture in change management. Families are the purveyors of culture (Moore and Asay, 2013; Wentworth, 1980), and this case study offers insights into the mechanisms that link culture with strategic change processes. We use Boyatzis's (2006) intentional change theory (ICT) to examine the progression of Juan Ramon Zapata from childhood to co-founder of a large cosmetic manufacturing and distribution company in Colombia. ICT provides a framework for examining change from a complexity perspective and allows us to highlight factors that lead to sustainable change.

Literature review

Change management in Colombia

Comparisons between technological advances in developed and underdeveloped countries and innovation studies in Latin America provide insight into the evolution of change management in Colombian industry (Malaver and Vargas, 2004). These studies indicate that change management in Colombia has focused on the roles of education, communication, commitment, negotiation, and teamwork (López-Duque, Lanzas-Duque and Lanzas-Duque, 2007) to generate changes in organizational culture, values, norms, traditional behavior, and knowledge (Acosta, 2002). Such approaches to change management have resulted in creativity and innovation, but the practice of change management is not widespread (Malaver and Vargas, 2004).

Family and culture in Colombia

Research on families in Colombia has shown links between family culture and values, entrepreneurship, and national economic development (Suárez-Restrepo and Restrepo-Ramírez, 2005). Families act as a source of support and advice for individuals (Viveros, 2007). Most families consist of a father, mother, and two or three children, but there are now more single and divorced parents raising young children. Traditional values continue to flourish in Colombian families, including solidarity, respect, honesty, work, and justice. These values, combined with more opportunities in the educational system, encourage the growth of entrepreneurship in Colombia. The vast majority of Colombian small and medium-sized enterprises are family-owned businesses (Suárez-Restrepo and Restrepo-Ramírez, 2005).

Intentional change theory

ICT differs from other change theories as it addresses change as a non-linear or discontinuous dynamic (Boyatzis, 2006). The theory is based on three features of complex systems that we use to analyze our data. These features are:

- tipping points, or events that spark recognition of abilities and beliefs that did not exist before;
- "self-organizing into patterns of equilibrium or disequilibrium" (Boyatzis, 2006, p. 608) or creating new dynamic processes; and
- "multileveledness" (Boyatzis, 2006, p. 608) or the interaction of different levels of social organizations.

Case study

Background

Juan Ramon Zapata was born into a wealthy, educated family living in Valle del Cauca, a region in southeast Colombia. His maternal grandfather had climbed the ranks of the German-owned company Bavaria, and had become a high-level executive. His paternal grand-father had been a college graduate and his son, Juan's father, was a lawyer who graduated from Universidad Javeriana.

Juan Ramon's favorite childhood memories are of the farm his father inherited and his mother cherished. His mother, Martha, took her seven children to the farm every weekend and holiday, often without Juan's father, Guillermo. Despite Guillermo's absences, the farm remains a symbol of family bonding for Juan as he recalls playing with his six siblings among the cows, horses, and other farm animals, and fishing and swimming in the river running through their property. Juan also fondly remembers the farm laborers who looked after the children and were an integral part of their bucolic life.

When Juan Ramon was 12 years old, his world collapsed. His father, an affable man, had a penchant for alcohol and infidelity. His absences from home became regular, his debt climbed, and he fell behind in paying his employees. Guillermo finally had to sell all his assets, including the beloved farm. Then Juan's parents divorced, his father ran off to the United States with his secretary, and Juan's mother was left with seven children and a handful of promissory notes with little value and a five-year expiration date.

This abrupt and disruptive change might have devastated the family if not for his mother's strength and guidance. A strict, well-organized, personable, and popular woman, Martha went to work in a construction supply shop where she was soon promoted to manager of a store. She also supplemented this income by selling real estate, which resulted in a working day that began at half past five in the morning and ended at nine in the evening. Her determination to provide educational opportunities for her children was inexhaustible. She admonished Juan's oldest brother who was studying in the United States, "You are not to come back. Even if we have to starve, you must graduate from the university." She then moved her other six children into a small apartment.

Juan Ramón recalls going to his mother's workplace after school during this time of transition to accompany her home on a city bus. Riding the bus was another example of Martha's socio-economic decline as she had always been provided with a car and driver. However, it also highlighted her fortitude in caring for her children and Juan's assistance was a sign of his deep devotion to his mother.

Eventually, Martha was able to buy a car and save money to open her own business. Her sister had opened a cosmetics shop in Bogota and Martha decided to follow suit. Martha's expansive social network included Don Francisco, the owner of a large cosmetics manufacturing company and he agreed to help Martha open her store. It was an instant success and a few years later Martha insisted that Juan attend college in the United States.

Appreciating his mother's struggle, Juan was a dedicated student in college. He studied industrial engineering while trying to master English, and he used his summers to advance his studies. When he graduated he was immediately offered a two-month scholarship to Japan, which his mother encouraged him to accept. Juan finally returned home at the age of 22 and was offered a job working in a prestigious multinational company that manufactured soaps. Juan's engineering skills and empathy for his co-workers helped attract the attention of his manager who mentored him and provided him with opportunities for advancement. Juan became the commercial manager and at the tender age of 28 the vice-president of the company tapped Juan to lead the development of an emulsion and detergent plant.

This appointment allowed Juan to demonstrate his bold and skilled business acumen as he led the creation of Coldequim (Colombian Chemicals) and subsequently led a merger with Stepa, one of the leading international manufacturers and distributors of Coldequim's product line. Juan discovered Stepa when he took the initiative to research worldwide industry leaders and found that Stepa had substantial plants in Brazil, France, the Philippines, and the United States. Juan traveled to Chicago with his manager to meet with Stepa's director of distribution for Colombia. He sold half of Coldequim to Stepa for the equivalent of the total investment in the company.

Like his mother, Juan was a multitasker. While working at Coldequim he partnered with his sister in a dressmaking company in a trade-free zone. His sister had just returned from studying in the United States and had been offered a good job with a multinational company. Juan convinced her to lead the dressmaking company instead and their company quickly grew from 3 to 60 employees as they received contracts from companies such as Benetton. Juan also started a fast food company with a friend and invested in his brother's business, growing African palm trees. Meanwhile, Juan encouraged innovation at Coldequim and often attended trade fairs with the vice-president of the parent company, looking for opportunities to grow and change.

Reflecting on his success in establishing Coldequim, Juan realized that he had entrepreneurial skills and decided to leave Stepa to build his own business. He had been offered the job of managing Stepa's largest Latin American plant in Mexico, but he felt his family needed him to stay in Colombia. One of his brothers had recently been killed in an accident, his sister had been diagnosed with cancer, and his father had returned to Colombia, penniless. Juan was 31 years old, unmarried, and had substantial savings since he had been living with his mother and had been frugal with his earnings. He went to visit his cousin, Jorge, in Bogata, who owned a small henna plant with about three employees. He offered to buy half of Jorge's company, Belleza Express, and explained his intentions to build it into a much larger business. Jorge, who had been running the company for about 18 months, agreed to Juan's proposal. After a few years, Belleza Express had grown such that another office was needed in Cali, Colombia's third largest city. Eventually, the office in Cali became their headquarters and the Bogata office became their sales support.

Over time, Juan and Jorge noticed that their company's dependence on imports made them subject to changes in the value of the US dollar and, in turn, changes in the international economy. Juan realized that owning their own brand would counter this effect and in 1999, armed with market knowledge and the support of Harold Eder, a friend and successful businessman in the sugar cane industry, they acquired Maricel, a Colombian-produced brand of toiletries and personal care products. They gradually introduced Maricel into their imported product line and in just one year their sales doubled. They soon eliminated almost all foreign products and further developed the Maricel brand. The company grew from 70 employees to 180 and has been growing ever since. Currently, Belleza Express is a national company employing over 1,000 people and 90 percent of sales come from their own manufactured products.

Business management and cultural values

The core principles of Juan Ramon's strategy are to expand through reinvestment and innovation, to build trust within and outside the organization, and, most importantly, to develop talent. He purchased Menticol, a perfume company in Cartagena, and has introduced other lines such as Arrurru and Stay-Off. Arrurru is the second most popular brand of toiletries in Colombia after Johnson and Johnson, and Stay-Off is the leading bug repellent. Belleza Express has also extended into product lines such as Depilex for hair removal, shampoos such as Nutrit and Bioherbal, and liquid soaps such as Aromasense. The company is successfully competing with multinational companies, including Reckitt Benckiser and Proctor and Gamble. Belleza Express's products are currently available in 10,000 drugstores and sales are expected to reach 143 billion pesos (COP) in 2015. In the last 10 years the company has sustained growth of roughly 15 percent per year. Their objective is to achieve an annual growth rate of 18 percent and triple sales by 2020.

Juan Ramon builds trust and loyalty within his company through frequent personal interactions, providing development opportunities for his employees, and addressing every day needs. Employees are encouraged to attend trade shows, including international fairs, and expenses are covered by the company. Educational programs, both in-house and outside, are also available to employees. Importantly, salaries are tied to corporate growth because of Juan's philosophical belief that "people have to feel they progress at the same time Belleza Express progresses." Additionally, Juan believes that employees will be more engaged and committed to Belleza Express if the company cares for both their corporate and private lives. Belleza Express therefore provides housing, employee credit programs, and a wellness program. Their wellness program includes flexible working hours, time off to attend to family needs such as graduations, marriage, and a death or illness in the family. The company also offers paid maternity leave and nursing rooms for lactating mothers. The holistic approach towards employees even includes half-days for special occasions like Halloween and vouchers for family activities. At Belleza Express, employees are considered the most valued asset as they define the culture and provide the company's competitive advantage.

Juan also develops talent by promoting a culture that favors the interests of the collective group over interests of an individual or small group. Within this framework he urges a culture of transparency where employees respect and encourage one another. Juan believes that this type of environment encourages collaboration and innovation, which leads to a corporate competitive edge and, ultimately, stronger performance. Belleza Express's supportive employee policies combined with financial success has made it a very desirable place to work. Thus, they are able to hire the most skilled, high achieving, and emotionally intelligent candidates.

Outside the company, Juan devotes 10 percent of his time to volunteer work with city and regional governments. In this capacity he proffers the same values – the importance of collective interests over individual interests, transparency, and interpersonal support. He seeks to ensure less corruption while helping to create more efficiency in the government. Unlike other business representatives who offer help, he refuses to capitalize on his civic duty. His behavior helps to build trust and is indicative of his mother's axiom: "Life isn't easy when you behave well, let alone when you don't."

Change management

Juan Ramon leads change by empowering those who are involved in executing change. Change initiatives may be generated by him or his employees. Juan diligently follows market conditions and trends and listens carefully to his well-trained management team. Typically, a change initiative will be led by a team of six managers who will meet with Juan both officially and socially. Juan evaluates risks and opportunities and, together with his managers, articulates an action plan. This strategic process evolved organically but was formally institutionalized in 2013 when the company moved from a medium-sized company to a large company competing with multinationals. Belleza Express's rapid growth made it imperative to design rigorous processes to align the visions and strategies of all actors. Juan focused on improving internal communication so that results and information are appropriately spread throughout the company. He formed interdisciplinary teams so that changes in the environment, market opportunities, competitive threats, and strengths and weaknesses can be identified and discussed within the context of company priorities, including short- and long-term goals.

Juan also recognized that leadership at all levels of the company were central to his strategic process and implemented an Imperative Leadership Competencies program. There are six competencies:

- Differentiated focus on consumers and clients (Foco diferenciador en el conusmidor y cliente).
- High-impact innovation (Innovar con alto impacto en el negocio).
- Strategic thinking (Pensamiento Estrategico).
- Over-achiever capacity (Capacidad de logro superior).
- Capacity for team work (Capacidad para trabajar en equipo).
- Ability to develop others (Capacidad para descarrollar personas).

These competencies are embedded in the company culture and are criteria used in recruiting and hiring. Workshops are offered at every level and support is available to help employees understand and implement these competencies. Juan believes that innovation and achievement are the product of beliefs and attitudes of individuals, compounded by perceived opportunities for collective and individual growth. The leadership competencies are intended to foster the types of beliefs and attitudes that encourage economic change.

Measuring success and suggestions for leadership training

In addition to reaching financial targets, Juan measures success according to the well-being of his family, the families of employees and business associates, and the welfare of his friends and community. As a community leader he advocates the same philosophies espoused in his company – placing the interests of the group above the interests of individuals, while simultaneously empowering individuals. He hopes that these ideals will help to create stability and prosperity. He states, "seeking the general well-being over the individual, encouraging cooperation and offering the necessary support – this means that you are successful."

Juan evaluates leaders according to their pragmatism and engagement. He is attuned to the use of meetings for grandstanding or selfish interests and considers these actions signs of lack of motivation and commitment. Conversely, he sees individuals who use meetings to advance projects with commitment, clarity, and simplicity as strong, effective leaders.

According to Juan, a strong educational program for leadership would emphasize values and emotional intelligence competencies, and lastly, technical knowledge. While technical knowledge is important, he argues that the essence of a human being, or their ability to relate positively to others, is a highly valuable discipline that leads to results. He believes that those who do not possess these interpersonal skills ought to be encouraged to acquire them and training programs could assess these skills and offer means to fill the gaps.

The future of the business

Juan Ramon strongly believes that family business succession plans should focus on the skills and abilities of next-generation leaders. He expects that his three daughters will participate in shareholders' meetings, but will only serve as board members if they have acquired and demonstrated the necessary skill sets. He is acutely aware of the families who depend on Belleza Express and aspires to ensure that the company is sustainable through generations. He is in the process of identifying strong individuals who may lead the company after he retires and is planning to train and empower managers in the company. He is also planning to create a strong corporate governance structure and nominate highly qualified individuals to assume positions in this governing body.

Family update

While his schedule is very demanding, Juan finds time to be with his family on the farm he purchased after his success in Belleza Express. He, his wife, mother, and family of young daughters may be found there riding horses, swimming in the river, and preparing meals. Juan tries to instill the same values in his daughters that his mother imprinted on him – care, love, and discipline. His philosophy is to "give them little and teach them a lot." He encourages them to appreciate their good fortune and to help those in need. He teaches them about his business and the commitments he has made and, like his mother, he wants his children to study abroad but return to Colombia. He realizes the education and contacts made abroad can bring opportunities to their home country.

Juan's mother, Martha, is now 85 years old and completely lucid. She is his neighbor, having closed her store three years ago and retiring. She claims her family has a "vein of entrepreneurs," a metaphor that may be based in truth. One of Juan's sisters lives in Boston, teaches, owns her own company, and appears on television. Another sister owns a handbag company and exports to the United States, and his brother is part owner of a successful agricultural business. Martha's sacrifices, discipline, courage, and deep love seem to have traversed through her children like veins from a mother's heart, creating prosperity and opportunities for the family and community.

Lessons learned

The purpose of this study was to discover the influence of culture on change management. Juan Ramon's narrative revealed that interconnected family and business systems provided pathways for culture in the form of values, preferences, and beliefs that helped guide strategic changes. An examination of tipping points and self-organization, the components of change processes (Boyatzis, 2006), highlights the role of culture.

Three major tipping points can be seen in Juan Ramon's narrative. The first occurred when Juan's parents were divorced. Juan perceived that his mother self-organized around dreams of sending her children to colleges in the United States and starting her own business in order to finance these ambitions. These activities suggest values and preferences such as family solidarity and support, personal development, and entrepreneurship.

The second tipping point occurred when Juan was offered a promotion to head a Stepa plant in Mexico. He refused the offer in order to help his family through a critical time and, instead, partnered with his cousin in Belleza Express. Juan self-organized by mirroring his mother's values and preferences – family solidarity and support, and entrepreneurship.

The third tipping point occurred when Juan assessed the risk posed by Belleza Express's dependence on imported products. Juan acquired a company in order to own their own brand and manufacture products domestically. While expanding his company, Juan created programs for his employees to attend educational events, offered complete health and wellness programs, and provided credit for necessities such as housing. His self-organizing principles again reflected his mother's preference for entrepreneurship and values such as personal development through education, and family support and solidarity. Juan also adopted governing principles reiterating his mother's values. His conviction that the needs of the group surpass individual needs is reminiscent of his mother's sacrifices for her children. Additionally, two Imperative Leadership Competencies – capacity for teamwork and ability to develop others – exemplify values similar to family solidarity and support.

Values, preferences, and beliefs, representatives of culture, were passed through a complex interconnected system. They moved vertically from mother to son, laterally from son to organization (in the form of human resource policies), and, finally, vertically from the human resource hierarchy to employees. They served as principles for self-organizing after tipping points, or discontinuous or non-linear events, that triggered change (Boyatzis, 2006).

Conclusion

This case study suggests the important role of leadership and the cultural attitudes and beliefs that drive corporate leaders through change processes. Perceptions of possibilities for change following tipping points and values asserted throughout change processes emanated from the highest hierarchical levels and reflected cultural beliefs and attitudes carried from the leader's family. The leader's dreams of building a business while valuing the collective efforts of individuals who function within a multi-level complex system resulted in the growth and success of Belleza Express.

References

Acosta, C. (2002). Cuatro Preguntas para Iniciarse en Cambio Organizacional. *Revista Colombiana de Psicología, 11*, 9–24.

Boyatzis, R. E. (2006). An overview of intentional change from a complexity perspective. *Journal of Management Development, 25*(7), 607–623.

López-Duque, E., Lanzas-Duque, A. M. and Lanzas-Duque, V. E. (2007). Administración de Cambio en las Organizaciones. *Scientia et Technica, 13*(37), 301–303.

Malaver, F. and Vargas, M. (2004). El Comportamiento Innovador en la Industria Colombiana: Una Exploración de sus Recientes Cambios. *Cuadernos de Administración, 17*(279), 33–61.

Moore, T. J. and Asay, S. M. (2013). *Family resource management.* Thousand Oaks, CA: Sage Publications.

Suárez-Restrepo, N. del C. and Restrepo-Ramírez, D. (2005). Teoría y Práctica del Desarrollo Familiar en Colombia. *Revista Latinoamericana de Ciencias Sociales, Niñez y Juventud, 3*(1), 1–28.

Viveros, E. (2007). Aproximación al Concepto de Familia en Desarrollo Familiar. *Revista Fundación Universitaria Luis Amigó, 10*(15), 25–32.

Wentworth, W. M. (1980). *Context and understanding: An inquiry into socialization theory.* New York: Elsevier.

4 The role of change management in Cypriot organizations

Marcos Komodromos

Cyprus has been undergoing an economic crisis in recent years. The financial crises in Europe and the United States (US), together with the global processes of social and economic change, have contributed to a large degree to the economic and political situation in Cyprus. The financial watershed in Cyprus involved the exposure of Cypriot banks to overleveraged local property companies, together with the Greek government debt crisis, the downgrading of the Cypriot government's bond credit rating to junk status by international credit agencies (Moody's and Standard and Poor's), and the weakness of the government to restructure the troubled Cypriot financial sector. The ramification is that Cyprus was unable to raise liquidity from the markets to support its financial sector, and requested a bailout from the European Union (Bank of Cyprus, 2013).

More specifically, on March 25, 2013, a EUR 10 billion international bailout by the Eurogroup was announced in return for Cyprus agreeing to close the country's second largest bank, the Cyprus Popular Bank (Laiki), in addition to imposing a one-time bank deposit levy on all uninsured deposits, and converting 47.5 percent of deposits exceeding EUR 100,000 in Bank of Cyprus to equity in order to recapitalize the bank. To survive in the competitive world like today, Cypriot organizations must be aware of the external demands of the environment, and organizational change is one of the strategies to adjust to the environment.

Due to globalization and the increased international trade between Cyprus and other countries, managers have had an increasing need to influence people from different cultures and demonstrate cross-cultural sensitivity to be effective (Javidan, Dorfman, Sully de Luque and House, 2006). That is one of the reasons that managers need to have a global mindset and develop global leadership capabilities, which can be adapted to strategic organizational changes, to be able to understand how people from different cultures view and interpret their actions. It is believed that different cultures give birth to diverse management practices and to different perceptions regarding the contributors and inhibitors of outstanding leadership (Kabasakal, Dastmalchian, Karacay and Bayraktar, 2012).

Following, an organization's structure influences the communication patterns within it. In the media organization under study, the communication process was dominated by downward communication, the transmission of information from higher to lower levels. Canary (2011) identified five general purposes of downward communication, which helped the organization until recently to operate successfully: implementation of goals, strategies, and objectives; job instructions and rationale; procedures and practices; performance feedback; and socialization. The downward flow of communication provided a channel for general management to provide directions, instructions, and information to organizational members. In addition, downward communication consisted of policies, rules, and procedures that flow from top administration to lower levels. Due to organizational changes though, that included strategic, operational, and technological changes, the organization was forced to also change the flow of communication and adopt face-to-face communication that increased cooperation and equity across situations, and thus be more effective in promoting the cooperative efficient outcome inside the organization (Frohlich and Oppenheimer, 1998).

Organizations need strategic change to expand and successfully compete in a dynamic market (Franken, Edwards and Lambert, 2009). This is what we will examine in this case study for a media organization in Cyprus undergoing a strategic change.

Not all changes are successful. In fact, almost 70 percent of the planned strategic change programs in organizations do not accomplish their desired objectives (Goksoy, Ozsoy and Vayvay, 2012). Negative employee reactions to organizational strategic imperatives have the potential for highly negative impact, significantly interfering with the intended gains of change (Fugate, Prussia and Kinicki, 2010). As such, it is essential that organizations implementing change better understand potentially negative reactions by employees to the process in the interests of effectively managing the outcomes.

Managerial efforts for strategic change and restructuring in organizations over the past few years have consistently failed in the absence of support from non-managerial employees and their resistance towards the strategic change itself (Bouckenooghe, 2010; Sitlington and Marshall, 2011). Employee dedication, sincerity, and loyalty with regard to the management of change largely determine its success or failure (Battilana and Casciaro, 2012). Leadership is generally associated with strategic organizational changes and renewal. In the case of the media organization under study, leadership has a functional approach, where managers can get critical system functions accomplished, which focuses on the systems rather than the personal qualities of those who lead. This influencing behavior is crucial in leading subordinate employees in the right direction in times of change, and reduces resistance to change. Employee resistance to strategic change leads to increased absenteeism, employee turnover, lackluster performance, feelings of dissatisfaction, and lower morale – all of which can create feelings of mistrust in employees towards management.

A key task of the managers (leaders) in the media organization undergoing change was practical, to create group identification, which was likely to increase productivity and effective performance. Management also recognized publicity and advertised the strength of their members and followers, targeting the setting of group norms, and created a degree of cohesiveness. There were many variables that seem to have influenced the decision of change, such as the content of change, the process of change, the context of the organization, and the people in the organization who were involved with the change. Thus, to facilitate the process of change, leaders in the media organization focused on finding the focal issue and choosing participants (employees) carefully and utilizing their energy and enthusiasm by creating a transitional space. Considering that the important variable in terms of the success of change is people, leaders tried to get the support of the people in every department of the media organization and ready them for organizational change, also identifying the variables that might increase people's commitment to change.

Management's role in the management of executing change is a critical issue for successful outcomes of strategic initiatives (Buss and Kuyvenhofen, 2011). Strategies for the management of change include communication to share information with employees while addressing their concerns to the management, and providing additional training when needed (Rouleau and Balogun, 2011; Self and Schraeder, 2009). Recent research investigated the role of middle management in implementing strategic change to highlight principles that can improve successful strategic implementation (Balogun, 2008; Buss and Kuyvenhofen, 2011). Management of the day-to-day functions of middle management is of great importance, and that through their behaviors and thoughts managers can contribute to strategy.

Among the many concerns organizations have, an important focus is employee perception of organizational justice given the role it plays in attitudes and behaviors of employees. Considerable research on organizational justice has evidenced that fairness perceptions are linked to outcomes that are important both to the employees and their employing organization; these include trust, job satisfaction, cooperative work behaviors, and organizational commitment (Colquitt and Rodell, 2011). The purpose of this case study is to examine how an organizational justice framework can be used to explore employees' perceptions of trust, fairness, and the management of change during a period of strategic changes for a media organization in Cyprus, and the role of leadership in these changes.

The management of strategic change in organizations

Scholars have argued that organizational change is necessary for organizations to survive and prosper (Carter, Armenakis, Feild and Mossholder, 2012). Researchers support that in cases where change is perceived as threatening, employee resistance may increase, and organizations need management to implement successfully the change procedure (Austin, 2009). Seminal scholars emphasized the important role that human resource (HR) practices can play in the management of change, to maintain trust (Saunders and Thornhill, 2004).

Globalization and economic instability have prompted an increase in organizational changes related to downsizing and restructuring as a means of improving financial performance and competitiveness (Fugate *et al.*, 2010). In organizational change research, there have been studies focusing on how to prevent, reduce, or overcome resistance to change, and how to prepare the organization for managing strategic change (Rouleau and Balogun, 2011; Self and Schraeder, 2009; Sonenshein, 2009). Researchers agree that managers' inability to fully understand what is necessary to guide their organizations through successful change can be a reason for failure (Self and Schraeder, 2009). Proper planning and management of change can reduce the likelihood of failure and promote change effectiveness, and increased employee morale (Self and Schraeder, 2009).

Research has shown that employees' behaviors in support of the proposed change are positively influenced by their commitment to change; however, organizations often have difficulty in successfully motivating the needed levels of employee commitment to change (Rouleau and Balogun, 2011). The management of strategic change can invariably create uncertainty and where such change involves people, this often proves problematic (Austin, 2009; Croonen, 2010). Where change is perceived as threatening, it is likely to meet with resistance, and thus requires careful implementation to overcome fears (Austin, 2009). Employees' feelings of threat are ameliorated when trusting relationships exist throughout the organization (Farndale, Hope-Hailey and Kelliher, 2010). HR practices can therefore be crucial in the management of change, whether it is incremental or continuous through the creation and maintenance of trust (Saunders and Thornhill, 2004). Therefore, making trust an integral aspect of employee–organization relationships can facilitate change sustainability (Kim, Hornung and Rousseau, 2011).

Researching employees' perceptions of trust, fairness, and the management of change using an organizational justice framework can have significant implications for HR management and leadership during a time of strategic change (Fuchs, 2011). The purpose of this qualitative study was to examine how an organizational justice framework can be used to explore employees' perceptions of trust, fairness, and the management of change during a period of strategic change in a privately owned media organization based in Cyprus. The aim was to increase knowledge regarding how an organizational justice framework could address the need raised by justice scholars (e.g., Colquitt and Greenberg, 2003; Mayer, Nishii, Schneider and Goldstein, 2007) for new, conceptually derived accounts of non-managerial employees' perspectives on organizational justice (Colquitt and Rodell, 2011; Heslin and VandeWalle, 2009) during periods of organizational change (Fugate *et al.*, 2010).

Results of the study

To acknowledge relevant perceptions of trust, fairness, and the management of change during organizational change in a media organization in Cyprus using an organizational justice framework, unique questions were provided in research results to indicate supporting themes that emerged from participant interview sessions. The results, findings, and summaries of participant responses described employees' perceptions of trust, fairness, and the management of change during a period of strategic change in a privately owned media organization based in Cyprus, using an organizational justice framework. This research focused on the following central research question:

Q1: How can an organizational justice framework be used to explore employees' percept-ions of trust, fairness, and the management of change within the context of strategic change?

The sub-questions derived from the central question are:

Q2: How can an organizational justice framework be used to explore employees' perceptions of trust within the context of strategic change?

Q3: How can an organizational justice framework be used to explore employees' perceptions of fairness within the context of strategic change?

Q4: How can an organizational justice framework be used to explore employees' perceptions of the management of change within the context of strategic change?

Employees believed that their attitude towards their organization had been affected, as related to trust, since the enactment of the strategic changes taking place in the media organization. Since the enactment of the strategic change the organization did not communicate with honesty with their employees, and thus trust eroded, leading to doubt and confusion internally. Specifically, one of the participants noted:

> In times of change, management needs to understand how and what it takes to create the vital elements of trust between managers and employees. I still do not understand why our management didn't establish and maintain the integrity by keeping their promises and telling us the truth and what's really going to happen. I do not trust the organization and the management anymore; they do not communicate their opinions and ideas to us, and my attitude has changed too towards the organization in a negative way. I'm not willing to work with passion as before. Management tells us half-truths, or nothing. How are we supposed to trust them?

Other participants mentioned the significance of information sharing in the workplace for employees to continue having trust in management, since communication supports the information and willingness to interact with employees during times of uncertainty and ambiguity. "Trust affects the quality of relationships and this is what we are experiencing now, since the attitudes of a lot of our peers have changed negatively towards management, and in some situations towards their colleagues," one of the employees said.

Study results reveal that some of the employees believed that their attitude towards their organization had been affected, in relation to the interactions they have with their manager, since the enactment of the strategic changes in the media organization. In addition, participants quoted commitment as one of the most important factors related to the success of strategic changes. Some participants believed that when employees feel committed in their workplace this helps in the development of a very good environment, especially in the context of change. One mentioned: "If I felt more committed I wouldn't want to leave the organization because of the changes taking place. Because I don't feel committed I'm more stressed and I don't want to go to work in the morning."

Related to organizational changes, tasks, and responsibilities, the following comments were noted:

> This change brought a lot of changes to my current job, like heavier workload and increased role ambiguity, because now I do everything; one day my manager may tell me to go to see some clients, and the other day I might be asked to do something totally different. This is a reason to be less committed, and less dedicated to my job.

> After change, it is more difficult for me to work in teams as I effectively used to do before. My work position requires teamwork because we have a wide range of responsibilities, such as cross-functional teams or self-managing teams, and the goal is to improve the production process. Teamwork was part of the culture of this organization because in my department we had some collective tasks where the team members were mutually regulating the execution of these collective tasks, which now I'm not willing to do. I do not blame my colleagues, I blame the management of my organization, but even if I don't want to behave like this, my attitude changed towards my peers too.

Other participants mentioned that their attitudes towards their peers have changed, as related to trust, and that the need for collaborative relationships in times of change could benefit the organization. One of the participants said: "I believe that my attitude towards my colleagues didn't change, and I always advise my peers that passive behaviors and neglectful activities will not help our organization to be successful in this change initiative, but will drive the organization to failure." Another participant noted:

> When employees trust their managers they will be very supportive of the organization during change, even willing to work for more hours without expecting more money. My attitude towards the organization changed because I don't trust the organization as before, and employees' relationships with the organization changed because there is limited trust. Management must sit down and examine why trust failed, which leads to negative organizational relationships.

A participant from the technical department stated:

> Senior management must recognize the actions that cause trust to fail between managers and employees. When trust erodes, employees feel insecure, they are less productive and committed, and organizational relationships with managers and employees erode

too. My trust towards the organization failed because management refused any kind of specific information and do not provide us with support and guidance when we needed it.

All participants believed that their attitude towards their organization had been affected since the enactment of the strategic changes in the media organization, quoting commitment as one of the most important factors related to the success of strategic changes. Some participants believed that when employees feel committed in their workplace this helps in the development of a very good environment, especially in the context of change. Specifically, a participant from the sales department stated:

I would be more committed to the organization if management showed more willingness to cooperate with us. We have no leaders in this organization, because if we had leaders, they would understand and promote commitment, which is an essential element for the effective implementation of the strategic change initiative. I also experienced some unfair situations that have to do with colleagues being promoted (during this time of changes) to positions that had nothing to do with their previous responsibilities, and this makes me less committed to the organization.

"Managing change means managing people's fear" – this was a statement from a participant who supported that change is natural and good, but employees' reactions to change can be unpredictable and irrational sometimes, when management is not able to effectively communicate this change to them.

Another participant commented:

At the beginning, I was positive to change, although I did not have any official communication from the management. Later, management started changing our roles and areas of responsibilities without asking us or at least having a short discussion before assigning us the new roles. I experienced anxiety, loss of control, and confusion. I was expecting to have clear information, but it was just a wish that was never implemented. Now, I'm very pessimistic about this change and my commitment to the organization is less. I don't feel positive about the change.

Most of the participants believed that the secret to successfully managing strategic changes, from the perspective of the employees, is definition and understanding. "Resistance to change comes most of the times from a fear of the unknown or an expectation of loss, and the front-end of an individual's resistance to change is as how employees they perceive the change in this organization," a participant from the media department elaborated.

Understanding is a two-way communication, and employees must understand what is changing and why. Management also needs to understand their reluctance, and communicate to them what is also not changing. One participant believed that:

In times of changes within the organization it is expected that employees' attitudes will be negatively changed if the organization keeps a distance from them and does not consider them in their decisions. … During this change I am more attentive to how I am treated by my manager, especially in regards to fairness.

On the other hand, another participant suggested that:

> After change, it is more difficult for me to work in teams as I effectively used to do before. My work position requires teamwork because we have a wide range of responsibilities, such as cross-functional teams or self-managing teams, and the goal is to improve the production process. Teamwork was part of the culture of this organization because in my department we had some collective tasks where the team members were mutually regulating the execution of these collective tasks, which now I'm not willing to do. I do not blame my colleagues, I blame the management of my organization, but even if I don't want to behave like this, my attitude changed towards my peers too.

Participant responses to one interview question – since the enactment of the strategic changes how do you perceive that your attitude towards your peers has been affected? – provided insights into three emergent themes, covering teamwork, trust, and communication. One participant said:

> Currently, I can't say that my attitude towards my peers has been affected nor it remained the same. Some years ago, we used to be a high-performance organization having a lot of power and influence in the media industry. This was because we were always working in teams, having great support from our managers, because our work requires a broader scope of knowledge, expertise, and judgment. What I can say is that the advantage of teamwork is significant in the increase in productivity, which requires creative resolution of different tasks, and I'm willing to work in teams like before with my colleagues. In times of change, teamwork must create an environment that can facilitate knowledge and information exchange inside our organization, something that is not implemented now.

Another participant stated:

> My attitudes have changed negatively towards my peers because now no one takes responsibilities, and many experience low levels of job satisfaction. Employees do not have direct participation in the organizational changes, and they are not willing to work in teams, or if they are obliged to get involved in teamwork, they are not productive.

On the other hand, a participant from the sales department commented:

> I understand that effective changes can only be achieved with trust among employees who are the driving forces that will facilitate and sustain effective change in an organization. My attitude towards my peers has not been affected to a large degree, but I feel that I don't trust them as before. The reason is that I see some behaviors inside the organization by my peers that prove that most employees look at how to save themselves, and are not willing to cooperate with their colleagues. I don't blame them, but how can my behavior not change when I see that their attitude towards me has changed, because of the changes that are taking place in the organization?

One participant noted:

> My attitude towards my peers, since the enactment of the MASC [management's agenda for strategic change], has changed because I feel insecure and this change is a threat, and

trust towards my peers has been reduced. I do not trust my peers as before because this change involves restructuring, job cuts, salary changes, and I see that my colleagues' attitudes changed too towards other colleagues. Before change, we used to be like a family, now we are trying to survive on top of others.

Most of the participants believed that since the enactment of the strategic changes in their organization, their attitudes towards their peers have changed, as related to the communication between them. "Since the enactment of the strategic change in the workplace a lot of employees acquired new attitudes and behaviors towards managers, and communication has been decreased," one of the participants stated. Another asserted:

> I think that employees who had positive attitudes before the enactment of any organizational change, and who adopt negative attitudes after change are not doing anything particularly wrong. I've noticed a lot of negative attitudes from our peers after change, but what I understand is that employees have this cynical and negative feeling because of the insecurity they feel in the workplace and because of the fact that the organization does not provide to employees a consistent communication. My attitude has changed to a relatively small degree towards my peers, but still we do not communicate on a regular basis as before the enactment of the change. I feel that we keep a distance between us, there is a lot of stress and in some situations some of my colleagues ignore me when I ask for their help in my work.

One participant noted:

> My attitude changed towards my peers because there is no communication between my peers in my department. My colleagues adopted new attitudes and they hold a distance between each other; I tried at the beginning to be friendly with them and show them that we can work through this change together as a team, as we were acting before the change, but it seems that that their attitude will not change if they do not feel secure about their job.

Following, participants were also asked to identify if they believe they have been treated with dignity and respect during the period of strategic change in the organization, and whether they feel that some of their peers have benefited more from the strategic change than they have. Most of the participants believed that when employees are treated in a way that they can express their views and feelings during organizational change, this might lead to organizational support and trustworthy behavior on the part of employees towards managers. One participant believed that employees' perceptions and feelings must be seriously considered by management, especially in times of change, and employees must be asked by management about these since they can solve any kind of disputes or conflicts within the organization. Specifically, one participant asserted:

> No one from the management asked us if we consider right or wrong the organization's decision, or even to listen to our suggestions. We weren't able to express our feelings regarding the organization's policies during this change. As a result, our reactions towards the organization were negative since any decisions were taken directly by the organization without our input, even to be able to express our opinions or ideas for this change. This is why a lot of employees are not willing now to offer support to the

organization in their try for change. I know employees who refuse to cooperate even with their colleagues.

Another participant, from the media department, added that transparency of the processes by which decisions are made can lead to fair outcomes for employees, when their suggestions are heard by the management, and this can lead to organizational support for organizational change. "If management have asked for our opinion during change then this change could have been turned to be successful in the long term, but I personally do not think that the change outcomes will be positive," a participant noted.

Another participant suggested:

Employees' views and feelings during MASC have a direct impact on organizational support from the employees towards the organization. The use of such fair procedures helps employees to have a say in the decision process in the workplace, and employees must have a voice to express their feelings in times of change. This promotes fairness in the workplace where employees express their perceptions of fairness regarding outcomes, and by this employees have more input in the appraisal process. Also, employees could support the organization when the management hears their "voice" and we could be more positive to this change and overall have positive impact on outcomes.

One participant asserted:

In times of change people get frustrated and organizations must have charismatic leaders. This currently does not happen in our organization, and it seems that management failed to keep together and united their employees. Management didn't ask about our views during change, they didn't even bother to communicate to us the reasons for the changes in a way that we can understand the context, the purpose, and the need. Now, they expect from us to support the organization in their effort for change, tell me how this is possible? And how fair does it sound to an employee who sacrificed 11 years of his life in this organization? They nearly destroyed our credibility towards the organization because they provide us incorrect and insufficient information, and the most important, they don't listen. And if they listen, answers are given too quickly, and rumor is already in action, which leads us not to trust them anymore.

Furthermore, most of the participants believed that when employees are treated in a way that they can express their views and feelings during organizational change, this might be a reason to positively change their behavior and adapt more easily to change. One participant said:

If management asked for our views and feelings, let's say on a weekly basis, then they wouldn't have a hard time dealing with change. Employees' behaviors would be more easily adapted to these difficult circumstances and we, as employees, could be more positive to these changes.

Another participant suggested:

The organization itself created multiple barriers between managers and employees, and now there is no collaboration and team work to the degree it had to be inside the organization and this makes it more complex for the management to achieve their goals. Employee behaviors changed negatively towards management and they rarely maintain interpersonal relationships to the level that is required to ensure success in the change initiative. Management should have been more close with employees and use us (as employees) to help them achieve the planned change, by changing the way we think, the way we react, and generally the way we behave in a positive way.

In addition, another participant stated:

Managers should hold individual meetings with each single employee from their department and ask them to express their views, because this one-on-one interaction helps employees to understand better the change strategy and adapt their behavior to this change, helping the organization to succeed.

Finally, some employees could express their opinions to the management during strategic changes. Some participants considered these actions as fair on behalf of management and an opportunity for employees to be heard and have their views considered. Following, one participant stated:

As understanding and acceptance are important determinants of an employee's behavior in times of change, by expressing our views it helped us increase our support towards the organization and our colleagues. We are willing to work more effectively in teamwork and help our organization implement this change successfully.

Another participant suggested: "The importance of feedback from employees to management, and communication between employees during change in the workplace, could help our organization to successfully implement this change."

Another participant asserted:

For the past nine months the organization stopped giving us any kind of information or asking for our opinion, and we were not able to express our feelings about the changes taking place. Here we are talking about strategic changes, structural changes, reductions in our salaries by 25 percent to 30 percent from one day to another, or even changing our tasks and responsibilities because they fired employees and we need to fill those positions too, with a lower salary. This has a negative impact on our behavior within the workplace, like lower productivity and performance (poor services), bad rumors, and lower quality of services in our work. A large number of dissatisfied employees are under physical disturbance such as tension, depression, and sleeplessness. Therefore, it is necessary for the organization to place the fairness of those actions in high consideration and give us more freedom of expression of our views and thoughts.

Conclusion

The present study examined employees' perceptions of trust, fairness, and the management of change using an organizational justice framework in a media organization in Cyprus undergoing strategic change. This is an area that has not been directly studied in the media organization field; therefore, the data from this research study can help to enhance understanding in this area and provide useful information for media organizations in the future. Some scholars support that organizational justice can act as an indicator for the effective implementation of a change initiative, be used as a contingency framework for understanding employees' perceptions of trust, fairness, and the management of change during strategic change, and enable effective action in the organizational environment (Cropanzano, Bowen and Gilliland, 2007; Folger and Skarlicki, 2001; Williamson and Williams, 2011).

Since organizational justice has been firmly linked with trust, fairness, commitment, citizenship behavior, customer satisfaction, and conflict resolution (Cropanzano et al., 2007), this study guides organizations in all aspects when implementing strategic change in such a way that the change implementation process never results in a failure. It also ensures that there are no adverse effects felt by the employees, customers, or even stakeholders who may be associated with it. Thus, this research expands the understanding of employees' perceptions of trust, fairness, and the management of change using an organizational justice framework for a media organization in Cyprus undergoing strategic change.

Globalization and competitive market environments force organizations to improve themselves every day. Therefore, organizations that are undergoing strategic change need to incorporate strategies and procedures that will facilitate the process. Since strategic change has become inevitable for organizations, this study will enhance understanding of how change in organizations can be successfully implemented, and how to forecast employee reactions so as to bring about the desired change (Balogun, 2008; Fugate et al., 2010).

Key findings from this study, aligning with relevant research, suggest that organizational justice can: act as an indicator for the effective implementation of a change initiative (Colquitt, Greenberg and Zapata-Phelan, 2005; Fuchs, 2011; Thornhill and Saunders, 2003); be used as a contingency framework for understanding employees' perceptions of trust, fairness (Bidarian and Jafari, 2012; Jones and Skarlicki, 2012), and the management of change during strategic changes (Austin, 2009; Self and Schraeder, 2009); and enable effective action in the organizational environment (Ali, 2010; Ambrose and Schminke, 2003). Other important findings suggest that non-managerial employees build their judgments of organizations on elements of fairness that can be observed (e.g., distributive, procedural, and interactional) (Croonen, 2010; Saunders and Thornhill, 2003, 2006), and all three organizational justice constructs are identified as moderators of employees' perceptions of fairness related to organizational change (Carter et al., 2012). Further findings indicate that organizations that are undergoing strategic change need to incorporate strategies and procedures that will successfully facilitate the change process (Jones and Skarlicki, 2012).

Research results further suggest that when management understands how the change in organizations can be successfully implemented, this will help them to forecast employee reactions and behaviors so as to bring about the desired change. Findings indicate that justice perceptions by non-managerial employees towards management in the specific organization under study are influenced by the development of close interpersonal relationships that are based on exchanges perceived as fair (O'Neill, Lewis and Carswell, 2011; Saunders and Thornhill, 2003).

Finally, findings will contribute to an enriched understanding of employees' perceptions of trust, fairness, and the management of change using an organizational justice framework within a media organization in Cyprus, enhance better understanding, and provide useful information to guide future research for such organizations. Media organizations may benefit from the study by understanding how employee perceptions of trust, fairness, and the management of change can facilitate change sustainability in the future.

References

Ali, H. (2010). A study of relationship between organizational justice and job satisfaction. *International Journal of Business and Management, 5*(12), 102–109.

Ambrose, M. and Schminke, M. (2003). Organization structure as a moderator of the relationship between procedural justice, interactional justice, perceived organizational support, and supervisory trust. *Journal of Applied Psychology, 88*(2), 295–305.

Austin, J. (2009). Initiating controversial strategy change in organization. *OD Practitioner, 41*(3), 24–29.

Balogun, J. (2008). Managing change: Steering a course between intended strategies and unanticipated outcomes. *Long Range Planning, 39*(1), 29–49.

Bank of Cyprus. (2013). *Annual financial report*. Retrieved from www.stockwatch.com.cy/media/fstatements_pdf/Annual_Financial_Report_ENG_not_signed.pdf (last accessed 12 December 2016).

Battilana, J. and Casciaro, T. (2012). Change agents, networks, and institutions: A contingency theory of organizational change. *The Academy of Management Journal, 55*(2), 381–398.

Bidarian, S. and Jafari, P. (2012). The relationship between organizational justice and trust. *Social and Behavioral Sciences, 47*, 1622–1626. doi:10.1016/j.sbspro.2012.06.873

Bouckenooghe, D. (2010). Positioning change recipients' attitudes toward change in the organizational change literature. *Journal of Applied Behavioral Science, 46*, 500–531.

Buss, C. and Kuyvenhofen, R. (2011). Perceptions of European middle managers of their role in strategic change. *Global Journal of Business Research, 5*(5), 109–119.

Canary, H. (2011). *Communication and organizational knowledge: Contemporary issues for theory and practice.* Florence, KY: Taylor & Francis.

Carter, M., Armenakis, A., Feild, H. and Mossholder, K. (2012). Transformational leadership, relationship quality, and employee performance during continuous incremental organizational change. *Journal of Organizational Behavior, 1*, 1–17.

Colquitt, J. A. and Greenberg, J. (2003). Organizational justice: A fair assessment of the state of the literature. In J. Greenberg (ed.), *Organizational behavior: The state of the science* (pp. 165–210). Mahwah, NJ: Lawrence Erlbaum Associates.

Colquitt, J. A., Greenberg, J. and Zapata-Phelan, C. P. (2005). What is organizational justice? A historical overview. In J. Greenberg and J. A. Colquitt (eds), *The handbook of organizational justice* (pp. 3–56). Mahwah, NJ: Lawrence Erlbaum Associates.

Colquitt, J. A. and Rodell, J. B. (2011). Justice, trust, and trustworthiness: A longitudinal analysis integrating three theoretical perspectives. *Academy of Management Journal, 54*(6), 1183–1206.

Croonen, E. (2010). Trust and fairness during strategic change processes in franchise systems. *Journal of Business Ethics, 95*(2), 191–209.

Cropanzano, R., Bowen, D. E. and Gilliland, S. W. (2007). The management of organizational justice. *Academy of Management Perspectives, 21*(4), 34–48.

Farndale, E., Hope-Hailey, V. and Kelliher, C. (2010). High commitment performance management: The roles of justice and trust. *Personnel Review, 40*(1), 5–23.

Folger, R. and Skarlicki, D. P. (2001). Fairness as a dependent variable: Why tough times can lead to bad management. In R. Cropanzano (ed.), *Justice in the workplace: From theory to practice* (Applied Psychology Series, vol. 2, pp. 97–118). Mahwah, NJ: Lawrence Erlbaum Associates.

Franken, A., Edwards, C. and Lambert, R. (2009). Executing strategic change: Understanding the critical management elements that lead to success. *California Management Review, 51*(3), 49–73.

Frohlich, N. and Oppenheimer, J. (1998). Some consequences of e-mail vs. face-to-face communication in an experiment. *Journal of Economic Behavior and Organization, 35*(3), 389–403.

Fuchs, S. (2011). The impact of manager and top management identification on the relationship between perceived organizational justice and change-oriented behavior. *Leadership and Organization Development Journal, 32*(6), 565–583.

Fugate, M., Prussia, G. and Kinicki, A. (2010). Managing employee withdrawal during organizational change: The role of threat appraisal. *Journal of Management, 2*(1), 1–25.

Goksoy, A., Ozsoy, B. and Vayvay, O. (2012). Business process reengineering: Strategic tool for managing organizational change an application in a multinational company. *International Journal of Business and Management*, 7(2), 89–111.

Heslin, P. and Vande Walle, D. (2009). Procedural justice: The role of a manager's implicit person theory. *Journal of Management*, 2(1), 2–25.

Javidan, M., Dorfman, P. W., Sully de Luque, M. and House, R. J. (2006). In the eye of the beholder: Cross cultural lessons in leadership from Project GLOBE. *Academy of Management Perspective*, 20(1), 67–91.

Jones, D. A. and Skarlicki, D. P. (2012). How perceptions of fairness can change: A dynamic model of organizational justice. *Organizational Psychology Review*, 19, 1–23.

Kabasakal, H., Dastmalchian, A., Karacay, G. and Bayraktar, S. (2012). Leadership and culture in the MENA region: An analysis of the GLOBE project. *Journal of World Business*, 47, 519–529.

Kim, T., Hornung, S. and Rousseau, D. (2011). Change-supportive employee behavior: Antecedents and the moderating role of time. *Journal of Management*, 37(6), 1664–1693.

Mayer, D., Nishii, L., Schneider, B. and Goldstein, H. (2007). The precursors and products of justice climates: Group leader antecedents and employee attitudinal consequences. *Personnel Psychology*, 60(4), 929–963.

O'Neill, T. A., Lewis, R. J. and Carswell, J. J. (2011). Employee personality, justice perceptions, and the prediction of workplace deviance. *Personality and Individual Differences*, 51, 595–600. doi:10.1016/j.paid.2011.05.025

Rouleau, L. and Balogun, J. (2011). Middle managers, strategic sensemaking, and discursive competence. *Journal of Management Studies*, 48(5), 953–983.

Saunders, M. and Thornhill, A. (2003). Organizational justice, trust and the management of change: An exploration. *Personnel Review*, 32(3), 360–375.

Saunders, M. and Thornhill, A. (2004). Trust and mistrust in organizations: An exploration using an organizational justice framework. *European Journal of Work and Organizational Psychology*, 13(4), 493–515.

Saunders, M. and Thornhill, A. (2006). Forced employment contract change and the psychological contract. *Employee Relations*, 28(5), 449–467.

Self, D. and Schraeder, M. (2009). Enhancing the success of organizational change: Matching readiness strategies with sources of resistance. *Leadership and Organization Development Journal*, 30(2), 167–182.

Sitlington, H. and Marshall, V. (2011). Do downsizing decisions affect organisational knowledge and performance? *Management Decision*, 49(1), 116–129.

Sonenshein, S. (2009). Emergence of ethical issues during strategic change implementation. *Organization Science*, 20(1), 223–239.

Thornhill, A. and Saunders, M. (2003). Exploring employees' reactions to strategic change over time: The utilization of an organizational justice perspective. *Irish Journal of Management*, 24(1), 66–86. Retrieved from Business Source Complete database.

Williamson, K. and Williams, K. J. (2011). Organisational justice, trust and perceptions of fairness in the implementation of agenda for change. *Radiography*, 17(1), 61–66.

5 Young, Estonian and female

A leader of the new generation

Mari Kooskora and Marta Piigli

This is a case study of a young Estonian female leader; we can call her Ms. Mirtel Piko, who has been able to build up a successful career in a big international corporation. Currently, she holds the position of CEO in the Baltic Business Unit operating in three countries. She also belongs to the corporation's management board, where she works side by side with managers from 10 countries. Her team consists of 80 members and the company employs more than 2,000 people.

Being a young, female Estonian in a high leadership position is not very common (yet) in Estonia; however, especially during recent years, things seem to have started to change and therefore we can see her as a good example of a leader of the new generation.

Leadership is said to be one of the most observed and least understood phenomenon on Earth (Burns, 1978), having presented a major challenge to researchers and generating as many definitions as there are authors who have covered the subject (e.g., Nirenberg, 2001). An even greater phenomenon seems to be female leadership (Eagly and Carli, 2003). Making up half of the work force and more than half of university graduates both in the European Union (EU) and the United States of America (US) there are many women in the lower level of organizations. The higher the level, the smaller the percentage of women to be found, eventually making up only 3 percent at the executive level (European Commission, 2013a). Although numerous studies have proven women's performance levels to be at least the same if not better than their male counterparts (Oakley, 2000; Eagly and Carli, 2003; Eagly, 2007; Carter and Wagner, 2011; Kooskora and Piigli, 2014; Zenger and Folkman, 2012), women's advancement is still lagging behind.

The recent EU-wide figure of women on boards is a mere 16.6 percent with an annual increase rate of 1.7 percentage points (see European Commission, 2013a). Moreover, we can see significant differences among different countries within the EU; as an example we can take two neighboring countries with both language and cultural proximity: Finland and Estonia. From the European Commission Report it can be read that Finland is leading the way with more than 29.1 percent of women on boards; yet the neighboring country, Estonia, with only 8.1 percent, is far lower than the EU average of 16.6 percent (European Commission, 2013b). As a comparison we can note that from outside the EU Iceland has 48.9 percent and Norway 41.9 percent women on the boards of large listed companies (European Commission, 2013a).

Surprisingly, the proportion of women on boards in Estonia has been falling progressively from 14.7 percent in 2003, whereas in Finland it has been rising steadily from just under 11 percent in 2003. However, especially during the most recent years, after the financial and economic crisis, the number of female leaders in Estonia seems to have increased at least in international companies and the number of women on corporate boards is increasing, albeit very slowly.

Many arguments about possible obstacles to women's advancement have been analyzed and much research has been conducted on the subject of female leadership, but women's advancement to higher positions is still moving upwards in a slow-mode. Research on the topic of female managers has addressed different obstacles, for example, the glass ceiling or the labyrinth metaphor (Bass, 1996, 1999; Carli and Eagly, 2001; Eagly and Carli, 2007; Pesonen, Tienari and Vanhala, 2009), the presence of a pay gap (Perry and Gundersen, 2011), or focusing on the comparison of leadership style differences of male and female leaders (Vinnicombe and Singh, 2002; Manning, 2002; Eagly, Johannesen-Schmidt and Van Engen, 2003; Prime, Carter and Welbourne, 2009; López-Zafra, Garcia-Retamero and Berrios Martos, 2012; Katila and Eriksson, 2013).

Yammarino and Atwater (1997) found a positive relationship between transformational leadership and female leaders' effectiveness, and Eagly *et al.* (2003) suggested that women are more transformational than men, as the characteristics of a transformational leadership style are related to feminine gender characteristics. Empirical evidence (Fernández Berrocal, Salovey, Vera, Extremera and Ramos, 2005; Palmer, Gignac, Manocha and Stough, 2005) indicates that the female gender possesses more and better emotional abilities associated with predicting transformational leadership behaviors (López-Zafra, Garcia Retamero and Landa, 2008). Being sincerely committed and passionate about their vision, which emanates through culture (Bass and Steidlmeier, 1999), enables transformational leaders to appeal to their followers and enhances the cultural change process towards a positive outcome. Therefore, it has been also proposed that female leaders might be even better as change agents within organizations.

Additionally, we can say that there is a need for female role models (Burke and McKeen, 1996) to help women's advancement to senior management positions, and therefore we have chosen a young successful female leader as the character for this case study with the hope that there will be more young female and successful leaders in the world soon.

The case study

This is a case study of one young female leader in Estonia, who as the CEO of the Baltic Business Unit is leading a group of 80 people in 3 countries.

Being an Estonian, young and female in a high-ranking position in an international corporation is something that is rather unique and was even considered impossible only about five years ago. When we asked Ms. Piko to tell us about her background and childhood, which might have shaped her leadership skills, she told us the following:

> When growing up I did not have a conscious thought that I will be a big boss so to say… I have however always had a tendency to take lead in groups already since kindergarten. I grew up as youngest in the family and my siblings were all 6 to 8 years older than me. Naturally they expected me to be at the same level as them and did not set me any lower standards. I think that this has kept me on my toes and helped me to develop the ability to build relationships or get people to act on my agenda without the possibility to tell them to do so. As a leader this skill has proven to be very useful as people rarely like to be told what to do, rather guided or negotiated into it.

She has been supported and her activities valued by her family and parents; this has given her confidence when taking the lead of other people and achieving set goals. Her background and interest in studies and music have enabled her to benefit from good education and creativity also in leadership activities:

Throughout my development I have always felt strong support from my parents and they have both believed in my abilities as well as always celebrated by achievements. My family has for two centuries been from one side professional musicians/teachers and from the other side managers of organizations. Good education and scholarliness was important for my family and seen as a base for a productive life. I think that music has helped me to develop my artistic side and creativity and on the other hand focus on education and results have taught me the importance of persistence.

She is a person who uses her positional power as a manger, but prefers to share and do things together with others. This leadership quality was considered as having a positive outcome on the follower's motivation and commitment already by Mary Parker Follett in the 1930s (Follett, 1995):

As I do love to create and envision, share it with others, and lead people to reach the goals, it has naturally directed my career to leadership positions. What appeals to me is that as a specialist you do it yourself, as a leader you do it with others and through others.

Ms. Piko's leadership style can be described as transformational (Kouzes and Posner, 2012); she pays much attention to the company's values and ethics at work. When leading others and making changes within the organization she encourages and promotes values relating to honesty, loyalty, fairness, justice, equality, and human rights (Kooskora, 2012), and strives to advocate, encourage, and support individual development while shaping strong relationships with her followers (Horner, 1997):

In any organization it is much easier to manage change or really any situation when you have defined common company values and or ethical values. It is especially essential in an international organization where people' values are affected by their cultural differences influenced by history, religion, social norms, and so on. I have experienced that people feel better and perform better when the uncertainty is taken out and they can evaluate whether their own ethical values are aligned with the company's values. With defined values everyone knows what is expected of them.

Cultural diversity (Cox, 2001) and considering different cultural backgrounds and characteristics are issues Ms. Piko faces every day. Being a CEO for people from neighboring countries that others might see as quite similar, she knows that in reality there are remarkable cultural differences and national attitudes that often have a strong impact on people's behavior and performance, especially in a multicultural environment (Bagshaw, 2004). Overcoming tensions between people from different nationalities and misunderstandings related to cultural and language differences is an important task for a leader in a multicultural organization:

In multicultural project teams as well as cross-cultural management teams one has to take notice of cultural differences and the effect these differences have to how people understand, react, and respond to tasks, goals, level of detail, understanding about time, urgency, or even at celebrating success. For instance, where more temperamental Lithuanians see Finns as too diplomatic and slow-motion then vice versa Finns may feel paralyzed by the "straight-to-the-point" communication and restlessness of their counterparts from the

Baltic countries. In order to make it work for multicultural groups you must generalize and at the same time localize the frames so that all parties feel positive stress needed to accomplish and yet feel motivated.

Success and failure go hand in hand. We can look at failure as the most powerful source for learning and understanding. It's always better and cheaper to learn from other's mistakes and failures, however when the leaders are able to admit their own mistakes and learn from these, it will help them to become stronger and better understand the situations and organizations. Great leaders are accountable for their actions and behavior, have enough courage to admit when they have made a mistake, take responsibility for the outcomes, and have the ability to learn from those situations (Kooskora, 2013).

Failure and making mistakes, especially in change management, is also known to Ms. Piko, but she has taken these as learning experiences that have encouraged her to make changes in her mind-set, activities, and behavior. These situations have shown her how important it is to be honest towards oneself and ones' values and most of all, to engage others and overcome their resistance with open and honest communication:

> In managing change you learn by experience of self and others. From my failures I have learned that in order to succeed in change you need honesty, communication, and engaging people in all stages. The key to leading people through change is to first believing in the change yourself. You then need to engage people in the process of planning the change in whatever needs to be changed – the way of working, processes, etc. Get people on board, get people to envision and plan the change themselves, recruit ambassadors, and make the fierce opponents of change your allies by giving them the role in executing and leading the change … There is no point in persuading people unless you get their real agenda and fears out of the way first. By this you get people to accept the situation and get them to the next stages. And then it is needed to have constant follow-up to prevent people to falling back to the resistance phase of change. The emphasis should be at all times on communication and honest communication in all stages. And when there is uncertainty then also be honest about that.

One of the central issues that has often interested researchers in leadership studies is how to define leaders' success and who is a successful leader. According to our own earlier research (Kooskora and Piigli, 2014), a successful leader is a person who hires valuable people for the company to benefit, respects the knowledge of people, and remembers to delegate and also to leave people room to act. The ideal leader has to be inspiring to get people to follow, but in order to be inspiring the leaders would first have to be aligned with their true self.

Ms. Piko sees success in "only one question needed to define whether a leader has been successful in leading organization through change successfully and that is 'do you as an employee recommend your company to other potential employees?'." She suggests that "when the answer is yes, then without much analysis needed one can conclude that the difficulties of change have been overcome and the frustration is not an issue."

Ms. Piko also wants to encourage other young (and especially female) potential leaders to take the lead and welcome the challenges of high positions within multicultural organizations. She also emphasizes the importance of considering differences in values and cultural understandings. She suggests "always to generalize the desired outcome and at the same time localize the execution of change process taking into account both cultural and other social capital variables that may define the group reaction and thus response to the change needed." As an example, she spoke about the differences in understanding and using the matrix system in different countries: "If in Scandinavia a matrix organization is widely accepted and efficient then in the Baltics a more traditional organization is accepted and matrix leadership can lead to confusion more often than not."

Concluding remarks

When we are talking about the good and successful leaders of today, we see that they support the people-oriented view enabling others to participate in activities and decision making, hiring the right people, fostering cooperation, and giving people enough room to act. The successful leader is able to see the big picture, visualize clear future targets, and is able to communicate it clearly and inspiringly to others. The successful leader is straightforward and direct in communication and able to give both positive and negative feedback; at the same time being patient, listening to others, and being able to balance directness using intuition and empathy to knowingly manage emotions and critical situations.

The leader has to consciously develop leadership skills, but be honest, self-confident, and stay true to oneself. It can also be concluded that in order to work efficiently, the values of the leader have to be aligned with the company's values and that both trust and networking are considered important leadership tools.

Using intuition and empathy to knowingly manage emotions and critical situations is an important characteristic of successful leaders and inherent to transformational leadership. As we may relate transformational leadership style used by successful leaders to female leaders, then, more than gender, personal characteristics and the way people are led play a role in a leader's success. However, the combination of both genders in the company and on managerial boards can contribute to whatever task.

Companies that want to be truly successful and sustainable have realized that the increasing demand for qualified and experienced managers can successfully be fulfilled by including more women in the candidate pool, and when there are more women in high managerial positions they are able to make more balanced decisions and consider different perspectives. Female leaders often bring needed collaborative and participative skills to the workplace; moreover, well-managed diversity, including gender diversity, is an inherent source of innovation and has been identified as a key factor in global competitiveness.

To conclude, we can say that to be a leader in the business world, politics, or any other field is traditionally related to being ambitious and taking great responsibilities and risks, and ambitiousness and risk taking have always been considered to be male characteristics and were not considered appropriate for women. However, today nobody can deny that female business leaders are succeeding at an unprecedented rate and their success has surprised many; but even with the significant increases over the last decades in women holding management positions, only few women have become top-level managers and moreover recognition of women's potential role in top business management has been painfully slow. Often, women are facing different barriers, and in order to overcome these obstacles, including gender stereotypes, lack of opportunities for women to gain the job experiences necessary to advance, and lack of top management commitment to gender equity and equal employment initiatives, successful female role models may prove useful to help and encourage young women to reach senior management positions.

References

Bagshaw, M. (2004). Is diversity divisive? A positive training approach. *Industrial and Commercial Training*, *36*(4), 153–157.

Bass, B. M. (1996). Theory of transformational leadership redux. *The Leadership Quarterly*, *6*(4), 463–478.

Bass, B. M. (1999). Two decades of research and development in transformational leadership. *European Journal of Work and Organizational Psychology*, *8*(1), 9–32.

Bass, B. M. and Steidlmeier, P. (1999). Ethics, character, and authentic transformational leadership behavior. *Leadership Quarterly*, *10*(2), 181–217.

Burke, R. J. and McKeen, C. A. (1996). Do women at the top make a difference? Gender proportions and the experiences of managerial and professional women. *Human Relations*, *49*(8), 1093–1104.

Burns, J. M. (1978). *Leadership*. New York: Harper & Row.

Carli, L. L. and Eagly, A. H. (2001). Gender, hierarchy, and leadership: An introduction. *Journal of Social Issues*, *57*(4), 629–636.

Carter N. M. and Wagner, H. M. (2011). *The Bottom Line: Corporate Performance and Women's Representation on Boards (2004–2008)*. New York: Catalyst. Retrieved from www.catalyst.org/system/files/the_bottom_line_corporate_performance_and_women's_representation_on_boards_%282004-2008%29.pdf (last accessed 12 December 2016).

Cox, T. (2001). *Creating the multicultural organization: A strategy for capturing the power of diversity*. San Francisco, CA: Jossey-Bass.

Eagly, A. H. (2007). Female leadership advantage and disadvantage: Resolving the contradictions. *Psychology of Women Quarterly*, *31*(1), 1–12.

Eagly, A. H. and Carli, L. L. (2003). The female leadership advantage: An evaluation of the evidence. *The Leadership Quarterly*, *14*(6), 807–834.

Eagly, A. H. and Carli, L. L. (2007). *Through the labyrinth: The truth about how women become leaders*. Boston, MA: Harvard Business Press.

Eagly, A. H., Johannesen-Schmidt, M. C. and Van Engen, M. L. (2003). Transformational, transactional, and laissez-faire leadership styles: A meta-analysis comparing women and men. *Psychological Bulletin*, *129*(4), 569.

European Commission (2013a). Report on women and men in leadership positions and gender equality strategy mid-term review. November. Retrieved from http://europa.eu/rapid/press-release_MEMO-13-882_en.htm (last accessed 12 December 2016).

European Commission (2013b). *National factsheet, gender balance in boards: Country: Finland*. January. Retrieved from http://ec.europa.eu/justice/gender-equality/files/womenonboards/womenon-boards-factsheet-fi_en.pdf (last accessed 12 December 2016).

Fernández-Berrocal, P., Salovey, P., Vera, A., Extremera, N. and Ramos, N. (2005). Cultural influences on the relation between perceived emotional intelligence and depression. *International Review of Social Psychology*, *18*(1), 91–107.

Follett, M. P. (1995). *Prophet of Management: A celebration of writings from the 1920s* (ed. P. Graham). Washington DC: Beard Books.

Horner, M. (1997). Leadership theory: Past, present and future. *Team Performance Management*, *3*(4), 270–287.

Katila, S. and Eriksson, P. (2013). He is a firm, strong minded and empowering leader, but is she? Gendered positioning of female and male CEOs. *Gender, Work & Organization*, *20*(1), 71–84.

Kooskora, M. (2012). Ethical leadership, the role of leader. In R. Pucetaite (ed.), *Cases in organizational ethics* (pp. 23–38). Vilnius, Lithuania: Vilnius University.

Kooskora, M. (2013). The role of (the right) values in an economic crisis. *Journal of Management & Change*, *2*(1), 49–65.

Kooskora, M. and Piigli, M. (2014). Comparative research on leadership profile of Estonian and Finnish female top executives. In M. Huseyin and H. Danis (eds), *EBES Conference Proceedings* (pp. 3–22). Berlin: Springer.

Kouzes, J. and Posner, B. (2012). *The leadership challenge* (5th edn). San Francisco, CA: Jossey-Bass.

López-Zafra, E., Garcia-Retamero, R. and Berrios Martos, M. P. (2012). The relationship between transformational leadership and emotional intelligence from a gendered approach. *Psychological Record*, *62*(1), 97–114.

López Zafra, E., Garcia Retamero, R. and Landa, J. M. A. (2008). The role of transformational leadership, emotional intelligence, and group cohesiveness on leadership emergence. *Journal of Leadership Studies*, *2*(3), 37–49.

Manning, T. T. (2002). Gender, managerial level, transformational leadership and work satisfaction. *Women in Management Review*, *17*(5), 207–216.

Nirenberg, J. (2001). Leadership: A practitioner's perspective on the literature. *Singapore Management Review*, *23*(1), 1–34.

Oakley, J. G. (2000). Gender-based barriers to senior management positions: Understanding the scarcity of female CEOs. *Journal of Business Ethics*, *27*(4), 321–334.

Palmer, B. R., Gignac, G., Manocha, R. and Stough, C. (2005). A psychometric evaluation of the Mayer–Salovey–Caruso emotional intelligence test version 2.0. *Intelligence*, *33*(3), 285–305.

Perry, J. and Gundersen, D. E. (2011). American women and the gender pay gap: A changing demographic or the same old song. *Advancing Women in Leadership*, *31*(1), 153–159.

Pesonen, S., Tienari, J. and Vanhala, S. (2009). The boardroom gender paradox. *Gender in Management: An International Journal*, *24*(5), 327–345.

Prime, J. L., Carter, N. M. and Welbourne, T. M. (2009). Women "take care," men "take charge": Managers' stereotypic perceptions of women and men leaders. *The Psychologist-Manager Journal*, *12*(1), 25–49.

Vinnicombe, S. and Singh, V. (2002). Sex role stereotyping and requisites of successful top managers. *Women in Management Review*, *17*(3/4), 120–130.

Yammarino, F. J. and Atwater, L. E. (1997). Do managers see themselves as others see them? Implications of self-other rating agreement for human resources management. *Organizational Dynamics*, *25*(4), 35–44.

Zenger, J. and Folkman, J. (2012). *A study in leadership: Women do it better than men*. Orem, UT: Zenger and Folkman. Retrieved from http://zengerfolkman.com/media/articles/ZFCo.WP.WomenBetterThanMen.033012.pdf (last accessed 12 December 2016).

6 Leadership and change management

Regards Croisés from small and large companies in France

Marina Niforos in collaboration with Ariane Cherel

La Lamaneur qui entreprendra, étant ivre, de piloter un vaisseau, sera condamné en cent sols d'amende and interdit pour un mois de pilotage. Dans le vrai, si cette article était pris à la lettre, les interdictions seraient si fréquentes et si multipliées, qu'il n'y aurait jamais de pilotes en exercice, tant les hommes de mer, sur les ports, sont sujets à s'enivrer.

Mais il est différents degrés d'ivresse; et ce qu'il y a de singulier, c'est qu'il est des pilotes et autres mariniers qui ne montrent jamais plus d'habileté, de courage et de prévoyance tout à la fois, que lorsqu'ils sont ivres à un certain point. Le meilleur est néanmoins de ne pas s'y fier, ne fut-ce qu'à cause de la difficulté de distinguer le degré d'ivresse qui ne serait pas dangereux; et à cela le remède est facile, le maître ayant la liberté de réfuter tout pilote qui sera reconnu ivre; si ensuite, il le laisse s'enivrer à son bord, ce sera uniquement sa faute.

(Extract from 'Nouveau Commentaire sur l'Ordonnance de la Marine Aout 1681')[1]

Semper Fidelis became the Marine Corps motto in 1883. Latin for "always faithful," it guides Marines to remain faithful to the mission at hand, to each other, to the Corps and to country, no matter what. It goes beyond teamwork – it is a brotherhood that can always be counted on. Marine Corps Officers also embrace the phrase Ductos Exemplo – "lead by example" – and are guided by three main values, Honor, Courage and Commitment.

HONOR: A code of personal integrity, honor guides those who do the right thing when no one is looking. It is not only a duty, but also a distinction, as those who possess honor are held in honor. It's found in one's beliefs, but exhibited through one's actions.

COURAGE: Is the guardian of all other values. It is there when times are toughest, when difficult decisions have to be made. It takes the form of mental, physical and ethical strength.

COMMITMENT: Is the spirit of determination found in every Marine. It is what compels Marines to serve our nation and the Corps, and to continue on when others quit. Commitment doesn't take breaks and it cannot be faked. It measures and proves one's desire, dedication and faithfulness.

(Excerpt from the US Marines Principles and Values)[2]

Success in the global marketplace depends on the ability of an organization and of its managers to provide effective leadership. But how do we define leadership across a global interconnected economy that is still marked by national and local idiosyncrasies, traditions, and norms that reflect specific cultural and historical trajectories? Are there universal principles of leadership and management that apply and can form the basis of a common learning platform for individuals and corporations? The meaning of leadership (Yukl, 2006), its formulation (Hamlin, 2004), and the way it is perceived across cultures (Heck, 1996; Pillai, Scandura and Williams, 1999; Sarros and Santora, 2001), while heavily researched, remain difficult to assess.

The difficulties, and often highly visible failures, faced by many multinational organizations, small and large, to adopt and execute uniform strategic objectives and policies across their global operations testify to the magnitude of the challenges facing the modern corporation. This case study compares two French companies, one large multinational with global operations in heavy industry and one small, but rapidly growing company in services that is expanding in new international markets. Through their contrasted experiences, we hope to shed some light on how best to deal with the challenges of globalization and cultural misalignment. First, we present a brief survey of some relevant research.

Culture and management: A literature review

The Global Leadership and Organizational Behavior Effectiveness Research Program (GLOBE) (House, Hanges, Ruiz-Quintanilla, Dorfman, Javidan, Dickson and Gupta, 1999) as well as empirical research (House, Wright and Aditya, 1997) has demonstrated that what is expected of leaders, what leaders may and may not do, and the status and influence bestowed on leaders vary considerably as a result of the cultural forces in the countries or regions in which the leaders function.

Geert Hofstede's work on national cultural dimensions (Hofstede, 2001) has served as a point of departure and a backdrop to this study. According to Hofstede's cultural dimensions theory, people from different cultures operate under different assumptions about what is appropriate behavior and react differently to organizational structures depending on their culture of origin. Hofstede surveyed approximately 40 national cultures and then plotted their cultural dimensions according to four main references.

1   Power distance: the extent to which the less powerful members of institutions and organizations within a country expect and accept that power is distributed unequally.
2   Uncertainty avoidance: the extent to which the members of a given culture feel threatened by ambiguous or unknown situations and have created beliefs and institutions that try to avoid these.
3   Individualism/collectivism: this dimension translates the socialization a person receives, either as an individual who stands on his or her own merit, whose well-being and happiness will result from his or her own doing, or as an individual who primarily stands as a member of a defined group (Hofstede, 2001).
4   Masculinity/femininity: the masculinity pole represents cultures that predominantly value assertiveness and material success, while the femininity pole values a more nurturing and consensus-building approach.

Within this framework (Hofstede, 2001; Trompenaars and Hampden-Turner, 1998), France ranks very high on power distance (score: 68; rank: 15/16; Hofstede, 2001) and is one of the highest uncertainty avoiding cultures (86%). In comparison, the United States of America (US) stands at the opposite side of the spectrum with low power distance (score: 40; rank: 41) and moderate/low uncertainty avoidance (46%).

Extrapolating from Hofstede's (2001) model, Mintzberg and Gosling (2002) provide more systemic analysis of organizational behavior and examine the nexus of organization and culture. They produce several organizational types according to their internal structures but also taking into account their interaction with their environment (culture). France appears as an example of the 'full bureaucracy' model (a 'machine' with a pyramidal structure), 'standardization of processes,' and 'technostructure model.' In the French profile, hierarchy is essential; the superiors are often inaccessible and interactions are more formal. Information flow is associated with power and therefore unequally distributed. Certainty is often reached through analytical work and concepts that can respond to the need for context and detail. In management structures, change is considered a source of anxiety; rules and security are necessary and their absence can create stress. French-style managers typically revert all decisions to the 'strategic apex' (top management) and constantly pass detailed information up the hierarchy (where failure is not tolerated). This stands in contrast to Anglo-Saxon and Scandinavian business cultures where hierarchy is only established for utilitarian purposes, superiors are accessible and engage in a more participatory decision-making process, and there is higher acceptance of failure and appetite for risk. Information is shared frequently and communication is informal.

D'Iribarne provides an in-depth interpretation and a historical perspective of the *manière française de vivre* (French way of living) with his work 'La Logique de l'Honneur' (1989), in which he underlines the existence of a considerable gap between the official and unofficial and where procedures are rarely followed to the letter. In his reading, everyone in society has a defined set of responsibilities from which one cannot escape without severe sanctions. Yet at the same time, people have an aversion to control. The seeming paradox between adherence to a hierarchical power structure and the aversion to submission to authority appears to be resolved by the individual's sense of pride and honor towards work where respect for duty is key. Personal relations are indispensable to ensure collaboration in a system where hierarchical constructs are complicated. Different groups of allegiance can help cement those personal relations and provide the conduit for collaboration. D'Iribarne's later work (2004, 2009) and other country studies (Budhwar and Sparrow, 2002; Dorfman, 1996; Ravasi and Schultz, 2006) explored the inherent limitations in transferring theories and managerial practices across cultures. His research project on the French multinational Lafarge (one of our subjects for this case study) supported the case for leadership researchers to 'fine-tune' their theories by investigating cultural variations as relevant parameters of those theories (Triandis, 1993).

The case study: French business culture in small and large enterprises

We have chosen to look at the experience of two economic actors that represent different segments and sizes of organization in order to find similarities or discrepancies that may testify to the influence of culture on organizational structure and performance, and in particular to how their culture or origin impacts their approach in the context of their international activities. For that purpose, we interviewed the CEO and founder of a small but rapidly growing company (Leaders League) that is expanding beyond the French market, as well as the former Executive Vice President and member of the Executive Committee of an originally French multinational with global operations (Lafarge).

The SME: Leaders League

Leaders League, a media and business services company, was founded in 1996 by Pierre-Etienne Lorenceau, still its current President and CEO, with the launching of *Décideurs*

('Decision-Makers') magazine, a quarterly publication (now monthly) on issues concerning current affairs, evolving business practices, and leadership, and targeting senior business leaders. Besides the *Décideurs* magazine, they produce rankings across a variety of industries and professions, they organize conferences and events, publish market intelligence reports, and develop web-enabling media. Their first international event was held in 2004. They now also have offices in Paris, Sao Paolo, Lima, and Rio de Janeiro, and they provide coverage of the US market and the rest of Europe via their Paris headquarters since 2008. Currently, one third of the staff is made up of non-French citizens.

Mr. Lorenceau was born in New York City to French parents and spent his childhood between Paris, London and Monaco. He was educated in Monaco by Jesuits, studied law at Paris-Assas University for five years, and completed a one-year Finance Masters at French business school ESCP. He then pursued an MBA at Harvard Business School. When asked to identify his primary culture affiliation, he claims to be bi-cultural French and American.

The influence of family

The history and culture of the company is closely linked to the personal evolution and family relationships of its founder. His father was a successful entrepreneur, but his grand-father is the dominant figure in his discourse, a man who was with the French resistance during World War II and was sent to a concentration camp where he was tortured for four years. This landmark event and the resilience of the grandfather strongly influenced Pierre-Etienne, providing for a dominant role model and an aversion to centralized authority and to command and control structures. Pierre-Etienne attributes his entrepreneurial drive and his unconventional way of finding new market segments, despite initial resistance, to the lessons learned from the grandfather and his struggle for survival and freedom. He also mentions the strong influence that his wife and partner have had on his evolution as a manager and leader:

> I learned a lot from my wife about change management and first of all about emotional intelligence. She has been my partner for several years and actually ran the company while I was doing my MBA in Boston. She has an uncanny ability to read the unspoken, people's behaviors, and body language, and to identify hidden animosities and alliances between people, and to interpret them.

However, when asked about his apparent appetite for risk, Pierre-Etienne responds: "I do not consider myself a risk taker, I seize an opportunity and I insure through meticulous planning that risks will be managed successfully."

The influence of education

Mr. Lorenceau decided to pursue an MBA at Harvard Business School a few years after founding his company. He describes this as a truly transformative experience, creating a before and after in his personal development and in his mindset as a leader and business owner:

> When I arrived and was placed in this extremely diverse, international setting of very talented people, I realized all my own shortcomings and the gaps I had to fill, for me and

for my business, particularly if I wanted to operate internationally. The learning process came more from the dynamic creative interaction with other participants than from the formal content. When I returned, I knew there were many things that had to change.

The multinational: Lafarge

Lafarge was created in 1833 in the Ardèche region of France. It is a construction and building materials conglomerate (cement, concrete, and aggregates) with an annual turnover of EUR 12 billion. Lafarge has undergone a rapid international expansion during the last 20 years, with an entry in China in the 1990s, acquisitions in the United Kingdom, in North Africa, and the Middle East in the first decade of the new millennium. In 2014, Lafarge merged with the Swiss company Holcim to create the world's biggest cement maker, with USD 44 billion in annual sales, with operations in 90 countries and 130,000 employees.

Christian Herrault is Executive Vice President Operations at Lafarge. He is a French national. He has been with the company for almost 30 years and served in various line and functional positions. He graduated from Ecole Polytechnique in 1969 and Ecole des Mines, two of the top academic and engineering schools in France. He began his career in the public sector and served for a time with the French navy. He joined Lafarge in 1985, taking over the role of strategy and development of the Bioactivities division. He has been at the head of different business units within the group, including in the US. In 1998 he became Executive Vice President of Human Resources and a member of the Executive Committee.

The influence of corporate values

Lafarge's humanistic culture and corporate values are central to Christian Herrault's narrative. Indeed, a very strong tradition of humanist values was formalized in the 1970s in the so-called Principles of Action, a set of guiding principles capturing the culture and spirit of the company and revisited every five to seven years since their inception. In 2003, the company launched an organization-wide project called 'Leader for Tomorrow' (LFT), a process of translating the Principles of Action to the local level. Mr. Herrault puts emphasis on their concrete, operational aspects and distinguishes them from simple 'values' that are more aspirational. "They are not mere values, but guidelines on the way Lafarge and its employees should behave on an everyday basis." They are meant to create an ecosystem where every individual can find their own identity, and to find respect and recognition for their efforts. A motivated employee is a much more efficient one. But they cannot remain just simple words for they would seem artificial. Lafarge's Principles of Action are actionable and 'lived.' On a personal level, Mr. Herrault's actions were rooted in those same core values: openness, integrity, respect for others, priority given to the interests of the group, commitment, and responsibility.

Culture and change: Challenges and insights

Leaders League

Mr. Lorenceau's return to France after his MBA in the US marked a turning point for the organization as well. He suddenly became aware of the limitations of the existing team and of the incumbent culture of the company:

I had gotten accustomed to a highly dynamic environment and to an accelerated pace of action. My team in France seemed to lack agility and initiative, expecting things to come from the top. I realized we needed to change dramatically if we were to advance.

Pierre-Etienne proceeded with a thorough process of transforming the business and its culture with recruitment as a key driver to implement his new convictions. He restructured entirely the team and recruited new people under new criteria, focusing on providing more cultural and linguistic diversity (for every French recruit there, a non-French one was also hired) and an affinity for a culture of openness and entrepreneurship.

Another major landmark was the physical move of the company to new offices, which allowed him to implement a full internal reorganization. He chose a completely open space to encourage people to interact with one another and to foster collaboration across the board regardless of rank:

> It was an occasion for us to decide how we wanted to function. For example, would you put the management team, CEO, and COO on the same open floor? We decided to proportion the space according to functions (e.g., event HR, publishing HR). Another change: we organized around products and customers (event and publishing). We continued to experiment to see which structure promoted more collaboration and better results.

According to Mr. Lorenceau, national culture is not a decisive parameter in corporate culture. For him, family culture and personal experience are more influential factors that shape our perspective and our approach in tackling change in a business environment. He cites frequently his grandfather as a role model, whose paradigm taught him "to take an unconventional approach to identifying and seizing opportunities in the market and breaking new frontiers, even when others thought it defied logic. From him, I have inherited the taste for independence, freedom, and distrust towards institutions, they are often ill-willed."

Lafarge

Lafarge had to tackle the issue of rapid international expansion, most of it in non-western markets and it was called on to answer fundamental questions of management and leadership in a multicultural global environment. How do Lafarge's universal values apply across different markets where they operate, with radically different national and local cultures? How do the Principles of Action translate at the local level and how do you strike equilibrium between adherence to principles and respect for local social norms?

They chose a process of reconciliation and equilibrium between the universal principles that are part of the company's DNA and the need to provide an actionable framework to which the local employees could commit and engage in the core corporate values. This resulted in the LFT program mentioned above, introduced as a way of implementing the Principles of Action across borders.

These were comprehensive, organization-wide initiatives that solicited the full participation of its employees and managers to ensure alignment and cooperation with the guiding principles. They then made important efforts to articulate those corporate values to the local/national level, being meticulous about language and form. Mr. Herrault affirms that this is a continuous work in progress to update and fine-tune the Principles of Action, complementing them with *ad hoc* change projects and initiatives (for example, the issue of gender being introduced, beyond diversity concerns that were part of the original objective), while remaining faithful to the original spirit.

In the research project that Philippe d'Iribarne conducted on the company (d'Iribarne, 2012) from 2004 to 2007, we see the real-life challenges in maintaining a core set of values and principles and adapting to the cultural sensibilities of multiple environments. A comparison between the US and France is telling. Certain principles of action are shared (focus on client service, employee engagement, and shareholder value), but the way they are interpreted varies from country to country.

The example of a plant shutdown of a seeds factory in Rochester, NY is indicative. The US Chairman (an Irish national who had lived many years in the US) had decided to close the plant after a long period of disappointing performance and poor future prospects. He "wanted to tell the staff over the weekend," quickly and without direct confrontation. As was customary in Lafarge culture, Mr. Herrault thought people deserved to have a more direct exchange with management and insisted that most of the corporate staff stay a few days to follow up with people and answer questions or concerns. He preferred to have a more managed process, with a carefully planned blueprint for action and insisted on having an open meeting with the workers during a workday and for several days to allow for a face-to-face exchange. This was done in the spirit of the company's corporate values to put the 'human' first. "This is in alignment with our principles of putting the person at the center of our decisions." Incidentally, this is also consistent with the structured, rigorous process orientation characteristic of a French large organization.

This, however, is not something within the business norms of US companies where more informal negotiated relationships are in place (and firing is quick and unceremonial). The process of letting the personnel go was so organized (an action plan, individual coaching, and direct announcement with management in place to answer questions), that some people felt somehow it was too premeditated. "I heard of complaints that they felt forced, that the process was so structured and managed that it did not even allow them to voice anger and protest."

A few years later, when the company had already confronted the possibility of having to close down a factory in Morocco, Lafarge put forward an action plan to manage the transition over a period of two years before the actual closing, putting together a program in collaboration with the trade unions to manage the staff's conversion and creating 226 small enterprises by the staff laid off. This allowed the people leaving the company to continue having an economic activity and gave them technical and financial support over a period of two years to ensure the sustainability of their new venture. "It was case of putting action into words and translating into practice the stated principles."[3]

Another anecdote testifying to the misalignment between values/intentions and final impact was the company's involvement in emergency relief in Indonesia after the tsunami:

> In the aftermath of the catastrophe, everything had to be rebuilt. We sent several equipped ambulances to assist the local authorities in the enormity of the task of disaster relief before them. Soon, however, we realized that our 'helicoptered teams' were undermining the credibility and authority of the local emergency relief forces and we had to take a back seat.

"We have to be Algerians in Algeria … and find local stakeholders in order for the impact to be sustainable," he said, stressing the need for managers to be continually "listening" and adjusting to the local needs.

Nevertheless, he stresses that managing across so many regions and cultural domains the manager/leader has to permanently put his/her own personal values and judgment to play. He/she develops cultural competence by being immersed in the context, in friction with the reality:

> One must know how to navigate and how to exercise one's judgment. One's compass should be to try and put oneself in the other's shoes, and listen; listening is fundamental to strike the right balance between values and local norms and customs. The cultural filter needs to be always activated.

Christian Herrault stresses that one's best tool is listening to opinion leaders, all across the company:

> A business leader cannot be naïve; she/he must be attuned to the signals of the 'trenches,' must understand the power relationships and be able to adapt accordingly. Leadership after all is interpreted very differently across cultures; in the West putting forward the model of the collaborative, 'coach' type of manager whereas in some Asian cultures the leader is expected to be the absolute reference and solution provider for the team. A process of change management is evolutionary, one cannot go from Negate to Commit directly, they must pass first from the stages of Oppose and Experiment.[4]

Discussion and conclusions

We chose to juxtapose the experience of two different structures rooted in the same national French culture. Both face the challenges of globalization, but their size, historical development, and corporate cultures vary significantly. On the one side, we have a small family business that has experienced rapid growth in terms of market expansion and has a flat start-up/entrepreneurial culture with many practices inspired by the US tech ecosystem and fairly diversified staff (more than 30% foreigners). On the other, Lafarge is a mature global player with strong roots in French business and its corporatist culture, but whose business comes predominantly from emerging markets and is managing a truly global workforce across 90 countries.

Their stories suggest that the experience of French management practices in a rapidly changing global environment is not uniform. While certain elements are common and can be attributed to national identity (their adherence to humanistic values, the structured approach to management, the stated respect for individual choice and freedom), we see that they have arrived through different paths to the similar conclusion that different subcultures and supra-cultures can and do coexist under that national umbrella or above it, creating hybrid cultural archetypes that transcend national identity.

Another important element coming through is that size does matter. A smaller structure is by definition much closer to the operational level and is able to adopt and adapt organizational structures with more suppleness. A large company needs a construct to maintain cohesion across the board, but this can also lead to a "vacuum towards the top" effect (Herrault), a tendency to suck the organizational process towards the top echelons. Herrault cautions vigilance against this effect and stresses the need to look at internal stakeholders down the pyramid for any change initiative to work. "A staircase is built from the bottom up but it is cleaned from the top down." Also, "top leadership needs to be accountable and understand the importance of the team in the company's success." Finally, the key ingredients underpinning any well-performing organization are trust and humility. Trust as a sign of mutual respect and acceptance of the 'the other,' and humility in abandoning our heroic archetypes of leadership and focusing on those of collaborative leadership and shared growth.

Mr. Lorenceau alludes clearly to a supra-culture that defies national barriers when he mentions that he identifies with the start-up culture rather than to a strictly nationally defined French or American one: "I do not identify with 'American' culture; I am choosing to set up shop in San Francisco because of its particular ecosystem (in media/tech) and culture; that does not mean I would choose to go to Iowa or Denver."

Christian Herrault refers to the existence of subcultures that exist within a national culture and which cannot be ignored without falling into stereotyping:

> It is impossible to have one set of measures to treat the cultural specificity across countries but also communities. Attempts to over codify can lead to empty corporate statements that can actually alienate people on the ground, as it can be seen as window dressing.

This echoes d'Iribarne's (2012) conclusion that it is possible for a company/group to deploy processes and benefit from collaboration across different cultures provided: (i) care is given to the delicate exercise of building management practices that allow for the coexistence of core principles with local values and references; and (ii) awareness exists that such exercise – though essential – takes time to produce results.

Limitations and further research

There are two elements that were explicitly or implicitly referred to in our interviews that deserve further study.

The first is the emergence of supra-cultures (for lack of a better term) – that is the cultural tribes that transcend national barriers and that are bound together by common interests, values, and experiences reinforced by the digital connectivity. Social networks and the immediacy of communication across borders is evidently having a critical influence on the way people, particularly younger generations, perceive national identity and belonging, especially when a major part of their socialization and sometimes even education happens through digital platforms.

The second element is the conflict between the accelerated pace of globalization and managerial focus on short-term results, on one hand, and the longer-term process of cultural understanding and collaboration, on the other, something voiced strongly by Christian Herrault. How do we strike a balance between our own values and those of others? Getting to know each other takes time, but will we have enough time to take these into consideration in the fast pace of globalization? How can we ensure managers acquire in a timely manner the necessary skills for cross-cultural competencies? In this regard, d'Iribarne (2009, 2012) as well as Mintzberg and Gosling (2002) advocate the use of more experiential learning methods in training people, ones that focus less on the formal tools and modelling of parameters and more on the capacity of people to listen. Hence, we need to further explore the connection between leadership in multicultural settings and emotional intelligence, and the capacity to listen, to motivate individuals and teams, and to create an environment where we develop the conditions for change to take place rather than try to over-manage it as a process.

Notes

1   See Valin (1760).
2   See www.marines.com/history-heritage/principles-values.

3   Abdelkebir Mézouar, from the film *L'emploi du Cœur: L'aventure de la création de 226 entreprises par des chômeurs au Maroc* (Collection Entreprise à Visage Humain, 2005).
4   This is a reference to the Change Curve, attributed to psychiatrist Elisabeth Kubler-Ross, frequently used in change management analysis and training.

References

Budhwar, P. S. and Sparrow, P. R. (2002). An integrative framework for understanding cross-national human resource management practices. *Human Resource Management Review*, *12*(3), 377–403.

D'Iribarne, P. (1989). *La logique de l'honneur*. Paris: Seuil Collection.

D'Iribarne, P. (2004). Face à la complexité des cultures, le management interculturel exige une approche ethnologique. *Management International*, *8*(3), 56–78.

D'Iribarne, P. (2009). *L'épreuve des différences: L'expérience d'une entreprise mondiale*. Paris: Éditions du Seuil.

D'Iribarne, P. (2012). *Managing corporate values in diverse national cultures: The challenge of differences* (Vol. 19). London: Routledge.

Dorfman, P. W. (1996). International and cross-cultural leadership research. In B. J. Punnet and O. Shenkar (eds), *Handbook for international management research* (pp. 267–349). Oxford: Blackwell.

Hamlin, R. G. (2004). In support of universalistic models of managerial and leadership effectiveness: Implications for HRD research and practice. *Human Resource Development Quarterly*, *15*(2), 189–215.

Heck, R. H. (1996). Leadership and culture: Conceptual and methodological issues in comparing models across cultural settings. *Journal of Educational Administration*, *34*(5), 74–97.

Hofstede, G. H. (2001). *Culture's consequences: Comparing values, behaviors, institutions and organizations across nations*. Thousand Oaks, CA: Sage Publications.

House, R. J., Hanges, P. J., Ruiz-Quintanilla, S. A., Dorfman, P. W., Javidan, M., Dickson, M. and Gupta, V. (1999). Cultural influences on leadership and organizations: Project GLOBE. Retrieved from http://globalmindset.thunderbird.edu/wwwfiles/sites/globe/pdf/process.pdf (last accessed 12 December 2016).

House, R. J., Wright, N. S. and Aditya, R. N. (1997). Cross-cultural research on organizational leadership: A critical analysis and a proposed theory. In P. C. Early and M. Erez (eds), *New perspectives on international industrial/organizational psychology* (pp. 535–625). San Francisco, CA: New Lexington Press.

Mintzberg, H. and Gosling, J. (2002). Educating managers beyond borders. *Academy of Management Learning & Education*, *1*(1), 64–76.

Pillai, R., Scandura, T. A. and Williams, E. A. (1999). Leadership and organizational justice: Similarities and differences across cultures. *Journal of International Business Studies*, *30*(4), 763–777.

Ravasi, D. and Schultz, M. (2006). Responding to organizational identity threats: Exploring the role of organizational culture. *Academy of Management Journal*, *49*(3), 433–458.

Sarros, J. C. and Santora, J. C. (2001). The transformational-transactional leadership model in practice. *Leadership and Organization Development Journal*, *22*(8), 383–394.

Triandis, H. C. (1993). The contingency model in cross-cultural perspective. In M. M. Chemers and R. Ayman (eds), *Leadership theory and research: Perspectives and directions* (pp. 167–188). San Diego, CA: Academic Press.

Trompenaars, F. and Hampden-Turner, C. (1998). *Riding the waves of culture: Understanding diversity in global business*. New York: McGraw-Hill.

Valin, R. J. (1760). *Nouveau commentaire sur l'Ordonnance de la Marine Aout 1681*. La Rochelle, France: Chez Jerôme Legier.

Yukl, G. (2006). *Leadership in organizations* (6th edn). Upper Saddle River, NJ: Prentice Hall.

7 It is not a way of making money; it is a way of life

The Apivita case

Maria Vakola, Dimitris Bourantas and Marina Karli

Apivita is a Greek natural cosmetics company, established 35 years ago, with an international presence in 15 countries in Europe and Asia (Spain, Japan, Hong Kong, the United States of America, Cyprus, Ukraine, Romania, Bulgaria, Belgium, the Netherlands, etc.). The company engages in the design, development, production, marketing, and sales of cosmetic products in Greece and abroad, the production of plant extracts used as raw materials in its products, and the trade of dietary supplements and bee products. It employs over 250 employees, produces approximately 300 different product codes, and has sold over 7.5 million items (Reguly, 2014).

Apivita was founded in 1979, but its story begins a few years earlier – more specifically, in 1972, when two pharmacists, Nikos and Niki Koutsianas, were preparing medicinal creams with bee products and herb extracts in their pharmacy. Inspired by the honeybee society, the biodiversity of Greek nature, and the holistic approach of Hippocrates to health, beauty, and well-being, they created the first natural cosmetics company in Greece. More specifically, the beehive is a super-organism that constantly generates value. Through pollination, it ensures the sustainability of ecosystems, providing precious beekeeping products. Greek nature, with its rich biodiversity, indigenous plants, and herbs of high biological value, is an invaluable natural treasure. Hippocrates was the first holistic physician, philosopher, and teacher. The name of Apivita is derived from the Latin words *apis* (bee) and *vita* (life), and means 'life of the bee.' It reflects the values that inspired its founders, which shape the philosophy of the company until today. Accordingly, the logo of Apivita is inspired by the 'Bees of Malia', a rare Minoan piece of jewelry from the Middle Bronze Age (*c.*1700 BC), representing fertility and harmony.

Apivita's founder vision is to become a leading, green, innovative company of the world (*kosmos*) in the market of natural beauty, well-being, and health, showing responsibility and respect towards nature and society. The fact that *kosmos* is a Greek word that stands for the Universe as a complex, well-organized system, characterized by order and balance is indicative of the holistic perspective of the company. Furthermore, the English words 'cosmetic' and 'cosmetology' derive from this word. This holistic perspective was integrated into its business strategy when Apivita was established, in 1979. It continues to be part of the strategy of the company to this day, and is reflected in Apivita's mission as well. More specifically, the key points of the mission of the company are presented here:

- to create and develop beauty products and services that promote a balanced and harmonious way of life, based on Greek nature and its rich biodiversity and on the unique honeybee society and its high biological value products;
- to adopt the holistic Hippocratic approach to beauty, well-being and health, which, coupled with scientific knowledge, supports and enhances nature's effectiveness; and

- to promote *kállos*, which is the classical Greek ideal of inner and outer beauty, high aesthetic value, balance, moderation, and well-being (Reguly, 2014).

Family and national cultural values in business practice

Apivita's founder was raised in a very poor family in a village. The whole family and the community were struggling for survival. As a young orphan child, he realized that only hard work can create opportunities to survive. This achievement orientation led him to do well at school and pass very tough university exams against all odds. Even today, that he is the owner of a very successful international business, he keeps working long hours and is involved in all business decisions. His family also taught him to earn his living in a fair and honest way. His family believed that earnings should come only from working hard in an ethical way. Cheating, overpricing, lying, gambling were not acceptable even when money was essential for the family's survival. These values are obvious throughout Apivita's founder's professional life. As a pharmacist, he was a member of their professional union and a member of the left party fighting for their code of practice and fair wages and rights. Also, Apivita's founder directed all his efforts towards developing products according to the highest standards as a way of building trust with customers. Apart from working hard and earn his living in a fair way, as a child he learnt to appreciate simplicity and the small things in life. He continues living with simplicity and modesty, avoiding big spending and a luxurious way of life. Apivita's founder is more interested in creating and leaving a legacy than creating a fortune for himself and his family. He says, "Apivita is not a way of making money, it is a way of life. I am not interested in making profit. I am interested in creating value."[1]

Apart from believing in himself, Apivita's founder values close family relationships. He grew up knowing that family is an invaluable source of support, especially in times of crisis. This is the reason why he decided to build his company along with his wife. He says, "If it wasn't for Niki, my wife, I would have never gone ahead with creating a business and establishing the business because I was more into the philosophical part of what I was doing." Their roles are distinctive in the company since he takes care of what he describes as "the roots" of the business, essentially its philosophy, and to help create the products, while Niki's role is branding and marketing (Hope, 2013).

From a very young age, he appreciated nature and was fascinated and inspired by bees. He grew up in a family of beekeepers. As a result, he developed a deep understanding of nature and appreciated its laws and balance. This love and passion for nature are critical for Apivita's evolution and success. During all the years of Apivita's life, he created products using nature's ingredients, such as black soap with propolis and thyme and therapeutic shampoos with herb extracts in glass pharmacist bottles. The key ingredient is propolis, a natural resin gathered by bees from the bark and leaf buds of trees, which they then use to protect and maintain their hives. Nature appreciation is present not only in the products, but also in the company's partnerships. Apivita established partnerships with local cultivators throughout Greece to ensure the best possible organic Greek herb ingredients. This passion and love for nature is also reflected in a series of business decisions. For example, he decided to invest in new company premises that are bioclimatic. The new Apivita headquarters and factory, a cement structure located on a former olive tree grove, is surrounded by herb gardens and an apiary and respects the natural environment. The care and nurturing of gardens and bees are a big part of the Apivita founder's everyday job. This passion inspired him not only to build premises but to create an organizational culture based on their values such as teamwork, togetherness, organization, and hard work.

Apivita's founder considers his business as a living organism like the bee; it never stops creating value for society, for the natural environment, and for the economy. At Apivita there is the belief that society, people, and culture are elements belonging to the same equation along with the environment, the planet, and natural resources. And that sustainable development is ensured when all of the above remain in complete balance. This holistic perspective characterizes the philosophy of Apivita, which is more specifically based on four elements, as presented here. Morale and sustainable entrepreneurship are regarded to coexist, providing value for society. Beauty and well-being are addressed in a natural, effective, and holistic way. The products and the services of the company are intended to utilize and to pollinate the long-standing knowledge of Greek flora, the beekeeping products, and the holistic approach of Hippocrates. The company is dedicated to respect, retain, and enrich the natural and anthropogenic environment. The philosophy of Apivita embodies values such as the following:

- 'think local, act global';
- emotional intelligence;
- transparency and integrity;
- priority to human resources;
- life-long learning; and
- *kállos*, the classical Greek ideal of inner and outer beauty, and balance.

The fact that human resources are placed among the values of the company stresses their importance for Apivita. The people of Apivita are expected to be characterized by nine virtues, which are translated into desired behaviors and which are incorporated into the performance evaluation system of the company. More specifically, these nine virtues are:

- learning, development, excellence;
- teamwork and synergy;
- creativity and innovation;
- effective change;
- leader–inspirer;
- emotional intelligence;
- accountability;
- knowledge–ecosystem–pollination; and
- strategic thought.

They are integrated with the philosophy, the values, the vision, and the mission of the company.

Managing change – The bright and dark side of values

Apivita's founder has managed many changes throughout company's history. His way of managing change is characterized by his own values. During these 35 years, Apivita's founder managed to build a successful international business through a series of decisions and changes. He managed to establish the first natural cosmetics company in the country, creating value for society, customers, and employees. He implemented a number of changes related to the company's strategy such as expanding in international markets, investing heavily in innovative products, opening experience stores where products and beauty services are offered, and investing in quality natural extracts as a competitive advantage. The last was an important decision that signaled a number of internal changes. Compared to other industries, the production process is rather complex and demanding, mainly due to the fact that specialized know-how is required for medicines and natural extracts. Instead of buying or importing lower-class raw materials, which would have led to lower prices of end products, he choose to insist on quality respecting the company's trust relationship with customers. All these decisions led to many changes in the company's functioning such as improving process, changing the production line, restructuring, and forming a new managing team.

The above successful changes and Apivita's sustainable success were based on its founder's management style, vision, competence, and business decisions. All these were shaped by his cultural and family values. As mentioned above, Apivita's founder was an orphan and raised in a very poor family. As a result, he learnt to believe in himself and survive in every circumstance. From a very young age, he became innovative as a way of moving forward, coping with difficult situations and making progress. This spirit and character can be seen in his constant desire for improvement and innovation. He created new products, supported international growth, and developed a new green product development platform. He notes, "People knew in 1979 … that the Earth is round … and the soap is white… I still had another idea for the soap. I thought of changing soap's composition and therefore its color. Thus we created the first black soap with propolis in the world." Being a beekeeper, Apivita's founder created an organizational culture based on bees' values. There is an emphasis of teamwork, hard work, and support. In times of crisis and change, Apivita's founder relied on positive relationships with his managing team and employees, trust, good will, proactivity, respect, and hard work.

However, there were a number of unsuccessful organizational changes implemented in Apivita. First, Apivita has acquired a pharmaceutical company to strengthen its position in order to enter a new market. Apivita's founder invested in his very good relationships with a vast number of pharmacists. He trusted that they would support his choice and become customers. However, this acquisition was not a success. The reason was that these two companies were incompatible in terms of branding, positioning, and organizational culture. He showed trust in people relationships and overconfidence in his abilities to succeed in every situation.

Second, Apivita was managed by two CEOs at different times. They didn't bring the expected results and at the end they both left the company. Apivita's founder appointed these two CEOs based on personal recommendations. Hiring through personal trust is quite a common element of Greek culture (Myloni, Harzing and Mirza, 2004). He chose to partially ignore the formal selection process as these two CEOs gained his trust very quickly. He showed overconfidence in his instinct, which was saying that these were the right people for his company. That wasn't the case in the end, and he admits that "you don't only need character but also you need specific skills to succeed in leadership."

Third, being a member of a left-wing party, Apivita's founder believes in fair wages and employee treatment. Following his beliefs, he was very sensitive to employees' rights, equal opportunities, and well-being. That contributed to employees' motivation and work engagement. On the other hand, Apivita's founder was prepared to accept low performance as he was very reluctant to let people go. In times of crisis and change, being protective of low performers can damage employees' morale and the company's future. There are perceived inequalities among employees and this has a negative impact on superior performance when it is most needed.

Finally, Apivita is a company with a strong philosophy, values, social responsibility, heritage, and an innovative outlook. It has evolved into a vast universe of people, products, aims, values, dreams, and new endeavors, which ensure its ongoing development. The mission of the company cultivates the notion that Apivita is a way of life. And it shapes the relationships of the company with employees in Greece and abroad, suppliers, beekeepers and cultivators, university teachers and researchers, and with pharmacists and customers throughout the world. Apivita has managed to find corporate success based on the abilities of the firm to adapt to the public demand for a greener way of being and by developing products that combine the natural, environmental, and social elements. As a result, Apivita can claim to be one of the few Greek companies to have emerged from the six-year recession not just intact, but also confident of its future (Reguly, 2014). Apivita's founder has remained true to his values and to his mission to promote a natural way of life and to inspire others through his vision.

Note

1   All quotations and some of the background information for this chapter are taken from personal communications with M. Vakola, dated April 15 and June 5, 2015.

References

Hope, K. (2013). Apivita: Bees provide key ingredient for cosmetics firm. *BBC News*, November 29. Retrieved from www.bbc.com/news/business-25124048 (last accessed 12 December 2016).

Myloni, B., Harzing, A.-W. and Mirza, H. (2004). Human resource management in Greece – Have the colours of culture faded away? *International Journal of Cross Cultural Management*, 4(1), 59–76.

Reguly, E. (2014). How a Greek company searching for 'common good' became a rare success story. *The Globe and Mail*, July 1. Retrieved from www.theglobeandmail.com/report-on-business/international-business/european-business/slow-and-steady/article19406734 (last accessed 12 December 2016).

8 Leadership and change management

An Indian perspective

Shefali Nandan

Introduction

India is a vast country with 29 states. It is the seventh largest country in the world. The country is unique in terms of culture as Indian culture is an assimilation of various cultures. Each Indian state has its own customs, traditions, language, dress, etc. Moreover, in the past the country was invaded and ruled by many foreign rulers like Muslims, Mughals, English, Portuguese, and Dutch, and each of them left a deep impact on Indian culture. Despite so much diversity, there are certain traditions, values, beliefs, and assumptions that are common in the Indian population.

According to Hofstede (1991, p. 263), culture can be defined in terms of "broad tendencies to prefer certain states of affairs over others." He used four dimensions to measure these tendencies: power distance, individualism vs. collectivism, masculinity vs. femininity, and uncertainty avoidance. India scored relatively high on power distance and masculinity (in terms of visual display of success and power). There is a deeply rooted hierarchical culture, according to which subordinates are expected to strictly follow the orders of superiors. Tolerance is a valued virtue in Indian culture and orientation is long-term. Indian society shows traits of both collectivism and individualism. Collectivism means that there is a high preference for belonging to a larger social group, and the actions of the individual are influenced by the opinions of members of their social framework, like one's family, work group, etc. Individualism results from the Hindu concept of *karma* (or the sum of a person's actions during their entire existence, which affect their destiny in this and future lives) and dominates religious and philosophical thought. People are, therefore, individually responsible for their actions and behaviors and the impact these will have on their rebirth (Hofstede, undated).

The Global Leadership and Organizational Behavior Effectiveness (GLOBE) project placed India along with certain other countries in the southern Asia cluster, finding it to be performance driven with a strong future orientation (Liddell, 2005). This cluster was also found to value charisma, team orientation, and humane leadership (Javidan and Dastmalchian, 2003). Cappelli, Singh, Singh, and Useem (2010) found that Indian leaders and their organizations take a long-term, internally focused view. They work to create a sense of social mission. They have a high concern for employee development and try to increase their engagement by looking after the interests of their families as well. Indian leaders have long been involved in societal issues, investing in community services.

Case study

The present case study is about a social entrepreneur coming from an academic background. Dr. Sunit Singh is working with 3,000 stonebreakers and agricultural labor families residing in rural areas of the Allahabad district located in southeastern parts of Uttar Pradesh, a northern province in India. The majority of these families are trapped in intergenerational debt bondage in lieu of the illegal loans taken from the contractors or moneylenders. Dr. Singh has organized these families into 250 self-help groups (SHGs) and other forms of community-based organizations, and then federated them at the district level. He has created a unique model of commercially viable social enterprise by combining social, financial, and business innovations at community level for ensuring sustainable freedom for the bonded families through collective ownership of enterprise.

By profession, Dr. Singh is an Associate Professor at Govind Ballabh Pant Social Science Institute (GBPSSI), a constituent institute of the University of Allahabad. Dr. Singh is also Founder President of the non-governmental organization (NGO) Pragati Gramodyog evam Samaj-kalyan Sansthan (*pragati* is a Hindi word that means progress). The NGO was formed by a group of young social entrepreneurs in 1986. Through his tireless efforts and visionary leadership for the last 25 years, Dr. Singh has led the NGO to move forward from one trajectory to another in a successful manner. Besides, he also supports a few grassroots organizations in an advisory capacity. A semi-guided interview was conducted, which was based on a literature review and an interview guide provided by this book's editors.

Early life

Dr. Sunit Singh was born in a middle-class family. His father was a professor, an idealist, and a man of strong principles. He was active in politics and believed in communist ideology. He was a hardliner, and the then government was against that ideology so he was arrested in early 1971. Dr. Singh was still studying at school in those days. It was a tough time for the family, which comprised his mother and his two younger sisters. There was no source of income. Their relatives and friends started avoiding them. His mother was not being hired for the same reason, despite holding the required educational qualifications. Those were very difficult days for the family that was once living a comfortable life full of friends, fun, and enjoyment. His mother did not lose heart and opened her own school. This helped in creating a flow of steady income, which could sustain the family. His father was later released from jail in 1972.

His early studies were completed in a school based on scouting principles. The teachers gave a protective environment to the students and tried to inculcate humane values in them, with an objective to produce good human beings who would lead in their respective fields. Later, admission into a bigger school for higher school studies led to an opening up of his personality. He then took admission in the University of Allahabad where he completed his graduation and post-graduation. It was during this period that the 'leader' in him began to show. He learnt many lessons of life at university. He took active part in student politics. India is a country where many religions are practiced and society is divided into an even larger number of castes. He is an idealist like his father and never used any undue means to achieve his goals. He never appreciated the politics of caste and religion. This value has also been inherited from his father, who himself has been secular in his beliefs. He says, "there were no differentiations ever made in the family on the basis of caste or religion."

The struggle that he faced in his childhood for ensuring a livelihood and the values received from his parents and teachers, coupled with exposure to various experiences in university, shaped his personality. Since he was actively involved in student politics, he learnt how to organize people with shared vision and manage affairs collectively to achieve common goals. The leader within him got a platform. While participating in various student activities, he learnt the lesson of democratic decision-making and how to accommodate dissent.

Change management

During his college days he was interested in working for the destitute and poor. Since he himself had experienced the pressures of making a living and making both ends meet, he was determined to organize initiatives for sustainable livelihoods for poor people. During his university days as a student, just out of sheer interest, he along with some like-minded friends decided to support laborers working in stone quarries. The stone contractors recruited these laborers. Because of poverty they often had to take loans and advances from their contractor. This put them in a trap to work on payment of only one third of the prevailing wage rates. These poor laborers were stuck in a state of abject poverty. They could not even think of sending their children to school as the entire family was forced to work in stone cutting. They worked very hard hoping that they may be able to repay their loan, which they never actually managed to do. They were, in fact, living like bonded laborers.

Dr. Sunit Singh and his friends were moved by the condition of these workers and wanted to bring them out of their bonded situations. They consulted District Rural Industry Centre and other senior functionaries of district administration, who offered a lot of support to their endeavor. In order to be able to do so formally, they got an NGO registered. This was an outcome of his entrepreneurial zeal. Through their NGO they wanted to train some of these workers for match manufacturing. They managed to procure a loan from District Rural Industry Centre and purchased machinery and sent some workers for training to south India. The machines had to be procured from specific government vendors. These machines were very expensive, yet old fashioned and using outdated technology, which did not work. Thus, their project was virtually a failure. Dr. Singh learnt from this failed endeavor that they themselves should have gone to inspect and check machines before purchasing them. The problems had arisen largely due to their inexperience. The enterprise failed to start up; however, Dr. Sunit Singh and friends repaid the loan of Rs 80,000 to the Centre personally. Through this experience he learnt that it is essential to do proper research and gain full knowledge about the business development plan before embarking upon any project.

Later on, Dr. Singh and his team realized that they needed to adopt a different approach if they wanted to uplift the lives of stone cutting workers. They realized that in order to free the bonded stone laborers, they should try to help the laborers in getting lease rights of stone quarries. They had the inherent skills in stone cutting and therefore they could move to their own sites from the contractors' sites without involving any gestation period. The major challenge was to arrange money for applying for a mining lease.

A credit innovation was introduced in the form of the Group Savings Fund. The laborers were encouraged to pool their meager savings among themselves through SHGs. The SHGs put together their savings with the Group Savings Fund. It was the starting point to mobilize resources required for getting a mining lease. Thus, this was the beginning of the formation of SHGs. Dr. Singh educated the workers about the benefits of forming SHGs. Finally, as a cascading effect, about 200 SHGs were formed. It was a significant innovation in creating community organizations among the bonded stone laborers. He went to meet officers at the National Bank for Rural Development (NABARD), who were very positive about this initiative. NABARD observed the work of the SHGs for six months and later decided to help them in getting loans from the local commercial bank branch. The district administration granted mining leases to SHGs and the workers started working freely on their own quarries. Their income increased by three to four times. Others workers observed this success and started forming SHGs and getting leases. Seven mining leases were granted. This was a big success on the part of bonded laborers and at the same time was a challenge to the monopoly of mining contractors. Throughout this entire initiative his entrepreneurial zeal was reflected, as this activity involved a lot of risk, innovativeness, and patience, which was exhibited during this experimentation.

After a few years, challenges related to management of the leases began to surface. The problems were largely due to lack of professional skills among laborers. The issues were related to accounting of revenues and expenses, day-to-day management of activities, such as transportation and supply chain management activities that workers had not earlier been responsible for and hence were not conversant with. Gradually, the problems began to multiply and ultimately the experiment headed into failure. Workers began to revert to their old contractors who had been awaiting this opportunity. Dr. Singh learnt another lesson. He realized the importance of professional skills for undertaking activities of this magnitude. Later, the disintegrated SHGs were reorganized. As a result of learning from previous failures, this time mining activities were managed by trained people, for example, professionally trained people handled accounts, and the effort proved to be successful. His experiences of overseeing the mining lease with workers' SHGs taught him the importance of transparency and accountability. There were lawyers who were ready to help him and they provided legal advice to the workers on various issues. After several rounds of discussions at GBPSSI with all the stakeholders, a Participatory Model of Responsible Mining was devised for new stone quarries – the Pragati Freedom Mining Site. The quarry business was operated successfully for five years from 2008 to 2013.

GBPSSI runs a two-year MBA Rural Development program with the aim to train young development professionals for bringing transformation in rural areas and to take up their careers as active change agents for community development. Dr. Singh had been in the sheet anchor role during the launch of this innovative and unique program in 2001. He was made the first coordinator of this program, because of his past experiences. At GBPSSI, he learnt to put practice and principles together and honed his researching skills.

Dr. Singh again came up with innovative ideas to bring about positive changes for community development. He motivated SHG members to take up organic farming. This seemed a feasible activity as it did not require much investment. The soil in forests around targeted villages was fertile. Here, farmers were trained to adopt low-cost organic farming systems to produce local variety food grains, fruits, and vegetables. It was good for soil health and agricultural sustainability. The produce was processed and sold with a tag of social value to free laborers from debt bondage. He facilitated in creating a producer company of reliable and responsible farmers leading the organic farming practices. At present, there are about 150 marginal and small farmers as shareholders. The majority of these shareholder farmers are freed bonded laborers. They are producing organic food grains, green vegetables, and fruits. He linked this producer company with a campaign on Food for Good Health. With these aims, the producer company is operating with a triple bottom line – ensuring freedom to the bonded, food for good health, and sustainable agriculture solutions. He motivated them to participate in trade fairs organized at different places and to sell their products.

The outcome of his relentless efforts has been that it has brought a big change in the lives of people. Workers who were not even able to send their children to school are now sending them to schools regularly. Two young boys have completed their law studies and have become lawyers. They chose to pursue this profession to remove legal vulnerabilities prevailing among them. Now they are running Legal Aid Centers. Inspired by these young men, other SHG members are also sending their children for higher education. SHG members are now living a dignified and free life, which was once a dream for them.

Leadership qualities

His biggest strength is his belief in his conviction and ability to articulate his vision. He does not wait for support to come. He believes in action with his ideas and support falls in. There have been times when his ideas were not supported by others. During such times he listens to his 'inner voice' to overcome resistance to change. The resistance he faced has never been at a personal level. It has always been related to work. Right from his college days he has taken resistance very positively. With his respect for others' opinions and his amicable ways, he has been successfully able to overcome resistance. He does not hesitate accepting another's point of view if he realizes that it is better for goal achievement than his own opinion. He has always analyzed the reason for resistance and feels that his ideas have been resisted when they were not right.

He strongly believes in collective decision making, with participation of all the members. He is a relationship-oriented leader and believes that it is important to understand the problems of others and to connect with them. He believes in working with shared vision. This has been his learning from community-based participatory processes.

He has always taken a lesson from his failed endeavors, so that mistakes are not repeated. He believes that a leader should be able to inspire others, despite his or her personal weaknesses. A leader should be self-motivated and should be there with a positive attitude for finding solutions, rather than just pointing out the problems. Dr. Singh is a transformational leader who believes in influencing others for accepting change by enhancing their motivation and morale. He believes that a leader should be oriented towards the future.

Another reason for his success in managing change is his capability to create a strong network. As the scope of his work expanded, many persons, professionals, and agencies started becoming associated with him. These include government organizations, NABARD and other banks, university and research institutes, a medical college and hospitals, a regional cancer institute, advocates, human rights organizations, and individual volunteers. All these bodies have actively helped him in carrying his mission forward.

Table 8.1 Analysis of beliefs/actions for change management and leadership qualities

Belief/action	Leadership qualities
Democratic decision making in team	Participative leadership
Strong belief in secular values and opposition to casteism	Belief in equality
Starting NGO	Zeal to bring a change in society
Starting match-making business	Risk taking
Coordinator of MBA (RD)	Ability to take challenges
Concern for people's personal problems	Relationship oriented
Motivating workers for SHG formation	Transformational leadership
Mustering support from persons/agencies working in different areas	Networking

Table 8.2 Socio-cultural context of a leader's change management style

Belief/action	Socio-cultural context of India
Participative decision making	Collectivism
Listens to his inner voice in times of uncertainty	Spiritual beliefs
Strong belief in secular values	Secular values in India
Believes in doing good to others	Belief in karma
Strong bonding with family	Family culture
Working to uplift poor and helpless	Poor economic condition of a large number of Indians

Conclusion

It may be concluded that there has been a profound influence of cultural context on the leadership and change management style of Dr. Singh. Family, school, and other social institutions have shaped his value system. He believes in taking a lesson from every situation of life, whether good or bad, which has helped him move ahead in life. He is a relationship-oriented leader. He never compromises on his principles and believes that this creates an identity and also helps in being recognized as a leader.

The mission of his life is to improve the lives of poor people and give them a life of dignity. He chose this particular cause as a mission of his life because he was moved by seeing poverty all around, and he made a resolution to make all efforts to improve poor people's lives. He considers that the biggest measure of his success in social terms is that his efforts have given the people a chance to live a life of dignity. The love and trust of people that he has won are his reward.

References

Cappelli, P., Singh, H., Singh, J.V. and Useem, M. (2010). Leadership lessons from India. *Harvard Business Review*, March. Retrieved from https://hbr.org/2010/03/leadership-lessons-from-india (last accessed 12 December 2016).

Hofstede, G. (1991). *Cultures and organizations: Software of the mind*. Maidenhead: McGraw-Hill.

Hofstede, G. (Undated). India. Retrieved from http://geert-hofstede.com/india.html (last accessed 12 December 2016).

Javidan, M. and Dastmalchian, A. (2003). Culture and leadership in Iran: The land of individual achievers, strong family ties, and powerful elite. *Academy of Management Perspectives*, 17(4), 127–142.

Liddell, W. W. (2005). Project GLOBE: A large scale cross-cultural study of leadership. *Problems and Perspectives in Management*, *3*, 5–9.

9 Leading an expatriate workforce

Simon Jones

Knowledge industries are a significant element of twenty-first-century economies. Over the last 25 years, universities – the original knowledge industry – have become increasingly important engines of growth and indeed economic enterprises in their own right (Breznitz, 2014; Lane and Johnstone, 2012; Shaw, 2013; Yusuf and Nabeshima, 2007). Many countries are trying to restructure and re-invigorate their higher education sector in order to ensure pertinence, wealth creation and social cohesion. As we move further into the Asian century (ADB, 2011; Blumenthal, Coblin, Dhume, Eberstadt and Scissors, 2015), the understanding that improvements in the higher educational system facilitate economic growth (Boys, 2014; Jayasuriya, 2012; Lane, 2014) has resulted in a wide range of new university models being implemented (Arab News, 2015; Yang, 2014).

These universities vary widely in form, content, and context, some emulating directly established models and others emboldened to create distinctive models that reflect the regional imperative (Haynie, 2015; Kamel and Kazi, 2015). As a result, there has been marked growth in the number of new universities, especially in the Middle East and North Africa, and central and southern Asia regions (Havergal, 2015; Plackett, 2015). These universities, at least in the initial stages, are largely staffed and led by expatriates. Often, they are from the English-speaking world and encompass a mixture of first-time expatriates, the wider diaspora, and self-declared citizens of the world. The challenge such institutions face is building a real system out of the imaginations of many different stakeholders. Universities, like many knowledge industries, require bricks and mortar, but it is the ethos, insights, and impact of the individuals who inhabit these spaces that produce value.

This contribution reports on the experiences of building *ab initio* Nazarbayev University, a 5-year old research university in central Asia (Nazarbayev University, 2015). Like many new universities, it has a largely expatriate faculty and a largely local non-academic workforce. The development of such an institution requires the leadership team of the institution to understand the dynamics and efficiencies of such a cross-cultural workplace in order to meet its goals.

After outlining the institution, the following sections address four specific examples of where the cross-cultural interactions impact the building of the organization and when and how the leadership of this largely expatriate faculty needs to take action. Finally, some tentative conclusions about the nature of expatriate leadership in knowledge-intensive enterprises are made.

Case study: Nazarbayev University, Astana, Kazakhstan

The Republic of Kazakhstan is almost 25 years old. One of the Commonwealth of Independent States (CIS) formed when the former Soviet Union dissolved in 1991, it has a large land mass (the ninth largest country in the world) and a population of around 18 million (CIA, 2015; Embassy of the Republic of Kazakhstan in US, 2015). Its main economic activity is based around oil, minerals, and agriculture. It is considered an upper-middle-income country. By the standards of the region, it has managed the transition from a collectivist economy well and is peaceful and productive (Aitzhanova, Katsu, Linn and Yezhov, 2014). The Kazakhstani 2050 Strategic Development Plan (Nazarbayev, 2012) has education, research, and innovation as key elements. The reform of the education system is an important aspect of that (Ministry of Education and Science of the Republic of Kazakhstan, 2011), and the creation of a new model university as an exemplar of best practice is one of the ways this will be delivered.

Nazarbayev University aims to create a research university in central Asia fit for the challenges of the twenty-first century (Nazarbayev University, 2015). It incorporates a university, science park, innovation hub, and closely integrated national research centers. It is based on the concept of partnership; in this case involving 6 of the top 30 universities in the world. Each partner is aligned with one of the schools of the university, and the institution is broadly but not exclusively focused on STEM[1]-based subjects and the professions (Nazarbayev University, 2015).

The partnership model allows each school to have access to outstanding support within their domain area. Typically, partners in the initial stages provide comprehensive support, including visiting faculty, curricula, graduate students admission, and faculty recruitment advice. Over a period of about three years this evolves in such a way that the university partner develops into an equal in the relationship rather than as a service provider. This partnership model is intrinsic to the project of building a new university in the Republic of Kazakhstan. We did not wish to create an overseas branch of a campus nor did we believe the academic city model such as that found in Qatar (Kumon, 2014; Neil, 2015; TAMU, 2015) to be right for Kazakhstan. The goal was and is to create an in-country capability shaped by the needs of the nation and a lasting part of the ongoing transformation of Kazakhstan's economy and society.

Wealth creation, knowledge generation, and education are given equal importance in the model. The bulk of the funding in the early stages comes from central government, but over the longer term it is anticipated that costs will be met broadly by an equal mixture of fees, endowment income, and research work.

Nazarbayev University is an aspirational institution. It admits 9 percent of those who apply and commits over USD 100 million a year in research projects and infrastructure. In 2015, the university has three large schools and four, smaller, graduate-only schools. The university currently offers 16 majors, 15 Master's programs, two PhD programs, and one MD program. All this has been put in place by the local staff together with 229 faculty, seven deans, and two vice-provosts recruited over the last 3 years from around the world. It now has approximately 3,000 students and graduated the first cohort in June 2015.

Nazarbayev University is uniquely independent of the Ministry of Education and Science of the Republic of Kazakhstan. Authorized by an act of the Kazakhstan Majilis, it has independent authority to award degrees. Its charter is remarkably similar to many western institutions, with a high board, a supervisory board, and a guarantee of institutional autonomy (Nazarbayev University, 2015). The University Charter has created Academic and Research Councils. These are faculty-led top-level bodies with powers to define and approve the university's research and education missions. They provide a best-practice and unique-in-Kazakhstan model that balances the academic and executive governance of the institution. They also guarantee the relevance and independence of our teaching and research. Governance as defined by the charter is similar to that of a typical North American university with faculty involvement and separation of powers among the president and provost.

The cross–cultural perspective

This contribution adopts a practitioner view of the implications and challenges of cross-cultural leadership. It tries to articulate these issues and challenges by highlighting four specific examples that are germane to new institutions and where policy, human resources (HR), academic needs, and local requirements all intermix. Each example is introduced within the context of Nazarbayev University and the challenges facing its employees.

An example: tacit assumptions

Higher education institutions, like many other organizations in the creative and knowledge sectors, operate on a vast array of tacit assumptions that 'everybody knows' and therefore nobody needs to communicate (Trowler, 2008). These are built up over a long period and sometimes reflect the stability of their mission and the certainty of their purpose. For example, Oxford University was up and running long before the Aztec Empire was established.

They operate in a devolved manner, where practitioners or 'creatives' are permitted significant autonomy in what they do and how they do it. Merit is recognized by peer review and change managed by a sometimes lengthy process of reaching consensus. It's all worked very well where time, tradition, and institutional culture have permitted it. Also, such institutions are selective and it is often highly competitive to obtain a faculty position there. As a consequence, they tend to admit those with a track record of effective working and a high level of alignment with their own tacit assumptions. New universities in emerging economies are less able to do this.

What about new institutions and indeed those in regions where such traditions either never existed or are quite different? Cardinal Newman's (in Newman Reader, 2001; Mongrain, 2013) vision of a university of self-governing scholars doesn't play well in a region where population is hungry for knowledge, where private and public sectors require systematic reform, and where the expectations for research are for going from zero to hero in less than a generation. It's too slow, too solipsistic, too expensive, and just too obscure for the rapidly expanding economies of the east and the south.

New universities need new models and new management. Emerging institutions in emerging regions need models of culture, values, and expectations that are articulated more explicitly than elsewhere and a leadership structure capable of implementing it. A frequently made mistake is to assume that transplanting an American or European model will succeed because it has succeeded elsewhere (Salmi, 2010). People involved in transplantation surgery will tell you the problem is not the donated organ: that's usually been chosen because it is healthy and strong. The challenge is in managing the recipient's response and the tendency of their own immune system to reject the graft. This analogy seems applicable to higher education.

Without being explicit about institutions' values, chaos can arise even when the individuals involved have an outstanding track record elsewhere. Entropy increases because tacit assumptions are not mutual; hence, suddenly people are vexed by the behavior of others, and unless clear intervention takes place, in the worst cases it can turn into something resembling *Lord of the Flies* (Golding, 1954) with PhDs. So, one of the ways of addressing this is by being explicit about the values of an institution right at the start and taking more time than one might imagine necessary to repeat and reinforce those values through individual, collective, and administrative words and deeds.

Of course, the first thing is to define those values. Surprisingly, in many other areas such as collegiality, excellence, and inclusivity, a new university with culturally diverse, multinational faculty will have at first sight few shared tacit assumptions. For example, and perhaps reflecting the author's role, age, and cultural background, civility seems a natural tacit assumption. If you've worked at an uncivil organization you'll readily appreciate it. However, it's not universally accepted; the American Association of University Professors (AAUP) considers civility as incompatible with academic freedom (AAUP, undated; Euben, 2002; Thorne, 2013). This seems a good example of the gap in mutual understanding that can be faced. One might be tempted at this point to throw one's hands up in exasperation and tackle something less Sisyphean, but perseverance can pay off. Working in groups with people will get you to see that it is not the values themselves that are askance so much as the motivation for those values and the way they are articulated. It is slow work, but careful debate and dialogue can steadily take you to a place where a new institution can state with clarity, 'This is who we are and this is what we believe in.'

Without talking this talk, institutions constantly stumble over themselves as beliefs and the expression of those beliefs continue to be misunderstood. It's a conversation that has to be had, yet too often we skip over it in the rush to lead expatriate-intensive organizations. The Nazarbayev University experience has been the dynamic between three different constituencies. Each of them valid and, at the start at least, each of them adhering to their own perspective.

The first is the western model of universities as being autonomous bodies of scholars and that if you give scholars freedom, then the maximum utility will be derived. The second is the Kazakhstani model of universities being centrally organized and the Education Ministry having close control over academic delivery. Furthermore, as context, in the former USSR, which defines the heritage of the local Kazakhstani higher education system, universities teach: they do not research. So, the linkage of research and teaching is both new and challenging. In an attempt to address this, a suitable first step some institutions are considering is the co-location of research centers and academic schools on the same campus. The third perspective is of the leadership of the university, who are there to represent the government's interest. An institution such as Nazarbayev University is a symbol and source of national pride.

Indeed, travelling through the regions, I am humbled by the trust and faith local populations have in my colleagues to deliver something of pride and value. It is expressed regularly and unabashedly. The university leadership perspective is to ensure political and consequential financial support for the institution by being responsive to the needs of the government and civil authority. This perspective can often result in mission creep, sudden changes, and unexpected intervention at multiple levels.

It is little surprise then that these beliefs interact with each other in both productive and less productive ways. For example, there is a view that faculty should do research within a research center and subject to the organizational constraints of that center. Most typically, this would include the center selecting the project. That is an unusual approach for some faculty. Another example would be the desire of faculty to work with faculty from other universities without obtaining the endorsement of the leadership of the institution.

However, there are also extraordinarily positive, not always serendipitous events. One example of this is the way in which research in the university can be directly communicated to senior governmental leaders and approval for further work very rapidly reached. All these examples constantly test the tacit assumptions that faculty, administration, and leadership have. The better organizations trust the skills and flexibility of their people to deal with this. The best explicitly acknowledge these issues and actively manage it.

An example: academic freedom

Academic freedom is a topic regularly discussed by faculty at universities. It's a term that is used loosely and is sometimes meant whatever it is convenient to mean. Given its importance to successful universities, this section contextualizes the way in which academic freedom is articulated by expatriate faculty and the ways in which it is of most utility to the wider stakeholders of a university.

Academic freedom as defined in the nineteenth-century Newmanian, Humboldtian, or United States (US)-led liberal arts models (Anderson, 2006; Rothblatt, 1997), namely a notional, arguably mythical university, is in practice a culturally defined concept. This means that the unthinking application of this at best partial and transitory and at worst mythical model to nascent institutions in very different regions can easily be misconstrued.

For newly emergent institutions in rapidly developing regions, the notion of academic freedom needs to be explored in a more nuanced way if it is to provide the bulwark and lodestone of excellence as it can often do in more settled circumstances. Institutions and especially their faculty representatives can bind themselves in lengthy debate on this topic, but fundamentally, academic freedom in the twenty-first century is better understood in its original incarnation (Menand, 1996; Nelson, 2010) as the ability of an institution to chart its own course without undue influence from outside bodies. Like it or not, that's the academic freedom most pertinent to emerging institutions.

Whether a university has academic freedom or not is a topic regularly brought up in faculty-administration debate. It is true in both settled and emerging universities that there may always be the case that at the outer edges of scholarship and pedagogy there may be constraints on approaches that can be taken and topics that are difficult to teach or study. This is always a topic of intense debate and individuals will legitimately adopt different positions depending on their background and role. In practice, the complications occur when those who perhaps have elevated the position above its utility argue that since one topic cannot be explored academic freedom therefore does not exist. It's an argument that is at best puerile and at worst corrosive. To use an analogy, you have the freedom to cough, but you do not have the freedom to cough in my face. I would argue it is pertinent to focus on what can be addressed and the utility it permits.

When expatriate scholars talk of academic freedom, they sometimes bundle together two distinct concepts. The first is the notion that researchers should be able to address any topic they like without fear or favor (but with adequate funding). The second is faculty governance. This undoubtedly works well for the elite universities of the world where top-class researchers and outstanding students work in a resource-rich and mission-sympathetic environment. Less selective, more nascent institutions may experience different outcomes.

Most universities are by definition not elite. New universities in developing countries are especially dissimilar from the top 40 world-ranked institutions. It is difficult to persuade funders of the proposition that scarce research money, in a country with so many other pressing needs, should be spent on expatriate researchers who are perceived to be of uncertain fealty and insufficiently aware of the needs of the country. Research agendas will be tightly defined and the institution will be expected to comply with this framework. In addition, it is certainly possible that the cultural and or religious context defines boundaries of debate and challenge.

The second element of this unbundled academic freedom is faculty governance. It's important. It is so important it needs to be implemented systematically through the structures and processes of every institution. The question then is, given very different institutions, in very different circumstances, and at very different stages of development, does a single size fit all? The answer to this rhetorical question is no. A well-established institution rich in tacit assumptions, settled in its operation, and with a regular and incremental pattern of development is quite different from an 18-month institution yet to graduate its first students and only half its schools operating (as was, for example, Nazarbayev University in 2012). The balance between the consultative, the executive, and the participatory elements of faculty governance clearly needs to reflect this.

Academic freedom is undoubtedly advantageous. The challenge that expatriate leaders have is to frame the abstract notion within a specific context to permit free thinking and doing in a new and still evolving university and region. This freedom has to acknowledge the investment the host country has made, the pride that the citizens of the nation have in such a bold endeavor, and the hope that through the creation of new knowledge, economic growth will result and employment opportunities will be found and prosperity generated. These are the freedoms the host nation is seeking.

An example: administrative misconceptions

It is not unusual, indeed sometimes expected, that in new institutions administrative procedures do not go smoothly. This is compounded by the fact that in expatriate institutions the employer plays a larger role in the housing, childcare, healthcare, and travel arrangements for faculty. Such issues can matter a lot to individuals, especially when in a novel environment. So, when it does go wrong, people feel upset, insecure, and sometimes angry. In a contemporary western environment, people are expected to acknowledge their own mistakes, apologize, and learn from them.

The act of apologizing usually brings the matter to an end in western cultures. In contrast, in central and southern Asia where there is a culture of 'face' (Drake, undated; Kim and Cohen, 2010), it is hugely painful and embarrassing for people to lose face by apologizing and they can sometimes go to lengths to avoid this. Furthermore, in such parts of the world there often exists a formal bureaucracy and a member of staff who has to apologize may have disciplinary sanctions or a financial penalty against him or her as a result. So, for both practical and emotional reasons, an apology is avoided.

It is possible to see an illuminating sequence with an expatriate member of faculty more and more intensely seeking a specific apology and the (usually more junior and likely less well paid) staff member evading this with increasing anxiety. One does not realize that an apology can end the matter and the other that an apology can imply much more to the apologizer than temporary embarrassment. It's a dance you may see repeated time and time again.

Part of the leadership response is the well-established recognition that a multicultural environment should be flexible, tolerant of ambiguity, and not over-reacting. That's certainly a right thing to do as it will mitigate the effects. There is a bigger challenge beyond this, however. Many international companies prepare their staff for expatriate employment well in advance of the start of the contract. The initial cross-cultural talks from HR and others deal with the issue from a practical first-day perspective (Chew, 2004; Vance and Paik, 2015). In some organizations, including universities, it tends to end there. What is needed is to see the task of adjustment as an ongoing one and a central part of the employees' duties and responsibilities. Regular workshops will help; buddying with local employees will help. However, for this to succeed the individual employees need to be personally accountable for this as an integral part of their duties and in their continuing professional development. Consequentially, their competencies in intercultural conflict resolution may need to be appraised in terms of their progress, for example, through the annual performance review. Many institutions are some way from this today.

An example: organizational development

Faculty at a university have three types of duties: teaching, research, and service. Teaching and research activities usually are similar to faculty members' prior experiences. At Nazarbayev University we expect faculty to spend some 20 percent of their time providing service, so it is a not a minor component of their responsibilities. Moreover, service in a new university involves contributing to the management or development of the institution's administrative activities. Given the nascence of the institution, the balance of activity is towards organizational development and not administering any existing system or process.

The faculty members of Nazarbayev University originate from 43 countries, as indicated by their current passport. While some represent the regional diaspora of the last 20 years, the bulk of the faculty have been trained in established universities based on the traditional western model. Furthermore, as is common with new universities in developing regions, the faculty tend to be at the start or end of their career. Independent of background or longevity, the unifying characteristic of our faculty is that the bulk of them come from time-honored universities that have long established their tacit and implicit values and exist in a society with a reasonably settled view as to what higher education should be like and look like. As a consequence, few of them have any experience in building an institution *ab initio* and consequentially lack insight to do so. Furthermore, not all are equally inspired to do so. This sets the scene for a particular organizational dynamic.

The dynamic commences with the legitimate request for a faculty governance model. To this is added the circumstance that there is often insufficient administrative capacity during the start-up phase. As a result, faculty, sometimes even the most junior, need to undertake service that involves designing and implementing core administrative processes of the institution. Some see this as part of the excitement of a new institution. Some do not. Whatever their predisposition or enthusiasm, it is not the usual role that faculty service plays in a university, but is unavoidable in start-up institutions. Moreover, the faculty of new institutions are mainly junior and while mostly enthusiastic, they naturally lack experience. The cross-cultural element informs all this: people arrive from different institutions with differing management ethoses. Ideas about accountability, deference to authority, and communication will vary widely.

The service element of new institutions with a multicultural faculty continues to be an unresolved challenge for my own institution and I suspect some others. Core administrative processes were designed and operated by those we had appointed to different roles. The consistency, quality, robustness, scalability, and interoperability of the processes we design are challenged by the rate of growth in student numbers and the stakeholder-requested broadening of our mission. There is no straightforward solution to this other than acquiring leadership and management capability faster than one acquires faculty. Some start-up universities have explicitly created the management team prior to admitting a single student or appointing faculty, hopefully eliminating or mitigating the above issues (ISIS-Innovation, 2014; Yachay University, 2015). We could not. Even in the circumstances of having a fully formed management team in advance, cross-cultural issues will continue to impinge. The balance between the executive and the consultative, the ways in which agreements are negotiated and implemented, the style of communication, and the perceived separation between the authority of the post and that of the post-holder all vary widely.

Particularly pertinent here is that the typical US university model is towards one end of the continuum. It is effective in that setting, but it is designed to maintain institutions, not construct them. Many emerging institutions are in regions without that tradition and almost always expect results quickly. It seems typical that a more managerialist view emerges from new institutions. This conflicts with the more devolved models many faculty are familiar with. Sadly, this can sometimes result in conflict between faculty and administration. A good deal of distrust can emerge from an administration that is genuinely trying to build the necessary core processes and a faculty used to considerably more autonomy, as permitted and enabled by a well-established and robust system.

For the author, it is most remarkable that even seasoned higher education specialists genuinely believe that faculty can create a new university. It is a little like believing surgeons, nurses, and osteopaths are the people best placed to construct a hospital. Over the longer term this can settle down. Once adequate processes are in place, the institution feels more settled and the requirement for this managerialist approach can slowly diminish. Furthermore, the type of faculty that join an established university is different; they are mid-career, experienced, yet still willing to learn new methods. This helps too. The initial stages, however, are certainly full of passion.

Concluding remarks

Rapidly developing knowledge-intensive institutions with a predominance of expatriate workers face challenges different in scope and scale compared to their more established equivalents. These challenges include, first, the work environment not being underpinned by a set of well-established tacit assumptions. Much of the effectiveness of the traditional informal, unstructured work environment of many knowledge-based institutions relies on these shared assumptions as a means of ensuring order and progress. Second, the traditional academic culture of deferment to subject expertise and the subsidiary role of service means that the rate of change needed by new institutions is not deliverable by models of faculty or shared governance. Third, the need to build new structures rather than evolve existing ones requires conceptually different skills and markedly greater effort than the well-established collegial consensus-based model can provide.

These three challenges lead to the paradox of expatriate leadership in knowledge-intensive industries, namely that the very things that are argued by faculty to provide the creativity, flair, and insight in universities are not compatible with the structures, processes, and timescale necessary to deliver that model. The challenge of expatriate leadership is therefore to resolve this paradox or at least acknowledge and manage its consequences. Leading expatriate knowledge-intensive industries requires a much more formal and project-oriented mindset than faculty are sometimes comfortable with. Furthermore, it is not entirely frank to claim that this is a temporary set of affairs and once fully developed the institution will resemble a traditional university model. First, this is because rapidly developing regions want a university fit for their needs, not one that fits an abstracted model. Their needs tend to be specific, short- or medium-term, and subject to revision or extension. This requires an action-oriented and directed approach. Second, the time scales to create a university that is considered internationally competitive is lengthy. Pohang University of Science and Technology (POSTECH) in South Korea (POSTECH, 2015) was founded in 1986 but took 25 years (and the shortest time on record) to break into the top 100 universities in the world, ranked 66th in 2015 (TimesHigherEd, 2015). So, it will be quite some time before an institution is considered research intensive. Thirdly, such entities usually require significant governmental resources, which imply scrutiny by media, political bodies, and governmental apparatus. This too increases pressures to have a more project-oriented and accountable organization. All these factors run counter to the collegial system where the balance between the consultative and the executive is strongly predisposed to the former.

So, what has to be done to resolve or manage this paradox? It is important to acknowledge and accept it rather than behave as if it were temporary or peripheral. Be clear and be public about this and encourage a debate around its implications at all levels of the institution. Moreover, the nascence of the institution, the faculty skillset, and the regional expectations require a much more explicit and managerialist approach to the construction, leadership, and operation of the institution. This will incur significant internal pushback from faculty and other academic stakeholders, but it needs to be done in order to maintain the positive growth path of the institution in a manner and timeliness that satisfies national and regional stakeholders. Finally, the leadership of the institution has to try and build as much of the organizational processes, leadership, and management teams before recruiting faculty or admitting students.

Leading expatriate universities is a race. It's a race to acquire faculty faster than you acquire students, acquire leadership faster than you acquire faculty, and acquire the organizational processes and methods faster than you acquire leadership. Experience at Nazarbayev University has shown if you win that race, your other problems won't matter much. And if you don't win, your other problems won't matter at all.

Note

1   Science, technology, engineering, and mathematics.

References

AAUP. (undated). Protecting academic freedom. American Association of University Professors. Retrieved from www.aaup.org/our-work/protecting-academic-freedom (last accessed 12 December 2016).

ADB. (2011). *Asia 2050: Realizing the Asian Century*. Asian Development Bank. Retrieved from www.adb.org/sites/default/files/publication/28608/asia2050-executive-summary.pdf (last accessed 12 December 2016).

Aitzhanova, A., Katsu, S., Linn, J. F. and Yezhov, V. (eds). (2014). *Kazakhstan 2050: Toward a modern society for all*. Oxford: Oxford University Press.

Anderson, R. (2006). *British universities: Past and present*. London: Hambledon Continuum.

Arab News. (2015). New university to solve problem of expats. *ArabNews*, April 21. Retrieved from https://en-maktoob.news.yahoo.com/university-solve-problem-expats-050244549.html (last accessed 12 December 2016).

Blumenthal, D., Coblin, A., Dhume, S., Eberstadt, N. and Scissors, D. M. (2015). Rethinking the Asian Century. *Washington Examiner*, June 8. Retrieved from www.washingtonexaminer.com/rethinking-the-asian-century/article/2565662 (last accessed 12 December 2016).

Boys, J. (2014). *Building better universities: Strategies, spaces, technologies*. New York: Taylor & Francis.

Breznitz, S. M. (2014). *The fountain of knowledge: The role of universities in economic development*. Stanford, CA: Stanford University Press.

Chew, J. (2004). Managing MNC expatriates through crises: A challenge for international human resource management. *Research and Practice in Human Resource Management*, 12(2), 1–30.

CIA. (2015). The world factbook: Central Asia—Kazakhstan. Retrieved from www.cia.gov/library/publications/the-world-factbook/geos/kz.html (last accessed 12 December 2016).

Drake, B. (undated). What is 'Face' in Asian culture and why should we care? Casey Research International Man. Retrieved from www.internationalman.com/articles/what-is-face-in-asian-culture-and-why-should-we-care (last accessed 12 December 2016).

Embassy of the Republic of Kazakhstan in US. (2015). Discover Kazakhstan. Retrieved from www.kazakhembus.com/content/discover-kazakhstan-0 (last accessed 12 December 2016).

Euben, D. R. (2002). Academic freedom of professors and institutions. American Association of University Professors (AAUP). Retrieved from www.aaup.org/issues/academic-freedom/professors-and-institutions (last accessed 12 December 2016).

Golding, W. (1954). *Lord of the flies*. London: Faber & Faber.

Havergal, C. (2015). MENA top 30 snapshot released as THE MENA Universities Summit launches. *Times New Higher Education*, February 24. Retrieved from www.timeshighereducation.co.uk/news/mena-top-30-snapshot-released-as-the-mena-universities-summit-launches/2018704.article (last accessed 12 December 2016).

Haynie, D. (2015). Top 10 universities in Asia. *US News & World Report*, June 24. Retrieved from www.usnews.com/education/best-global-universities/slideshows/top-10-universities-in-asia (last accessed 12 December 2016).

ISIS-Innovation. (2014). New Muscat University to open doors in 2016. Retrieved from http://isis-innovation.com/new-muscat-university-open-doors-2016 (last accessed 12 December 2016).

Jayasuriya, K. (2012). Reinventing the public mission of the research university in the Asian Century: A gateway approach. *The Indo-Pacific Governance Research Centre, Policy Brief*, Issue 6, December. Retrieved from www.adelaide.edu.au/indo-pacific-governance/research/policy/Jayasuriya_2012_PB6.pdf

Kamel, E. and Kazi, S. (2015). Qatar's universities are too expensive for many expats. *Al-Fanar Media*, March 8. Retrieved from www.al-fanarmedia.org/2015/03/qatars-universities-expensive-many-expats (last accessed 12 December 2016).

Kim, Y. H. and Cohen, D. (2010). Information, perspective, and judgement about the self in face and dignity cultures. *Personality and Social Psychology Bulletin*, (36), 537–550.

Kumon, S. (2014). Qatar spends big to build academic hub. *Asian Review*, November 29. Retrieved from http://asia.nikkei.com/Life-Arts/Education/Qatar-spends-big-to-build-academic-hub (last accessed 12 December 2016).

Lane, J. E. (2014). *Building a smarter university: Big data, innovation, and analytics*. Critical Issues in Higher Education 3. Albany, NY: SUNY Press.

Lane, J. E. and Johnstone, D. B. (2012). *Universities and colleges as economic drivers: Measuring higher education's role in economic development*. Critical Issues in Higher Education 1. Albany, NY: SUNY Press.

Menand, L. (1996). The limits of academic freedom. In L. Menand (ed.), *The future of academic freedom* (pp. 15–19). Chicago, IL: University of Chicago Press.

Ministry of Education and Science of the Republic of Kazakhstan. (2011). State program of education development in the republic of Kazakhstan for 2011–2020. Retrieved from http://planipolis.iiep.unesco.org/upload/Kazakhstan/Kazakhstan_State_Program-of-Education-Development-in-the-Republic-of-Kazakhstan_2011-2020.pdf

Mongrain, K. (2013). *Newman's idea of the university-Today*. Center for Catholic Studies, Seton Hall University, Paper 10. Retrieved from http://scholarship.shu.edu/cgi/viewcontent.cgi?article=1009&context=catholic-studies (last accessed 12 December 2016).

Nazarbayev, N. A. (2012). Kazakhstan 2050. Retrieved from http://strategy2050.kz/en (last accessed 12 December 2016).

Nazarbayev University. (2015). About us. Retrieved from http://nu.edu.kz (last accessed 12 December 2016).

Neil, M. (2015). Harvard, Northwestern help Qatar open law school that will award a JD degree. *ABA Journal*, March 3. Retrieved from www.abajournal.com/news/article/harvard_northwestern_help_qatar_open_law_school_that_will_award_a_j.d._degr (last accessed 12 December 2016).

Nelson, C. (2010). *No university is an island: Saving academic freedom*. New York: NYU Press.

Newman Reader. (2001). John Henry Newman: The idea of a university. Retrieved from www.newman-reader.org/works/idea (last accessed 12 December 2016).

Plackett, B. (2015). The top five research universities in MENA? Maybe. *Al-Fanar Media*, February 3. Retrieved from www.al-fanarmedia.org/2015/02/top-five-research-universities-mena-maybe (last accessed 12 December 2016).

POSTECH. (2015). Founding tenets. Pohang University of Science and Technology. Retrieved from http://home.postech.ac.kr/eng/about-postech/introduction-to-postech/founding-tenets/ (last accessed 12 December 2016).

Rothblatt, S. (1997). *The modern university and its discontents: The fate of Newman's legacies in Britain and America*. Cambridge: Cambridge University Press.

Salmi, J. (2010). Nine common errors when building a new world-class university. *Inside HigherEd*, September 22. Retrieved from www.insidehighered.com/blogs/the_world_view/nine_common_errors_when_building_a_new_world_class_university (last accessed 12 December 2016).

Shaw, C. (2013). John Cridland: 'Universities are employers – they are businesses'. *The Guardian*, September 2. Retrieved from www.theguardian.com/higher-education-network/2013/sep/02/john-cridland-universities-economic-growth (last accessed 12 December 2016).

TAMU. (2015). Texas A&M University at Qatar, Huawei and Ooredoo build global education alliance. Retrieved from www.albawaba.com/business/pr/texas-am-university-qatar-huawei-and-ooredoo-build-global-education-alliance-701434 (last accessed 12 December 2016).

Thorne, A. (2013). Can civility and academic freedom coexist? National Association of Scholars (NAS), September 25. Retrieved from www.nas.org/articles/can_civility_and_academic_freedom_coexist (last accessed 12 December 2016).

TimesHigherEd. (2015). World University Rankings 2015: Pohang University of Science and Technology. Retrieved from www.timeshighereducation.co.uk/world-university-rankings/pohang-university-of-science-and-technology?ranking-dataset=1083 (last accessed 12 December 2016).

Trowler, P. (2008). *Cultures and change in higher education: Theories and practices*. New York: Palgrave Macmillan.

Vance, C. M. and Paik, Y. (2015). *Managing a global workforce* (3rd edn). New York: Routledge.

Yachay University. (2015). About. Retrieved from www.yachay.gob.ec/yachay-university (last accessed 12 December 2016).

Yang, C. (2014). New universities in Asia outranking young colleges in the West. *New York Times*, September 28. Retrieved from www.nytimes.com/2014/09/29/education/new-universities-in-asia-outranking-young-colleges-in-the-west.html (last accessed 12 December 2016).

Yusuf, S. and Nabeshima, K. (eds). (2007). *How universities promote economic growth*. Washington, DC: World Bank. Retrieved from www.usp.ac.fj/worldbank2009/frame/Documents/Publications_global/383330Universi101OFFICIAL0USE0ONLY1.pdf (last accessed 12 December 2016).

10 Leadership and change management

Case study of a manufacturing firm in Lebanon

Janine Saba Zakka and Renee Sabbagh Ghattas

Introduction

A prevalent form of businesses in Lebanon is the family business established and owned by a member of or the whole family. The family finances the business, and family members, usually the men, manage it. Hence, interdependence exists between the family and business. Family relations, culture, leadership, and traditions affect and sometimes constrain change that affects continuity in family business. Family businesses are distributed among the following sectors in Lebanon: agriculture, manufacturing, trade and services, Lebanese banks, and operating banks. This case study presents an overview on the survival of a small family-owned manufacturing firm (MF) during the civil war in Lebanon and up to 2015 with an emphasis on the role of education, leadership, and internal culture in achieving positive change that led to the development of the business.

Historic review of Lebanon

Lebanon, a small country on the eastern side of the Mediterranean Sea, suffered a demolishing civil war that lasted from 1975 to 1990. The infrastructure and economy of Lebanon were destroyed. In addition, Israeli wars against Lebanon in 2006 and the political and security instability that had been prevailing in Lebanon affected the economy and small family businesses in the country. Nevertheless, and despite all these turbulent events, Lebanon was rebuilt and regained its prewar economic status. Although Lebanon was not directly affected by the 2008 global financial crisis due to the wise legislation by the Central Bank of Lebanon, Lebanese organizations had to face and adjust to this crisis and to the political instability in the neighboring Arab countries called the "Arab Spring." Hence, the country and its people lived a continued adaptation to changing environmental conditions and circumstances.

Leadership

Productivity, change, growth, and innovation occur with the support of individuals (leaders) who have the power to assemble resources and affect others to support the new approach (Bartol and Martin, 1998; Jones and George, 2011). Luthans and Doh (2012) consider leadership as the process of influencing people to group their efforts toward the achievement of particular goals. However, leadership is credited for the success or blamed for the failure of business (Kanter, 2011). Hence, to be effective, leadership needs to implement rational business strategy designed to meet different possible future changes in the organization (Gill, 2002).

Transformational leadership replaced the notion of leadership as a series of transactions within a given cultural context (Robbins, 2001). As employees are major players in the organization, leaders are responsible for helping the workforce understand the effect of change and the way the organization is to respond (Strategic Direction, 2015). Transformational leaders establish supportive-culture that enables all employees to understand the influence of organizational change on improving operational performance (Birasnav, 2014). This culture, Birasnav (2014) adds, also ensures the involvement of employees in the change management process, which attracts certain individual or group benefits.

In order to manage production processes, firms, which strive to achieve as well as sustain competitive advantage, should focus on human resource development (Birasnav, 2014). The author notes that firms must also effectively implement the change management process, and human resource development.

Investment in production processes is notably higher than for other functions of organizations (Birasnav, 2014). Birasnav concludes that the suitable leadership style to be executed by top-level and middle-level leaders be involved in the manufacturing process to increase efficiency and lower production cost, thus improving financial performance, customer satisfaction, and sales growth. Key components of manufacturing strategies that improve performance are: flexibility during uncertainty period; product and services quality; speed and reliability of delivery; and reduced cost (Strategic Direction, 2015).

Internal culture

Culture is the sum of beliefs, values, meanings, and assumptions shared by a social group that shape the ways in which the members respond to each other and to their external environment (Ogbonna and Harris, 2002). The values embedded in a culture influence the behavior of leaders and other people working in an organization (Covey, 1999) and affects managerial attitudes (Kelley and Worthley, 1981). On the other hand, Luthans and Doh (2012) state that culture is acquired knowledge used to explain experience and cause social behavior and that it affects how people think and behave.

Culture and leadership are linked together because leaders generate culture through the groups and organizations they create (Day, Harris, Hadfield, Tolley and Beresford, 2000). The interconnections of love, money, and power might create family disputes and conflicts with solutions that differ based on culture and the family.

However, culture can be a liability when the shared values do not agree with those that will enhance the organization's effectiveness (Abdennur, 1987). When the organization's environment is rapidly changing, its culture may not be appropriate (Robbins, 2001).

Cultural values vary among countries. Cultural values in the Arab countries in general, and Lebanon in particular, are demonstrated through strong family ties, respect of parental guidance, and older generation authority. These cultural values govern family businesses in Lebanon.

Change in management

Change management is a continued process of renewing the organization's direction, composition, and abilities to serve the changing needs of the marketplace, the organization, and employees (Moran and Avergun, 1997).

Moran and Avergun (1997) add that the rate of change today is greater than at any other time in business history due to the rapid changes in the marketplace and the competitive field:

"Alliances and structures transform daily. Everything in the organization is open to scrutiny. Basic operating assumptions are questioned. Traditions are challenged. The cost of failure is greater than ever before, and so is the tension within the workforce" (Moran and Avergun, 1997, p. 146).

According to Johnson (1998), institutions that want to survive and be competitive must change. Companies must always be aware of changes in their internal and external environments and change accordingly (Anderson, 1998). On the other hand, Waddel and Sohal (1998) point out that with change comes the resistance to change, which is a complex prodigy that can affect change either negatively or positively. People do not resist change just for the sake of resisting; they actually resist the uncertainties in the process of change and its outcome, thus pointing out disadvantages and weaknesses and even mistakes in the process (Waddel and Sohal, 1998).

Moran and Avergun (1997) suggest that the following must take place in order to make the change process work in an organization:

- A clear definition of purpose, understanding the business of the organization, and identifying the customer.
- New performance requirements should be clear to and understandable by the employees who are to implement them
- Updated roles and responsibilities that indicate the new performance requirements. Hence, it follows that clear definitions of behaviors, values and expectations of the new workplace are provided.
- Timely and useful information is needed to enable customer-focused and cost-effective decision-making to take place at all levels.
- Core processes must be aligned with organizational goals.
- Leaders and employees must have the necessary skills in leadership, creativity, problem solving, continuous improvement, team effectiveness, and customer service.
- Reshape the organization's culture in ways that motivate all employees to serve the business as if it were their own.

The case study

The business's history

MF is a small family-owned manufacturing firm located in an industrial suburb in Beirut. Mr. F established MF in the early 1960s with the help of his elder son E who was named as a partner in the business. Later, the younger son Y was also made a partner in the business. Both sons were university graduates. As the firm grew in size, the sister was admitted as an employee in the business. In 1975, when the civil war erupted in Lebanon, the firm was hit by rockets and was completely destroyed. After the death of the father and the elder brother, Mr. Y took possession of the firm and MF changed from a partnership to a single ownership. Mr. Y is still owner and manager of MF and he has incorporated a lot of changes to the business.

The pre-war period

Mr. Y remembers the period during which MF was established and how it grew to a successful business:

I remember when my mother used to iron at home products of the business to have them ready for sale in the business. My father and my deceased brother used to go to work at five o'clock in the morning and they would stay till late at night. The whole family was committed to the business, which contributed to its growth. Every one of us, including the employees, was highly committed to the success and survival of the business. The employees were willing to work overtime. They never complained because they felt that they belong to the family and the business.

I believe that managing a small family business was and still is a challenge. The joint effort of all members of the family enabled the business to survive and to grow. I was young when I started working in the business. At that age I felt I could design and produce anything I want. The innovation that I introduced to the business created a high demand for the products, which resulted in an easy growth for MF.

The strong family culture in Lebanon had a great influence on defining the behavior of the family towards the business in general and me in particular. I was happy with the success of the business but all has a price. I could not spend much time with my family and my children complained about this situation and they even started to hate the business. My son went to the extent of refusing to work with the family.

The war and post-war period

With all the success that MF was having, my brother and I did not want to slow down. Even though the civil war had started, there were still opportunities to move ahead. Unfortunately, our father was not a risk taker. He refused and forbid us to borrow money from banks, which resulted in losing many opportunities. When my father grew older and got sick, my brother and I took over the business. We borrowed money and used it to add new machines that could produce new lines of products, which enabled MF to compete internationally. Unfortunately, MF was hit by rockets and destroyed. We lost everything: the business, which was declared bankrupt, money, and family ties. Conflicts broke between my brother and me, and between us and our sisters and children. There were no communications between family members. The worst was to come: My father died at that time from old age. He was striving to rebuild the business. Then my brother died from a heart attack. I was alone now to face all these problems. I hate to think about those days.

I would not have been able to manage and reconstruct the business without the help of the family; the family provided me with a loan with no interest. Here the family culture prevailed. In addition, when the business was destroyed, managers and employees joined forces and tried to repair the damage. The war environment gave people a sense of belonging. The strength of the business at that time was in the unity of its people, managers and employees. We met frequently to discuss the problems of that period. We were determined to go on no matter what happens. We managers and employees could not afford to lose the business forever. We were looking for solutions to salvage the business.

At this time I was willing to change. I felt as if a door was opening, not really for the MF family, although it benefited each one of them later when the war ended. At this point I decided to change. This entailed adding new product lines, buying modern machines, in order to produce a product with better quality and design and sell it at a higher selling price. My aim was to sell quality and not quantity. I believed that flexibility and competitiveness were the tools I needed to meet the new market demands. I felt that this is the way to compete in a global village.

However, the support and loyalty of my employees were a necessity to successfully implement this change in MF. I even gave the keys of the business to two old female employees to open the business in the morning and close it at night. My employees are like family to me, I trust them and I know that I can delegate work to them because of their ability to understand and implement new work requirements. I allow them to share in the decision-making process. I know that they care about the welfare of the business. Now the focus was on growth, which should be fast to make up for the lost time during the war. Clear job descriptions for the employees were written. I delegated authority and responsibility among the employees. Rewards were offered to excelling employees as an incentive to do more for the business.

The current period

Unfortunately, the culture of the business changed in the current period due to the economic and political situation prevailing in Lebanon and its neighboring countries. The strong team spirit that was a major asset during the war period was lost. People work only for the money. There is no solidarity anymore. Job insecurity prevails among the employees. Because of the heavy workload, I have no time to sit with my employees. I meet with them for business matters only. Our relation is getting to be official.

As my children expressed their resentment of my work, they refuse to work with me and later take over the business. As I am getting older, I cannot tolerate the idea that the business will close. It is part of the family that should go on. Hence I sit sometimes and deliberate about the future of the business. I have a strong feeling of transferring it to a shareholders' company and then I would sell part of the shares to outsiders who would continue running the business and maybe expand it. This way I feel that the family heirloom is continuing and in that would make us all in the family proud.

Conclusion

The case study above describes different leadership styles, cultures, and change management situations. The father was an authoritarian. The sons could not argue with him and had to obey him even though it meant the loss of opportunities to the business. The son used a transformational leadership style. He explained change to his employees, and shared with them the decision making process. There was a strong group feeling of belonging that provided security to the employees and contributed to the survival of the business. Everyone worked towards a main goal. The leadership style after the war emphasized achievement of predetermined objectives. The internal culture changed. It became more formal. Employees lost commitment and loyalty to the business. The business underwent a lot of positive change due to the transformational leadership style of the son and the strong internal culture of the family and the business. Even though the business is still profitable, the current situation in the country has had its toll on everybody including MF.

References

Abdennur, A. (1987). *The conflict resolution syndrome: Volunteerism, violence, and beyond*. Ottawa, Canada: University of Ottawa Press.

Anderson, T. D. (1998). *Transforming leadership: Equipping yourself and coaching others to build leadership organization*. Washington, DC: St. Lucie Press.

Bartol, K. M. and Martin, D. C. (1998). *Management*. Boston, MA: McGraw-Hill.

Birasnav, M. (2014). Relationship between transformational leadership behaviors and manufacturing strategy. *International Journal of Organizational Analysis, 22*(2), 205–223.

Covey, S. (1999). *Living the seven habits*. New York: Fireside Books.

Day, C., Harris, A., Hadfield, M., Tolley, H. and Beresford, J. (2000). *Leading schools in times of change*. London: Cromwell Press.

Gill, R. (2002). Change management – Or change leadership? *Journal of Change Management, 3*(4), 307–318. doi:10.1080/714023845

Johnson, S. (1998). *Who moved my cheese?* New York: G. P. Putnam's Sons.

Jones, G. and George, J. (2011). *Contemporary management*. New York: McGraw-Hill.

Kanter, R. M. (2011). The cure for horrible bosses. *Harvard Business Review*, October. Retrieved from https://hbr.org/2011/10/the-cure-for-horrible-bosses (last accessed 12 December 2016).

Kelley, L. and Worthley, R. (1981). The role of culture in comparative management: A cross-cultural perspective. *Academy of Management Journal, 24*(1), 164–173.

Luthans, F. and Doh, J. (2012). *International management*. New York: McGraw-Hill.

Moran, J. and Avergun, A. (1997). Creating lasting change. *The TQM Magazine, 9*(2), 146–151.

Ogbonna, E. and Harris, L. (2002). Managing organizational culture insights from the hospitality industry. *Human Resource Management Journal, 12*(1), 33–53.

Robbins, S. (2001). *Organizational behavior*. Upper Saddle River, NJ: Prentice Hall.

Strategic Direction. (2015). Transformational leadership: The impact of its behaviors on manufacturing strategy. *Strategic Direction, 31*(2), 25–27. doi:10.1108/SD-12-2014-0169

Waddel, D. and Sohal, A. (1998). Resistance: A constructive tool for change management. *Management Decision, 36*(8), 543–548.

11 *Te toka tū moana*

Māori leadership in Aotearoa New Zealand

Franco Vaccarino and Steve Elers

Ko rātou ngā toka tū moana.Ka ākina rātou e ngā ngaru o te moana.
Ka ākina e te tai, ka ākina e ngā hau.
Engari ahakoa p hea ka tū tonu, ka tū tonu.

They are the rocks standing in the sea.They are bashed by the waves of the ocean.
They are dashed by the tide.They are struck by the winds.
But no matter what hits them they stand and they stand.[1]

Introduction

Globalization is not a new phenomenon, but has increased and evolved significantly since the beginning of the twentieth century (Friedman, 2005), and even more exorbitantly in the twenty-first century as it is increasingly driven by technological advances where time and space between nations and cultures are less clearly defined. With globalization there is an increased interconnectedness and growing interdependence of different groups of people around the world, where national, economic, and cultural boundaries become less important. Due to this "international interconnectedness" (Baylis, Smith and Owens, 2008, p. 17), many countries around the world experience increased mobility and changes in demographics, resulting in changes in the multicultural and ethnolinguistic make-up of communities (Vaccarino and Dresler-Hawke, 2011). Globalization impacts on leadership and particularly on contemporary indigenous leadership, which needs to embrace the different elements and dynamics of the modern twenty-first-century world. Turner and Simpson (2008) point out that "indigenous leadership embraces a complex overlapping set of practices that weave together Indigenous and Eurocentric cultural practices" (p. 5), and this entails having leaders who know the indigenous ways of living and who are also acquainted with the dominant way of how the world functions. Culture plays a significant and integral part in leadership as it is "both a dynamic phenomenon that surrounds us at all times, being constantly enacted and created by our interactions with others and shaped by leadership behavior, and a set of structures, routines, rules, and norms that guide and constrain behavior" (Schein, 2004, p. 1).

This chapter focuses on Māori leadership in Aotearoa New Zealand. Before presenting the two leaders in this case study, it is important to provide an overview of leadership from a Māori perspective as this impacts on how change is managed. We have chosen to interview two leaders as they represent different contexts and situations that show the changes in Māori leadership over the years, and how they have managed change.

Literature review

This brief literature review provides an outline of traditional Māori leadership, the political changes that Aotearoa New Zealand has undergone, and contemporary Māori leadership in the twenty-first century.

Traditional Māori leadership

Māori started arriving in Aotearoa by *waka* (canoes) from East Polynesia and settled in tribal groups in various parts of the country, with tribes having their own histories and genealogies. During their migrations to Aotearoa, leadership was assigned mainly to the *waka* captains. Over the years the population grew and the *waka* leadership was substituted by three social units, namely *iwi* (tribes), *hapū* (clans or subtribes), and *whānau* (family and extended family) leadership (Katene, 2010). Although traditional Māori society promoted no distinctions between workers and leaders, but rather "all worked together as a collective," leadership was class-based and hierarchical (Te Rito, 2007, p. 52). Traditional Māori chieftainship and leadership were based on ancestry, and determined by *mātāmua*, or primogeniture, and usually based on the first-born male (Pfeifer and Love, 2004) and *whakapapa* (genealogy) (Henry, 1994; Winiata, 1967). Mead, Stevens, Third, Jackson, and Pfeifer (2006) state that the Māori system of leadership "is based on cultural criteria such as kinship ties, alliances with other kinship groups, appropriate whakapapa (genealogy)" (p. 4).

Winiata (1967) details four types of key leadership positions in traditional Māori society, namely *ariki* (highborn chiefs), *rangatira* (tribal leaders), *tohunga* (experts), and *kaumātua* (elders). The primary focus of *ariki* was to lead the *iwi*, but they could not be involved in all the day-to-day activities and this "collective perspective" that leadership is shared "represents the infrastructure of traditional leadership, orchestrated by hereditary chiefs (ariki/rangatira), assisted by highly trained priests (tohunga), and complemented by heads of whānau (kaumātua)" (Te Rito, 2007, p. 53). The *ariki* (paramount chief) was "the most senior family's first-born male in any generation" (Pfeifer, 2006, p. 50) and was the head of the *iwi* (tribe). The *rangatira* was the prominent leader of a *hapū* (sub-tribe) and provided political, social, and economic direction for the *hapū* (Pfeifer, 2006). The term *rangatira* consists of two words: *ranga* means to weave, and *tira* means a group; so *rangatira* literally means 'to weave a group of people together', thus guiding them to reach their full potential (Harmsworth, Barclay-Kerr and Reedy, 2002). This highlights the interdependent and collectivist nature of Māori society, where it is not about being an individual leader, but rather taking up one's responsibilities and obligations to the greater group. Te Whata and Kawharu (2012) highlight that a leader does not act out of self-interest, but in the interests of all, "in a caring and nurturing way, with the people close at heart, being accountable to them and thus in turn enjoying their respect and support" (p. 3). Skerrett (2010) asserts that Māori leadership is "distributed leadership" (p. 45). Central to the Māori worldview is therefore the concept of collectivism, where Māori identity is a collective identity and Māori values are seen as collective values that are "expressed in terms of collective action and responsibility" (Patterson, 1992, p. 154). In collectivist cultures, "people do not see themselves as isolated individuals but as interdependent with others, in which responsibility is shared and accountability is collective" (Liu, Volcic and Gallois, 2011, p. 101). Wolfgramm and Henry (2013) add that "collective social identities come from identification with a group, an organisation or a social category. This implies a merging of self and group, to ascribe group defining characteristics to the self and to take the collective's interest to heart" (p. 19). Wikitera (2011) highlights that Māori leadership "is not conducive to wielding power and control over others but rather it is about being servants to their whānau, hapū, iwi and wider communities they relate to" (p. 2).

The third type of leader was the *tohunga*, who could be defined "as a specialist in some field of knowledge and expertise" (Nga Tuara, 1992, p. 7) and who provided expert guidance in areas such as agriculture, hunting, fishing, warfare, weaving, conservation, woodcarving, and tattooing. The *tohunga* also performed sacred rituals and was regarded as "the religious expert or ritual leader" (Mead, 1997, p. 197). Katene (2010, p. 5) notes that "their knowledge, experience and skills were critical for the wellbeing of their people." Finally, the *kaumātua* (male elder) and the *kuia* (female elder) of a *whānau* (extended family) were the leaders who "made the decisions concerning the working of the family land, and control and use of family property, and the rearing and education of children" (Walker, 1993, p. 1). These leaders looked after the administrative side of village affairs, and were also involved in ceremonial duties, etiquette, and procedures (Te Rito, 2007).

Māori cultural values relevant to leadership

In her research, Pfeifer (2006) discusses some key Māori values that have been identified in the literature as being important and very relevant to leadership: *whanaungatanga*, *mana*, *tapu*, and *manākitanga* (or *manaakitanga*). Each one will be discussed briefly, although it is important to remember that these terms do not have the exact same meaning in a different culture and language and therefore cannot be translated directly. *Whanaungatanga* indicates a Māori way of thinking about relationships, kinship, and a sense of connectedness and belonging. It encompasses relationships between people, relationships between people and the world, and relationships between people and *atua*, or spiritual entities. *Whanaungatanga* strengthens kinship ties (Pere, 1982) and, as Pfeifer (2006) maintains, *whanaungatanga* can be seen as "the glue that joins together whānau, hapū, or iwi groups" (p. 44). Wolfgramm and Henry (2013) state that *mana* "refers to the spiritual power and authority that can be applied to people, their words and acts" (p. 16), and *mana* and *tapu* are closely linked as the one affects the other. *Mana* can be defined as prestige, authority, and influence, and is closely linked to the western concept of charisma. The more admired and prestigious a person or object is, the more it is surrounded by *mana* and *tapu*. Durie (2003) asserts that while there are many modern interpretations of *tapu*, "most emphasise a sacred quality and are linked in some way to gods or divinities" (p. 232). Wolfgramm and Henry (2013) state that "tapu is the sacred and sacrosanct in all things" (p. 16). As Te Rito (2007) points out, "Māori leadership is immersed in mana and tapu" (p. 54). The fourth cultural value is *manaakitanga* and is an important aspect of Māori custom and identity, as it is about how people make others feel welcome when in their company. It encompasses caring for others, treating others with respect, showing kindness, creating self-worth in others, nurturing relationships, and hospitality. Pfeifer (2006) points out that "expressions of manākitanga through aroha (love), hospitality, generosity, and mutual respect, acknowledge others' mana as having equal or greater importance than one's own" (p. 48).

Radical changes

With the arrival of European settlers in the early nineteenth century, there were significant changes in Aotearoa, including traditional Māori leadership. European capitalism, missionaries, and imperialism and colonization increasingly undermined the *mana* of traditional Māori leaders (Walker, 1993), which resulted in significant adaptations to the traditional Māori social and political structures (Pfeifer, 2006). With the "clash of cultures," there was a need for a radical transformation in traditional Māori concepts of leadership (Katene, 2010). Pihama and Gardiner (2005) assert that the growth of western colonial establishments "pre-empted the emergence of new forms and models of Maori leadership" (p. 35), in order to "respond to the unique challenges" (Katene, 2010, p. 6).

Contemporary Māori leadership

Since the times of early trade when goods and products were exchanged, globalization has steadily been bringing countries from around the globe closer. Globalization in the twenty-first century, however, has been expedited by the rapid pace of global integration due to advancement in technology, science, industry, and communications. As the world becomes more interwoven with an increase in interdependence and interconnectedness among countries, the social, political, economic, and cultural aspects of life are affected. The contemporary leader needs to operate within this ever-changing global village. Katene (2010) highlights that "Māori have the added challenge of negotiating the dynamically interacting influences of traditional Māori values and leadership principles and those of mainstream contemporary society" (p. 9). Wikitera (2011) talks about Māori leaders having to balance and negotiate their way through an increasingly multifaceted society.

Te Rito (2007) highlights that "the spectrum in which Māori leadership operates means that leaders are often between two different worlds, one based on Māori cultural parameters and the other based on western philosophies" (p. 43), thus operating within "two distinct, and often conflicting systems of values" (Winiata, 1967, p. 136), or as Walker (1993) points out, "a contradictory mix of tradition and modernity" (p. 22). Te Rito (2007) states that this creates fresh opportunities for a new type of leader to emerge who is familiar with both environments. Mead *et al.* (2006) refer to transcultural creative leaders, who are "people who can learn how to transcend their childhood acculturation" (p. 14) and interact and engage in diverse cultural contexts. Māori leaders have to therefore negotiate "the dynamically interacting influences of traditional Maori values and leadership principles and those of mainstream contemporary society" (Mead *et al.*, 2006, p. 14).

In contemporary society, although there have been changes to traditional Māori leadership, "the values and principles associated with traditional Māori leadership still have meaning today" (Te Rito, 2007, p. 55). From research it appears that Māori business leaders have retained certain traditional characteristics of leadership in contemporary business practices (Henry, 1994; Love, 1991). Mead *et al.* (2006) point out the importance of cultural criteria in contemporary society, but say that these are not applied as strictly as they used to be, and "many of the values held to be essential in traditional times are still meaningful today" (p. 4). The four key Māori leadership values discussed earlier, *whanaungatanga, mana, tapu,* and *manākitanga,* are still very relevant in Māori leadership today.

Douglas (2001) states that in traditional times, the transmission of leadership skills to succeeding generations was done by "association, learning by observation and participation and through the sharing of knowledge and skills and actively promoting opportunities for younger people to take the lead locally or nationally" (p. 5). However, as the world of the Māori has changed significantly, Douglas highlights that more deliberate leadership training is required. In the 1970s, leadership discussions "centred more on the qualities and characteristics of leadership with a recognition of the complexity and diversity of Maori communities" (Pihama and Gardiner, 2005, p. 27). Katene (2010) describes the emergence of tertiary-educated Māori who have brought about a new dimension. He states that these new Māori leaders were professionals who became "the latter-day tohunga because they could articulate the benefits of Māori values to Pākehā[2] and conversely, they could translate to Māori the Pākehā ways. Their education was good preparation for leadership" (p. 8). Contemporary society in Aotearoa New Zealand has also seen the emergence of Māori leaders who are skilled in business practice and "have responded to the need to create a new economic infrastructure to adapt to capitalism and industrialisation in order to survive and integrate with the mainstream system" (Pfeifer, 2006, p. 59).

Case studies

Sir Edward (Eddie) Taihakurei Durie, KNZM, of the Ngāti Kauwhata, Rangitāne, and Ngāti Raukawa *iwi* (tribes), was "the first Māori to be appointed to the High Court bench in New Zealand" (Palmer, 2011, p. 470). Born in Feilding (Deverson and Kennedy, 2005), Durie received his high school education at Te Aute College, Pukehou, Hawkes Bay, a Māori boarding school for boys that is renowned for producing leaders (Graham, 2009). After graduating from Victoria University of Wellington, he worked as a lawyer and later became a judge of the Māori Land Court in 1974, chairperson of the Waitangi Tribunal in 1981, judge of the High Court in 1988 (Deverson and Kennedy, 2005), and New Zealand Law Commissioner in 2004 (Law Commission, 2004).

Having led the Māori Land Court and Waitangi Tribunal for more than two decades, Durie currently sits on the board of the Crown Forestry Rental Trust (Crown Forestry Rental Trust, 2012) and is the co-Chairperson of the New Zealand Māori Council (Waitangi Tribunal, 2015). The Crown Forestry Rental Trust was established by statute in 1989 (Crocker, 2014) and is the "primary provider of research services to claimants to the Waitangi Tribunal" (O'Malley, 2001, p. 144). The research services are funded by the rental of Crown forest land (Crocker, 2014). Likewise, the New Zealand Māori Council was also established under statute to "represent Māori views on various issues of importance, such as Crown commitments to the Treaty of Waitangi" (Te Puni Kokiri, 2013, p. 8).

In our interview, Durie mentioned that when he qualified as a lawyer there were only a few Māori who obtained law degrees, so if you were at a *marae* or if you were talking somewhere, a law degree could give you priority of attention. He said that this added some *mana* and status and people would say "this chap must know something. He's got a Pākehā law degree." He continued by saying that in those days there was just a handful of Māori who had *Pākehā* qualifications, so "they could make decisions really quick and really easily … and people would frequently let them lead." Durie added that nowadays there are many people with degrees "and everybody wants to talk, and you can't get agreement so quickly." He said that now there is more competition and "I sort of feel it's harder for them in a way. It was much easier for us. People listened to what we said. Now you can have all the degrees in the world and people are not going to listen to what you say; they'll debate."

The modern change of leadership structures and the modern way of doing things is basically because the educated young Māori are taking what they have learnt at university, including the values, and implementing this new western learning within the roles in any given organization, including leadership roles. He also added that "the old Māori way was based on personal mana – that was their leadership." He pointed out that in the past the *hapū* leaders spoke from a common cultural base, but now as people are more dispersed, they are speaking from a range of cultural values from different communities, schools, and universities. He continued by saying that "you can't get the original dynamic to work so you've got to find other ways of handling it now. This generation is going to have to handle it in another way because their cultural values are different."

This is a significant shift within the last 50 or so years. Durie finds that people who have come out of a university business school, for example, can be extraordinarily efficient in western terms, but extremely difficult to work with "because their thinking is so different from what we were brought up to think." He considers that the business school concept of best practice is frequently in stark contrast with Māori best practice (or *tikanga* Māori). This links with Katene's (2010) statement of the emergence of tertiary-educated Māori who have brought a new dimension, and who have "responded to the need to create a new economic infrastructure" (Pfeifer, 2006, p. 59) in order to adapt to the twenty-first century. Durie also added that Māori are losing their identity as "we are having to depend more and more on books which tend to prescribe appropriate conduct rather than upon just following how our aunts and uncles and parents managed situations, drawing upon a smorgasbord of sometimes conflicting norms."

In the Māori Council, Durie points out that "people generally speak by the same rules" as they are operating in one traditional system; so for example, "people will broadly follow the rule that you will pick up what the previous speaker has said before you start to express your own idea." In addition, "people regularly start off by paying respect to the other tribal groups that are represented" at the meeting and they will spend a lot of time saying how they are connected to them or have worked together. At the end of the meeting people feel very comfortable with one another where they have reached a common decision. Durie highlights that this process takes a very long time, but "it's great because we reach really good decisions … which are not necessarily the best decisions in a commercial sense, but are good in that they keep relationships right between people, because the whole Māori focus is to maintain relationships between all the groups." Relationships are very important and respecting other people and maintaining the *mana* of all those attending a meeting is a cultural expectation, and keeps people together and feeling that they have all been respected.

Durie provided an example of the importance of maintaining relationships in Māori culture, so that others should not walk away from a meeting feeling aggrieved. It is important to have various *mihi* (introductions) at the beginning to greet one another and acknowledge common interests together. It is also important to have a meal together after an event, as this shows *manaakitanga*, or hospitality. Durie said that when he was a judge in the Māori Land Court there was a meeting among the members of a large tribal group who proposed a major forestry enterprise in respect of a particularly large area of land. There were numerous owners, but of those present, all generally agreed except for one family that farmed in the area. The leader of the meeting and most of the family heads spoke in support of the forest, as the land was marginal and most of it unutilized. But the family farming in the area spoke against this as the project would force them to leave the land. When the leader had to sum up, he said, "the forestry scheme does not go ahead" even though 90 percent of those at the meeting agreed that it should. He added, "the forestry scheme won't go ahead because this particular family will be disadvantaged and we can't do that." The people accepted this decision, and everyone went and had *kai* (food). The particular family that farmed there, then stood up at the meal to declare that they would support the forest project. Their *mana* had been respected. They said, "it's going to be hard on us. We will have to leave the land, but we will leave the land because of the respect that you have shown us."

Durie pointed out that when addressing issues around leadership in a Māori context, it is important to have a few people sitting around talking so that one can get an exchange of ideas, rather than just one individual's ideas. Again, this highlights the collectivist approach in the Māori culture. Durie provided an example of this when he was chairing the Waitangi Tribunal. The system required individuals to step forward to give evidence. One of the *kaumātua* (elders) of the Tribunal would switch it around when people came up and gave their evidence. He would start by asking the room, "Well, what do you think of this?" and immediately provide an answer by saying, "Well, among my people, we do this or we do that." Suddenly the whole room would start talking and say "Oh no, no. We don't do it like that; we do it like this." What he had here was the evidence coming forward, not from the individual, but from the group, and that was the Māori way of giving evidence, and it was a very effective way. The *kaumātua* took the view that to get an opinion of a person on a local custom or practice, you do not interview the person but the people because then you'll get a feeding in of ideas and you'll also help to keep that person honest because he's having to speak in front of his peers. Durie said that "it's a different way of handling interviews. But I would say the traditional Māori way of handling an interview is actually not to go to the individual, but to go to the group to which that person belongs."

Our other leader is Rangimarie Naida Glavish (Naida Glavish), ONZM, JP, of the Ngāti Whātua *iwi* (tribe). She has "spent her adult life as an advocate for Māori people" (Hayden, Gelsthorpe, Kingi and Morris, 2014, p. xvi). Raised in Kaipara, Glavish is of both Māori and Croatian ancestry (Families Commission, 2011). Fluent in both the Māori and Croatian languages, it was not until Glavish attended school that she learnt English (Te Rau Matatini, 2008). In 1984, Glavish, then known as Naida Povey (Mead, 1997), entered the national spotlight while working as a telephone operator at the post office when her supervisor ordered her to stop using the Māori greeting *kia ora* (Hayden *et al.*, 2014; Tuuta, Irwin and Maclean, 2011). The incident gained widespread national media attention and instigated public debate about "the place of the Māori language in the national culture" (Kukutai, 2010, p. 66). After the *kia ora* incident, Glavish became a Māori language teacher at Henderson High School (Hubbard, 2013), but is currently employed as the General Manager and Chief Advisor for Māori customs and protocols at the Waitemata and Auckland District Health Boards (Hayden *et al.*, 2014). Her curriculum vitae includes a list of 19 organizations where she holds leadership positions or is an advisor (Māori Party, 2014), including the New Zealand Police and Te Rūnanga o Ngāti Whātua (Māori Trust Board of Ngāti Whātua tribe), among others. However, she is probably best known for being the current President of the Māori Party, one of seven political parties that currently hold seats in New Zealand's parliament.

The Māori Party is a "political party founded to represent the strong and independent voice of Māori within parliament for the best interests of Aotearoa" (Bird, 2012, para. 1). In the 2005 general election, the Māori Party won four Māori constituency seats (Lansford, 2014), and thus "became the first Māori political party to enter the House of Representatives" (Lublin, 2014, p. 142). Glavish was elected President of the Māori Party on 13 July 2013 (Ngāti Whātua o Kaipara, 2013). Glavish has been at the helm of the Māori Party during significant organizational change, including the retiring of co-leaders Tariana Turia and Pita Sharples and the loss of their respective seats in the 2014 general election to the Labour Party (Roughan, 2014).

The Māori Party was formed in July 2004 by Tariana Turia. Pita Sharples joined her and they became co-leaders (the Māori Party constitution requires both male and female co-leaders). After the 2008 election, the Māori Party supported a National Party-led government and Turia and Sharples became ministers outside cabinet. In 2012, Turia announced that she would resign as party co-leader before the 2014 election. In 2013, Sharples resigned as male co-leader and was replaced by Te Ururoa Flavell, who became Minister for Māori Development (outside cabinet) following the 2014 election. In the general election in 2014, Marama Fox became the Māori Party's first List Member of Parliament and, as the Party's only female MP, under the Party rules automatically became the female co-leader. Managing these changes in the Party was Naida Glavish, who became the Māori Party's President in July 2013.

In our interview with Glavish we asked her how she managed the changeover after Turia and Sharples left as co-leaders. She said that it had been easy in that she has a good reputation and a public profile, which includes being an Iwi Chair for Te Rūnanga o Ngāti Whātua (a body corporate and a Māori Trust Board that is the sole representative body and authorized voice to deal with issues affecting the whole of Ngāti Whātua. Ngāti Whātua is an *iwi* (tribe) based in New Zealand's largest city, Tamaki Makaurau/Auckland). Glavish is also well known in the political field as well as at the flax roots level among Māori people. She said that one of the things that's often underestimated is perception, and the Māori community and political leaders have a perception of confidence in her leadership. She added that there is a willingness to support, with regard to the Iwi Chairs and the relationships that she has with the Iwi Chairs. Even though they daren't cross boundaries in terms of political affiliations, they still have respect for each other. Similarly, this applies within the political spectrum as well.

Glavish added that any changes within the Māori Party leadership, whether it be with the MPs, the Chairs of the Electorates, or the President, have always been one of team effort. She added that "it's totally a team effort and has to remain a team effort otherwise we'd be no different from any other party." When questioned about her leadership style being different to other political parties, Glavish said that her style is collective and has to be so otherwise it'll be just like any other party. She said "it wouldn't be a Māori Party if it wasn't collective." She added that regarding the collective, they are currently having discussions to ensure that policies are in place before the next election. They are looking at leadership at the ground level, at the flax roots level with regards to the strengthening of the branches, and holding their national executive meetings so that they are all in agreement as to the direction they are going. Thus, in terms of Glavish's leadership style, it's a collective movement forward, rather than a top-down approach, and to use a Māori metaphor, everyone needs to be on board the *waka* (canoe). Linked to this collective approach to leadership is also her personal *kanohi ki te kanohi* (face-to-face) approach, which assists her to remain in touch with people. Of course, such an approach needs "a mountain of resources to be able to go out to those communities and be seen in those communities." The Party is grateful that Te Ururoa and Marama are able to visit communities as they have travel discretions. However, she added that "if at the flax roots there's not a strong financial background, then it's a struggle, definitely a struggle."

When Glavish was asked whether there had been anything that she discovered in terms of her leadership style within the last few years since the significant changes in the Māori Party, she said that at any time in a leadership position, there will always be that moment where one has to make crucial decisions. She said that these are crucial decisions that have to be made in the interest of the multitudes, even though at times you know that you will be heavily criticized for making those decisions. What she discovered about herself is that she was able to make those decisions, even though they caused some sleepless nights. She continued, "our people can be in positions of vulnerability – political vulnerability – and those of us who understand and work daily with those who are vulnerable and those in positions of vulnerability, you develop a sense of strength to advocate on their behalf." Glavish has found that she is a "really good advocate," particularly for those who are vulnerable.

Glavish was asked whether she thought there was a different way in which Māori manage change in organizations compared to non-Māori; for example, how change is managed in the Māori Party and how it is managed in the Labour Party or National Party. She believes there is a difference, and the reason for this is that change in the Māori Party takes into account *whānau* (family and extended family), *hapū* (sub-tribe or clan), and *iwi* (tribe). She said the Māori Party, for example, takes into account the poverty line, and takes into account those who are members of the Māori Party who are struggling in the areas of housing and struggling in all the areas in which wellness – or *ora* in Māori – should apply and doesn't. Therefore, the decisions the Party makes are "based on that inside knowledge about being who we are and where we've come from and where we would like to be and go."

In terms of changes in Māori leadership over the years, Glavish was asked whether current Māori leadership has adopted more of a *Pākehā* model of leadership. She said that unfortunately, to a certain degree, it has, and that is because there have been changes at the *whānau* (extended family) level, for example the *tuakana–teina* relationship. This was an integral part of traditional Māori society that provided a model for buddy systems. In this relationship, an older *tuakana* helped and guided a younger *teina* in specific teaching and learning contexts. Glavish said that the older *tuakana* who supported the younger *teina* in the *whānau* would also have applied this in the workplace; however, it is no longer practiced in the *whānau*, and clearly not in the workplace either.

One of the challenges that Glavish mentioned was that members of the Māori Party were not aware of the benefits to them of the Party sitting at the table with government. Past influences and past assumptions had been that if you partner with anybody, you're in bed with them. And Glavish has said no to this: "We are not in bed. We are sitting at the table. And we're sitting at the table because that's usually where kai (food) is dished up." She believes that this is where the Māori Party ensures that what belongs to them actually goes to them. She added that the Party is not good at this yet, but it needs to be learned before the next elections, and people need to say, "these are the things that sitting at that table has achieved for us."

Conclusion

As globalization has impacted on contemporary indigenous leadership, leaders have had to embrace the different elements and dynamics of the twenty-first-century world. In this chapter we have presented two prominent Māori leaders who are respected in their communities and in the organizations they represent. From the literature it is clear that there have been significant changes in how decisions are made in the twenty-first century and how this impacts on how change is managed in any organization. The leaders have also highlighted significant changes, yet the core Māori cultural values are still evident in contemporary leadership. Turner and Simpson (2008) point out that "indigenous peoples are part of, indeed integral to, the evolving global community, and that the wellbeing of our communities depends on how well our leaders can effectively participate in this complex, often challenging world" (p. 2).

Notes

1   This metaphor was used to describe strong leaders and has come from the heritage of the Māori people, and it is also applied to the leaders of the future.
2   New Zealanders who are of European descent.

References

Baylis, J., Smith, S. and Owens, P. (2008). *The globalization of world politics: An introduction to international relations*. New York: Oxford University Press.
Bird, P. (2012). *Māori Party submission on the review of MMP*. Retrieved from www.mmpreview.org.nz/sites/default/files/submissions/uploads/Maori%20Party%20submission%20on%20MMP.pdf (last accessed 12 December 2016).

Crocker, T. (2014). History and the Treaty of Waitangi settlement process. *Journal of New Zealand Studies*, *18*, 106–117. Retrieved from https://ojs.victoria.ac.nz/jnzs/article/viewFile/2184/2025 (last accessed 12 December 2016).

Crown Forestry Rental Trust. (2012). Media releases. Retrieved from www.cfrt.org.nz/about/mediare-leases.asp (last accessed 12 December 2016).

Deverson, T. and Kennedy, G. (2005). *The New Zealand Oxford Dictionary*. Oxford: Oxford University Press.

Douglas, E. T. K. (2001). *Foreword: The 2001 Hui-a-Taiohi – The Young Māori Leaders' Conference in a Developmental Context*. Retrieved from www.firstfound.org/Vol.%207New_Folder/foreword.htm (last accessed 12 December 2016).

Durie, M. (2003). *Ngā kāhui pou: Launching Māori futures*. Wellington, New Zealand: Huia Publishers.

Families Commission. (2011). *He ara whakamua: Building pathways together to the future*. Retrieved from www.superu.govt.nz/sites/default/files/building-pathways-pipitea-report.pdf (last accessed 12 December 2016).

Friedman, T. L. (2005). *The world is flat: A brief history of the twenty-first century*. New York: Picador/Farrar, Straus and Giroux. Retrieved from www.uic.edu.hk/~kentsang/powerst/Friedman_the%20world%20is%20flat.pdf (last accessed 12 December 2016).

Graham, J. P. H. (2009). Whakatanga kia kaha: Toitū te whakapapa, toitū te tuakiri, toitū te mana – An examination of the contribution of Te Aute College to Māori advancement. Doctoral dissertation, Massey University, Palmerston North, New Zealand. Retrieved from http://mro.massey.ac.nz/bitstream/handle/10179/1254/02whole.pdf?sequence=1&isAllowed=y (last accessed 12 December 2016).

Harmsworth, G., Barclay-Kerr, K. and Reedy, T. (2002). Māori sustainability development in the 21st century: The importance of Māori values, strategic planning, and information systems. *Journal of Māori and Pacific Development*, *3*(2), 40–69.

Hayden, A., Gelsthorpe, L., Kingi, V. and Morris, A. (2014). *A restorative approach to family violence: Changing tack*. Farnham: Ashgate Publishing.

Henry, E. Y. (1994). Rangatira wahine: Māori women managers and leadership. Unpublished Master's dissertation, University of Auckland, Auckland, New Zealand.

Hubbard, A. (2013). 'Kia ora lady' still an agent for change. *The Dominion Post*, July 20. Retrieved from www.stuff.co.nz/dominion-post/news/politics/8943523/Kia-ora-lady-still-an-agent-for-change (last accessed 12 December 2016).

Katene, S. (2010). Modelling Māori leadership: What makes for good leadership? *MAI Review*, *2*, 1–16.

Kukutai, T. (2010). The thin brown line: Re-indigenizing inequality in Aotearoa New Zealand. Doctoral dissertation, Stanford University, Stanford, CA. Retrieved from http://ejournal.narotama.ac.id/files/A%20DISSERTATION.pdf (last accessed 12 December 2016).

Lansford, T. (2014). *Political handbook of the world 2014*. Thousand Oaks, CA: Sage Publications.

Law Commission. (2004). *Report of the Law Commission*. Retrieved from www.lawcom.govt.nz/sites/default/files/nzlc%20annual%20report%202003-2004_0.pdf (last accessed 12 December 2016).

Liu, S., Volcic, Z. and Gallois, C. (2011). *Introducing intercultural communication: Global cultures and contexts*. Thousand Oaks, CA: Sage.

Love, M. (1991). Ropu kaiwhakahaere. Unpublished Master's dissertation, Massey University, Palmerston North, New Zealand.

Lublin, D. (2014). *Minority rules: Electoral systems, decentralization, and ethnoregional party success*. New York: Oxford University Press.

Māori Party. (2014). Our president: Rangimarie Naida Glavish. Retrieved from http://maoriparty.org/president (last accessed 12 December 2016).

Mead, H., Stevens, S., Third, J., Jackson, B. and Pfeifer, D. (2006). *Māori Leadership in Governance*. Hui Taumata Action. Scoping Paper. Retrieved from https://moodle.unitec.ac.nz/pluginfile.php/85322/mod_resource/content/0/Readings_day_four/Maori_Leadership.pdf (last accessed 12 December 2016).

Mead, S. M. (1997). *Landmarks, bridges and visions: Aspects of Māori culture: Essays*. Wellington, New Zealand: Victoria University Press.

Nga Tuara. (1992). *Nga Toka Tu Moana, Maori leadership and decision making.* Wellington: Te Puni Kokiri.

Ngāti Whātua o Kaipara. (2013). *Candidate statements.* Retrieved from http://kaiparamoana.com/sites/kaiparamoana.com/files/documents/candidate-profiles-nwok-cps-compiled.pdf (last accessed 12 December 2016).

O'Malley, V. (2001). Treaty-making in early colonial New Zealand. In J. Binney (ed.), *The shaping of history: Essays from The New Zealand Journal of History* (pp. 129–145). Wellington, New Zealand: Bridget Williams Books.

Palmer, G. (2011). Judges and the non-judicial function in New Zealand. In H. P. Lee (ed.), *Judiciaries in comparative perspective* (pp. 452–473). Cambridge: Cambridge University Press.

Patterson, J. (1992). *Exploring Māori values.* Palmerston North, New Zealand: Dunmore Press.

Pere, R. R. (1982). *Ako, concepts, and learning in the Māori tradition.* Working paper no 17. Hamilton: New Zealand: Department of Sociology, University of Waikato.

Pfeifer, D. M. (2006). Leadership in Aotearoa New Zealand: Māori and Pākehā perceptions of outstanding leadership. Master's dissertation, Massey University, Wellington, New Zealand. Retrieved from http://mro.massey.ac.nz/bitstream/handle/10179/246/02whole.pdf?sequence=1&isAllowed=y (last accessed 12 December 2016).

Pfeifer, D. and Love, M. (2004). Leadership in Aotearoa New Zealand: A cross-cultural study. *Prism, 2,* 1–14. Retrieved from www.prismjournal.org/fileadmin/Praxis/Files/Journal_Files/Pfeifer_Love.pdf (last accessed 12 December 2016).

Pihama, L. and Gardiner, D. (2005). *Building baseline data on Maori, whanau development and Maori realising their potential – Literature review: developing leadership.* Final report prepared for Te Puni Kokiri by Auckland UniServices. Retrieved from www.rangahau.co.nz/assets/te_puna_kokiri/developing_leadership_literature_review.pdf (last accessed 12 December 2016).

Roughan, R. (2014). *John Key: Portrait of a Prime Minister.* Auckland, New Zealand: Penguin Books.

Schein, E. H. (2004). *Organizational culture and leadership* (3rd edn). San Francisco, CA: Jossey-Bass.

Skerrett, M. (2010). A critique of the best evidence synthesis with relevance for Māori leadership in education. *Journal of Educational Leadership, Policy and Practice, 25*(1), 42–50.

Te Puni Kokiri. (2013). *Discussion paper on proposed changes to the Māori Community Development Act 1962.* Retrieved from www.tpk.govt.nz/docs/MCDA-discussion-paper.pdf (last accessed 12 December 2016).

Te Rau Matatini. (2008). *Puna Hua Rangatira conference proceedings report.* Palmerston North, New Zealand: Te Rau Matatini.

Te Rito, P. R. (2007). Māori leadership: what role can rugby play? Master's dissertation, Auckland University of Technology, Auckland, New Zealand. Retrieved from http://aut.researchgateway.ac.nz/bitstream/handle/10292/42/TeRitoP.pdf?sequence=2&isAllowed=y (last accessed 12 December 2016).

Te Whata, R. and Kawharu, M. (2012). *Transformation of entrepreneurial tribal Māori leadership.* Ngā Pae o te Māramatanga. Retrieved from http://web.its.auckland.ac.nz/maramatanga/sites/default/files/12-IN-03%20Web%20ready.pdf (last accessed 12 December 2016).

Turner, D. and Simpson, A. (2008). *Indigenous leadership in a flat world.* Research paper for the National Centre for First Nations Governance. Retrieved from http://fngovernance.org/ncfng_research/turner_and_simpson.pdf (last accessed 12 December 2016).

Tuuta, C., Irwin, K. and Maclean, S. (2011). *Mātiro whakamua: Looking over the horizon.* Wellington, New Zealand: Families Commission.

Vaccarino, F. and Dresler-Hawke, E. (2011). How you doing, mate? The perceptions of benefits and barriers in forming friendships with international students: A New Zealand perspective. *Intercultural Communication Studies, 20*(2), 177–189.

Waitangi Tribunal. (2015). *Whaia te Mana Motuhake – In pursuit of Mana Motuhake: Report on the Māori Community Development Act Claim.* Wellington, New Zealand: Waitangi Tribunal.

Walker, R. (1993). *Tradition and change in Maori leadership.* Research Unit for Maori Education/Te Tari o te Matauranga Maori. Auckland, New Zealand: The University of Auckland.

Wikitera, K.-A. (2011). Travelling, navigating and negotiating Māori leadership challenges in the 21st century. *MAI Review, 2,* 1–4.

Winiata, M. (1967). *The changing role of the leader in Maori society: A study in social change and race relations.* Auckland, New Zealand: Blackwood & Janet Paul.

Wolfgramm, R. and Henry, E. (2013). *A relational dynamics approach to leadership based on an investigation of Māori leaders in the screen industry.* Paper presented at the ILA Oceania Conference, Auckland, New Zealand, July. Retrieved from www.nzli.co.nz/file/Conference/Papers/engaging-a-relational-leadership-approach.pdf (last accessed 12 December 2016).

12 Living the Shell core values

Andrea Santiago

The Shell Companies in the Philippines (SCiP) is not just an organization; it is a family. This is the premise of its Country Chair, Edgar Ocava Chua, as he describes his role in the company:

> In the Philippines, the father is head of the family. Thus as the most senior, [the employees] see me as their father figure. There is an expectation therefore that as father, I am there to listen, guide and protect. That is what parents are there for.[1]

About Shell

Shell is a global group of energy and petrochemical companies (Shell, undated a). It is a result of a merger between Shell Transport and Royal Dutch Petroleum in 1907. The merged company, Royal Dutch Shell Group, operates in over 70 countries and employs 94,000 people (Shell, undated b).

Shell first entered the Philippines in 1914 as a trading office. It took almost half a century before the Royal Dutch Shell Group decided to set up an oil refinery. From then on, there was no stopping the growth of the company in the country. Already trading for 100 years in the Philippines, the operations of Shell in the country include Pilipinas Shell Petroleum Corporation (managing the refinery, oil depots, and retail stations), Shell Exploration Philippines BV (oil and gas operation), Shell Business Service Centre–Manila (business processing center of Shell companies worldwide), and Pilipinas Shell Foundation Inc. (corporate social responsibility arm). These fall under SCiP. "Organizationally, we have moved from local to regional to global," the Country Chair stated.

SCiP is governed by the same business principles as all other Shell companies around the world. The three core values are honesty, integrity, and respect for people. Emanating from these core values are the companies' business principles, code of conduct, and code of ethics. To care for the environment and society is considered of equal importance as earning profits.

Shell was one of the pioneering members of the Philippine Business for Social Progress, a network of corporate foundations in the Philippines founded in 1970. In 1982, Pilipinas Shell Foundation Inc. (PSFI) was organized to initiate various social development programs for SCiP. Over 30 years, PSFI has touched the lives of over 10 million people through programs in education and livelihood as well as with technical and vocational skills training and employment. It also engages in various programs in environmental stewardship, leadership enhancement and attitude development, as well as in health, sanitation, and safety (Shell, undated c).

The constancy of change

Edgar Chua, a 36-year-old veteran in SCiP, and Country Chair for the last 12 years, relayed how change is part of the psyche of the Shell "family."

> The world is changing and so change is something people should always expect … especially for us, almost every year, there is a major change happening in our organization. It has been quite dynamic. Unlike when I first joined the company, the set-up is the set-up for five to ten years. It does not change much. I guess technology has enabled changes; so has globalization. All these things are imperatives for us to change as well … People are smart, they see these things happening. We are very explicit in telling people that change and dynamic change is there to stay with us.

Ed (as he is more popularly known) has had to deal with changes since he assumed the top post at SCiP. He saw through a decision of his predecessors to close a base oil refinery, but he has had to initiate and see through other changes. Two that immediately came to mind were the closure of a business unit to give rise to the business processing entity and the most recent is the impending closure of the Pandacan oil depot in the heart of Manila, the capital city of the Philippines.

Transitioning to Shell Business Service Centre–Manila

Ed explained how he had to disestablish an existing customer service unit at then Pilipinas Shell Petroleum Company to establish a spin-off, the Shell Business Service Centre–Manila:

> I was moving it [the customer service unit] to another entity. Effectively, I was asking everyone to accept a lower pay since the current pay structure was not sustainable. When I benchmarked outside, our cost was double or triple. Thus, the decision was very difficult.

The Country Chair had to deal with only 21 employees, but his legal advisers made him understand that if only one of the employees refused, the move could not be implemented. Thus, Ed had to handle the situation delicately:

> So, I had to sit down with them. It was not a big group … Everyone was in a different situation. Some had more years with Shell, while others had only a few years. It was less difficult to explain to those with many years with Shell that even if they would receive a lower salary, they would still have a job and they have their redundancy pay to invest the funds and augment their salary. That argument would not work for those who did not have enough years because even if they received a redundancy pay, it will not be a big amount.

Ed realized that he had to manifest his compassion. As "father" to the Shell employees, he had to show that he cared for their welfare. Since the closure of the unit was a major change initiative that he undertook in his early years as head of SCiP, how he handled the situation would lay the ground for future changes he would have to implement:

> I was only a year or two into the job … I came from sales. I knew some of them but not all of them. Those I did not know, I had no emotional capital to draw from. They saw me as this guy who is heartless, who is new, who wants to reduce costs.

Ed explained how he had to find "influencers," people who had moral suasion over those he did not know personally. It was a strategy that he felt was very effective when dealing with Asians, in general, and Filipinos, in particular:

> In western countries you talk to a person – that is okay. They agree or disagree. That is it. But in our culture if I can see you are struggling, I will look for someone who is close to you, and I will talk to that person. I would say: she has this problem, can you help me reach out to her? That, to me, is back channeling, and I had to do that to those employees I had no emotional capital with.

Ed recognized the value of communicating and establishing relationships. This, he felt, was very Asian:

> That's where I had to establish relationships by having frequent meetings with them. Every other week, I would listen to them. Just listen for an hour. It was informal, over snacks, where we shared stories. We discussed their concerns and I would say: this I do not have an answer for, but this, we will look into it. We worked together. When they saw that management was really sincere, they no longer resisted.

As a result of the discussions, Ed was able to close the internal unit and establish a separate entity in 2004. More than a decade later, the Shell Business Service Centre–Manila employs about 4,500, the biggest of 6 such business centers of Shell across the globe.

The impending closure of Pandacan Oil Depot

There were three oil companies that managed oil depots in Pandacan. However, the Supreme Court declared unconstitutional and invalid with finality, a city ordinance that allowed the oil companies to maintain oil depots in the area (Feliciano, 2015). Chevron Philippines, Petron Corporation and Pilipinas Shell Corporation have started removing the facilities from Pandacan. "The Pandacan decision is very unfortunate. We are not relocating the facilities. To us, it is a closure."

The closure of the Shell Pandacan facilities would mean the loss of jobs. There are many employees who had been with the company for a good part of their lives. Reiterating his role as "father" to the family, Ed relayed how he has reached out to those employed in the facility in preparation for its closure:

> I met with them 4 to 5 times already, almost on a monthly basis, sometimes twice a month. I listen to their concerns. For example, we have a scholarship program for deserving children of staff. So their question was: my kid is only first year college, or second year college, I am being redundated, so I am no longer an employee next year. What about the scholarship of my child? For me, we give scholarships to lots of people, so I said: the scholarship will continue as long as their child continues to meet the requirements such as minimum grades. That is a big thing for them. So, they ask other things. If it is a reasonable request which we can give, we give. That [meeting with them] enables them to feel they are valued – the company thinks of them not just as numbers or statistics, but as people who have served the company well. And that is true at Shell.

Learning from failures

Ed shared how he learned from failures he had witnessed and even personally experienced, as a recipient of streamlining initiatives. He admitted that some change management processes were better managed than others because of the element of communication: "The failures I have seen were those where there was not enough communication. Or that communication was very simple, such as we need to cut cost, this is it, and so we need to reduce, streamline."

It was in fact being a recipient of that change that made Ed realize the value of constant and personal communication. Years before he assumed the top post in the organization, Ed's position had been declared redundant. He looked forward to a separation package, but he was asked to stay on. Even then, he was not satisfied with the explanation given to him and to all others affected by the streamlining. To him, the rationale and objectives of the streamlining as well as the separation packages were not well articulated. This led him to conclude that one can never over-communicate when there is a change process going on:

> What do I mean by that? Sometimes even if there is nothing new to say, I engage people. I sit down and listen to their concerns although I have nothing new to tell them. And they know that I have nothing new, no new development. Yet, I am here because I promised we would have regular sessions. It can be monthly or every other week; it depends on the change process, on how quickly to implement. The shorter the lead time, the more I meet them. The staff appreciate that because when they see the most senior person taking time to sit down with them and listen, they realize that, hey it is important to management because the boss is here, the top guy is here to listen to us.

Ed acknowledged that his approach is influenced by culture. He explained that western cultures are highly individualistic, while Asian cultures, especially the Philippines, are not individualistic:

> We work on consensus. We also have a high regard for authority. Authority, whether seniority because of age, or seniority because of position ... we respect authority ... What's also important is even if the news is bad news, so as long as you spend time, find time and ways and means to assist, that is greatly appreciated. And then, as I said, you have to look for influencers.

In any change management, Ed believes that sincerity and authenticity are very important elements. He explained that sincerity and authenticity lead to credibility:

> When you are credible, when you say things, they will say: I believe that. At a certain point of time you don't have to explain too much since you established a certain level of credibility. Going back to my analogy – parents: we trust them, we love them. They sometimes ask us to do some things where we don't ask why. We just do it. But it is of course always good to explain the why so there is full understanding.

Strengthening the Shell family

Ed wants to make sure that the employees at Shell feel they are part of the family. He finds reasons to interact with employees and for the employees to interact with other senior managers:

Every month, we have a birthday breakfast for the birthday celebrants. Sometimes, there are 20 celebrants, other times there are more. Anyone who is available comes … It is a time for them to be able to engage senior management in a very informal manner and for senior managers to get to know them … It is really reinforcing the message we are family … Lately, we included a small part to recognize long service awardees.

Ed is also present in socio-civic activities like house building under the Gawad Kalinga Community Development Foundation:

The young people are very idealistic. They want to work for a company that is there not just to make money but to help the country. We have many of our staff in our BPO [Shell Business Service Centre–Manila] who are tired because of their night shift. Yet they will join our Saturday trip to Gawad Kalinga where we will build houses. We are about three buses. And they like it. I am there. We break bread together.

The sense of community is strong at Shell. In the strongest typhoon that hit the world – Typhoon Haiyan – Shell raised and contributed USD 4 million, one of the biggest corporate donations. SCiP received USD 2.5 million from the head office, but the balance was generated locally, through the help of the staff.

Indeed, the sense of family goes beyond the productive life of Shell employees. Ed explained that everyone who has worked with Shell is considered part of the family even when they retire:

We also have a very active retirees association which we continue to support. People see that even after Shell, you are considered part of the Shell family. After all, people have given the best years of their life with Shell. We believe we owe it to them even when they are no longer working with Shell for as long as they are not working with competition. We give them support. We have a Good Samaritan Fund, for those who become ill and are financially challenged. We organize summer outings and Christmas get-togethers.

Other Shell companies across the globe have retiree groups, but Shell in the Philippines is different:

Other shell companies, they have a retirees group … but not many are as active as ours. It is a Filipino thing, because as we said, it is family. In the western culture when parents become old, normally they go to a retirement home. For us, they stay with the family. We take care of them. This is also similar with the company. We continue to take care of our retirees, within limits, of course. But, whatever we can do to help, we help.

Ed is committed to fulfilling his role as father even to those who retired:

Before I took over [as President], the company decided to stop some of the support [to the retirees association]. Like, they were given free office space. I remember I was still Vice President then and the company was about to recall the office space. I strongly lobbied the Chairman at that time to allow the organization to keep an office here. And he agreed. Then, when I became President, I have been providing some additional funding for that group. And, they have also been getting support from the other managers. On a personal basis, retirees who are well off also give money or in kind support. For instance, someone has a resort, so it is used as a venue for activities for free. It is very Filipino. You can see that everyone is pitching in, the sense of community and family is there.

The "father" of SCiP

Ed has been and will always be a people person. He has been described to be humble and well-grounded (Dela Cruz, 2014). He is mindful of his roots and remains thankful for the opportunities he received:

> I come from very simple, humble beginnings. I grew up in a small fishing village. I can make it sexy by saying I lived near the bay, but it is actually a fishing village. I was sent to St. Andrew's in Paranaque, a Catholic school run by the Belgian missionaries and then to La Salle for college, again a Catholic school run by the La Salle brothers. My family, the schools, helped shape me to be one where I can identify with those who have less in life.

Ed was able to finish his college through the generosity of his relatives, after his father suffered a stroke. While at school, he became president of the Chemical Engineering Society and also became active in the school's Council of Student Organizations. He worked briefly for two fast-moving consumer goods companies before he joined Shell. Ed began his career in sales but was rotated to other functional areas (Dela Cruz, 2014). His exposure to finance, audit, trading, operations, and many other areas, including an assignment overseas plus executive training at INSEAD, served him well when he became President of Pilipinas Shell Petroleum Corporation and then Country Chair of SCiP:

> I saw the company [Shell] was a great company; that's why I stayed for so long. It is very good. It has a welcoming culture, very informal. It is not perfect, but no organization is perfect. In fact for any organizational structure, it is people who will make it work. So, there are structures which maybe more conducive to certain things. At the end of the day, if it is clear to everyone what we are trying to do, we can go around the structures.

In 2013, Ed was a recipient of the Management Association of the Philippines (MAP) Management Man of the Year. He was cited for his exemplary leadership and his continued support for nation building. He received accolades for "his contribution to reshaping national values by setting an example for Filipino professional managers through his track record of unblemished integrity, professional competence, and strong leadership in his management career" (Philippine Daily Inquirer, 2013). He noted, "my view, it is important for a company to not just be seen, but to really be a contributor to nation building."

In 2014, Ed was awarded CEO of the Year under the category of Diamond SABRE (Superior Achievement in Branding Reputation and Engagement) Awards for Excellence in Public Relations in the C-Suite. He was cited for "his outstanding and effective use of communications to advance the reputation of the energy and gas technology company in the Philippines, as well as for his strategic use of communications and public relations as a management function" (Manila Bulletin, 2014).

Education for change management

Ed is Country Chair of the local operations of a global company. He received training in the Philippines as he did in other parts of the world. He recognizes that an approach to change management is dependent on culture. Thus, any course in change management must take into account cultural differences: "First of all, understand culture. Simplistically, western culture is individualistic, while Asian culture is consensus building and family-oriented. Depending on where you are, that's the starting point."

Ed concedes that he is no expert in cultural management. He only knows there are differences that need to be learned and appreciated: "There are many aspects of culture … At the start, you need cultural immersion. After understanding the culture, how does one become effective in a change management program?"

Ed suggests that in Asian cultures the head of the family does the speaking. It may not be 100 percent of the time but the head must identify critical engagement periods and be there:

> The other element … because we [the Filipinos] are consensus-seeking, you have to find influencers for a particular person who may prove to be a challenge. In an individualistic culture, you can be assured that one-on-one would actually be more appreciated. You can deal straight. But that will not work here … Really, you have to dig in and understand the culture.

Apparently, Ed does understand the Filipino culture quite well. A low-key individual, holding a powerful position, he continually influences people to live Shell's core values of honesty, integrity, and respect for people – values that resonate his own beliefs. Not to forget, that in the Philippines, love for family is highly regarded and in Shell, they are one big family.

Note

1   All quotations from Ed Chua are from an interview conducted with him by the chapter author.

References

Dela Cruz, J. P. (2014). Edgar Chua: The subtleties of strength. *People Asia*, December 2013–January 2014 issue (reposted on Shell website on April 21, 2014). Retrieved from www.shell.com.ph/aboutshell/media-centre/news-and-media-releases/2014/edgar-chua-the-subtleties-of-strength.html   (last accessed 12 December 2016).

Feliciano, C. A. M. (2015). Clock ticks for petroleum firms to move facilities out of Pandacan. *Business World Online*, March 11. Retrieved from www.bworldonline.com/content.php?section=Top Story&title=clock-ticks-for-petroleum-firms-to-move-facilities-out-of-pandacan&id=104169 (last accessed 12 December 2016).

Manila Bulletin (2014). Shell Philippines head Chua named communications CEO of the Year. *Manila Bulletin*, October 10. Retrieved from www.shell.com.ph/aboutshell/media-centre/news-and-media-releases/2014/communications-ceo-of-the-year.html (last accessed 12 December 2016).

Philippine Daily Inquirer (2013). Shell's Ed Chua is MAP Management Man of the Year. *Philippine Daily Inquirer*, December 1. Retrieved from http://business.inquirer.net/154717/shells-ed-chua-is-map-management-man-of-the-year (last accessed 12 December 2016).

Shell (undated a). Who we are. Retrieved from www.shell.com/global/aboutshell/who-we-are.html (last accessed 12 December 2016).

Shell (undated b). Our people. Retrieved from www.shell.com/global/aboutshell/who-we-are/our-people.html (last accessed 12 December 2016).

Shell (undated c). PSFI Programmes. Retrieved from www.shell.com.ph/environment-society/shell-in-the-society/psfi/programs.html (last accessed 12 December 2016).

13 Leadership and change management

A cross-cultural perspective from Russia

Natalia Vinokurova, Vyacheslav Boltrukevich
and Alexander Naumov

Leadership is freedom; to be a leader is to fulfill one's potential.

(Sergey Filippov)

This chapter is devoted to Sergey Filippov, the former Director General of one of the largest aluminum plants in the world, the Bratsk aluminum smelter. Filippov became famous as a successful Russian practitioner in introducing effective production systems. His ways to run a plant are hotly debated in the Russian business and academic communities. In fact, his management ideas have been victoriously implemented by other plants and have gotten expected results.

This case study is based on personal interviews with Sergey Filippov. The authors also used his book, with the self-explanatory title *Break the stereotype!*, together with articles and interviews published in the media.[1]

The executive style of Sergey Filippov is a good example of implementing leadership to manage organizational changes successfully. Conventionally, leadership is being studied by using the following approaches:

- explaining leadership qualities or skills;
- defining different leadership styles; and
- studying situational and contingency leadership.

The first approach explains the early formation and development of Filippov's leadership skills, which were formed long before he began to work, and the experience that he gained from his managerial positions. The second one closely connects his leadership and intellectual qualities with his strong character traits. The third approach shows how he chooses the right leadership style to solve problems at the Bratsk aluminum smelter. Real leaders can be defined by their abilities to lead their companies and employees with changes through crisis to survive and achieve business success. One important thing is to determine what leader's behavior would be effective in the current context. It could include three key factors:

1   the leader's ability for vision and to convey this vision through communication to followers;
2   the understanding of what he or she is actually doing in the business; and
3   the ability to get power from "below" – from followers.

Sergey Filippov is a successful person in the Russian sense. In Russia, someone's success is usually based on self-realization, including the recognition of their activity by the surrounding community. Success also means the capacity to build effective social communications in the competitive output of production. This is an important Russian cultural trait. Given severe environmental conditions, and the social, political, and economic instability in the country's national development, Russian business people pay a lot of attention to developing different communication skills. All social connections are important to help overcome the challenges of difficulties in a new environment. Good social links and existing social capital promote better chances for doing business well. Business in Russia itself is mainly perceived as a process of interpersonal interactions rather than a process of producing a competitive product or service (McCarthy, Puffer and Vikhanski, 2005). Russian business culture is more focused on understanding business as a communication process, as the most efficient way of building personal relationships with the local authorities, as they concentrate both administrative and financial resources (Vinokurova, Kratko, Raskutina and Nazarenko, 2012). Hence, there is a special nuance in how the Russian word "success" is understood; it is "caught" as something short-run and temporary. When success is caught, even if for a short time, it allows the individual to improve and strengthen social communications and relationships. A situation of uncertainty does not allow for any planning – not only for business succession, but also the support of the operational and tactical activities of companies (Polyakov and Vinokurova, 2011). Thus, social capital gives a person the opportunity to obtain in an unstable environment a variety of physical and monetary resources along with so-called administrative support. Today, this is more important than money or profits. Using administrative resources, a business person is able to prepare a more favorable environment for their enterprise and to compete with less business management efforts.

This hypothesis is confirmed by data collected from a Russian opinion poll, conducted February 16–17, 2013, which polled 1,600 people in 130 towns and cities in 42 regions, districts, and republics across Russia. The sample represents the urban population of Russia. The statistical error does not exceed 3.4 percent. This study shows that 26 percent of Russians define a successful person as one who has achieved their own goals, publicly known. For a leader, this success includes achieving their interest too, and only then does success mean material prosperity. Russians know that in their cultural, social, political, and economic environment, a successful person is able to achieve their goals only with the aid of social contacts, and thus the successful person is one who continuously develops their social net. Only 21 percent of respondents equated success with being prosperous (GT Market, 2013).

Filippov's ability to understand people, to motivate them to stand at the forefront of industrial development, and to set up achievable and measurable goals helped him to gain recognition as a leader in Russia's largest aluminum plant. All plant changes were implemented by him gradually, step by step. The term step here denotes new, changing targets in Filippov's new production system. Step means a radical change in personnel management, production management, finance, and marketing, with the hope to break stereotypes. The first step was a transformational leadership decision, which is the most difficult to make in view of the conservative thinking that prevails in Russian culture (Naumov and Puffer, 2000). This step, according to Filippov, could affect the jobs of 1,000 or 2,000 people. So, those 1,000 or even 2,000 people could be unhappy and disagree with the change, and the leader must have the confidence and resilience to survive severe pressure both from below (discontent of the workers, former colleagues) and from above (dissatisfaction by top management). At this time of total isolation, the leader must have special vitality and absolute confidence in the proposed change, as well as a willingness to take responsibility. The pattern of leadership-like behavior and qualities was formed in early childhood and strengthened by working and managerial experiences.

Filippov's effective communication and personal leadership style began in his childhood when his relationships with both peers and adults were distinguished by openness and common sense judgment. His mother played a major role in forming his character by constantly asking him to put and keep things in order. Paying attention to details makes him able to observe and evaluate circumstances. The young man learned to notice those traits that attracted the attention of others and allowed individuals to stand out from the crowd thanks to their bright personalities. His courage and strong desire for expressive freedom in his adolescence and young adulthood were supported by his ability to defend his own opinion, regardless of other people's disagreements, which were sometimes even supported by fighting. In his childhood and adolescence he also gained a strong sense of morality and responsibility. Remembering the regular, thorough Saturday house cleanings, he noted that even though he hated those Saturdays, he clearly understood he alone had to do the cleaning. This principle would later be applied to workers: authority could be delegated only to a person who takes responsibility.

Observation, perseverance, and goal achievement were enriched in the future by working and managerial experiences, specifically in human relations, that helped Filippov to make profound transformations through small but predictably effective steps. A distinctive feature of his leadership style was the ability to understand and evaluate a specific situation and to get fast feedback. A leader's personal characteristics determine whether he or she can understand an organizational state, and then, using their strengths, act successfully on that understanding. The leader moves from self-knowledge, self-improvement, and elaboration of personal leadership skills to understanding where, how, and when their personal style of influence can best be applied in the organizational environment. He or she also learns how personal potential can be used in assessing external factors for interacting with the community outside the organization.

Sergey Filippov began using his personal potential to build effective organizational and interpersonal communications as soon as he started working. He believes that the main resource of any enterprise is its people and not the product or technical means of production. "Our main asset is our people. Their quality determines the strength and power of the business. Therefore, the accent should be on the staff. Everything starts with people. Profit is made by people too!"

It is impossible to make key changes within an organization without motivating its employees. Any new system of control is at first supported only by those leaders who developed it. Improving the working conditions and wages of the workers was the starting point of his creating a team that supported the conversion. During informal conversations with workers, he tried to interest them in improving the quality of their working lives. Taking the next step associated with changes, he consulted with workers about the main production strengths of the plant. Higher responsibilities and improved material resources were distributed among the workers after an unnecessary supervisory level of management had been deleted. Workers were encouraged to communicate and cooperate in a new way, to assume more responsibility, and to build their own effective team management. Since low-level workers were the main production component of the organization and their salaries were directly dependent on the enterprise's production rate and profit, they were very interested in changes that could improve profits.

Distributing responsibility and power among the workers was a very important step in developing the production system; this step helped form a team. Understanding and knowledge of the system of interpersonal relations inside the working environment allowed Sergey Filippov to draw various conclusions.[2] Team leaders usually enjoyed the greatest authority among the workers at hazardous production facilities. In an emergency, the team leader and members would always help. Working in a team, the team leader sees everything; they control the situation. Effective control demands from three to five people per team. One of the main methods of security is: I see my partner, my partner sees me. The team became a mechanism for implementing self-control and mutual assistance. Such a team does not need top-down control, as a rule. Power is distributed throughout the team. The team provided self-monitoring and this became the basic element of the Bratsk smelter's production system.

The biggest challenges of change management according to Filippov were new attitudes towards people. He had responsibility for high-quality products and workers' attitudes towards their jobs. The most vulnerable point in a metallurgical enterprise is safety standards. The ability to organize a safe production process is the key competence of a leader. If it is not done properly, all of the leader's accumulated authority can be automatically undermined. A tragic accident at the plant, the death of three experienced workers who ignored safety standards to increase production rates, was Sergey's most striking negative memory of the failure of governance. His response to this tragic situation was prompt and simple: first piecework pay (pay for performance rate) was abolished, then stringent standards of production were established, and strict sanitary controls were introduced.

Actually, the essence of the change at the Bratsk aluminum smelter was the improvement of attitude towards workers directly employed in the production process, and this led to the construction of a new management culture that was not based on old stereotypes. The transformation initiative came from the leader, from the top, not the bottom. When Filippov came to the Bratsk aluminum smelter there were 6,000 employees; when he left in 2012, there were only 4,000. However, during that period, the smelter's production rate increased from 150 to 250 tons per person on an international level. Wages increased from 10,000–15,000 rubles per month to 60,000–65,000 rubles per month, approximately $2,000 at that time period's rate of exchange. So that wage was close to international levels too.

Filippov created a middle-class, skilled, and well-paid worker force, which itself did not violate safety for production, and technological standards, and also did not allow others to break them either. Since the plant had been commissioned in 1966, 1,578 people had been injured and 72 people had died. The number of accidents decreased from four to two per year after Filippov's basic transformations. In 2008, the Bratsk aluminum smelter produced more than 1 million tons, with a planned production capacity of 920,000 tons. This was a world record for one plant at that time. The planned production capacity of the plant was kept at a record level despite the 2008 world economic crisis. Every day, the plant began with presentations by employees who recommended ways to improve inefficient methods of production. For the first time, leadership respected and needed initiatives from the shop floor.

Filippov's leadership style largely corresponds to the famous model of leadership described by American Joseph S. Nye (2006). In contrast, the hard methods of management in organizations include an emphasis on the technical features of the production process and compliance with the formal rules of security techniques, an unnecessarily high reliance on administrative resources, a substitution of respect relations for authority relations based on fear, a misunderstanding of the role of culture in effecting changes inside the organization, and a lack of development of organizational communications. This was never Filippov's management style; he preferred the consultation style of production management, understood the real needs of production personnel, and created a new environment and organizational culture. Persuading, motivating, and inspiring people by his own example and results, he gradually went from the hard power style of leadership (control and centralization of management), which is widespread in Russia, to the soft power style (distribution of power and allocation of responsibility). This changed the staff's attitude to the production process completely. For the first time, the production process began to be understood as the process of creating real wealth, and the final result was a profit fairly distributed among the active participants in its creation. Filippov noted that to get really serious results, it is first necessary to change the production culture in every working site.

The success of a leader depends on the effectiveness of their activities; each event should have maximum importance for all members of the team. Every activity requires energy, otherwise there will only be formalism and failure. A leader must constantly receive feedback so that he or she can keep employees focused on the results of the transformation. A failed leader is one whom people don't notice or quickly forget.

Building a new ethic for the worker–leader relationship is to create an atmosphere of trust and cooperation. Teams and initiatives work best if rules are shared and understood by each team member. Creating a proactive environment, in which leaders can implement effective production processes and other positive changes, is the main goal of organizational culture and ethics. The foundation for these relationships is the principle of justice (for example, the same standard of safety regulations for all employees), transparency of incentives and layoffs, and respect for the worker as the main actor in the process. "When talking with a worker, we always have to respect him, we must ask his name and patronymic (the use of both names is a sign of respect and formality in Russia). Arrogance must be punished." The ability to get the feedback needed to build relationships with employees begins with respect for those who can provide this feedback.

Filippov's management style includes the ability to set up and implement specific goals through effective communication. It also includes observing and quickly responding to complex contingencies and problems. As a result, he managed to overcome such typical shortcomings of Russian traits in organizational culture as: levels of production standards that are low by international standards, low levels of performance discipline, low levels of initiative, lack of feedback, fear of taking responsibility and misunderstanding its role, badly structured work, and frequent crisis mode in a company's operation.

In the framework of developing a training program, "the leader and organization" in business schools, Filippov advised starting from a personal, individualized approach to learning. "Teach the program leaders in your organization, those people who have a real ability for leadership," he said. It is unproductive to teach effective communication or leadership skills to a person who doesn't have this ability. An effective training program should be built by studying the personal characteristics of the leader and the problems of the relationship between the leader and the corporate environment. The skills needed to plan global changes in the company should also be studied, especially the problem of leadership and the external environment. A leader needs to have time and a place to implement positive change effectively.

Russian business leaders demonstrate traits of the national character in their behavior (Naumov and Petrovskaya, 2011). However, not all of these can be directly associated with leadership behavior. The analysis of research produced by Russian and foreign authors on the subject and its applications to Filippov confirm a number of the most typical patterns of a leader's behavior.

Notes

1   Sergey Filippov was Managing Director of Vyksa metallurgical plant since June 2012 (United Metallurgical Company) to June 2015. He began working at Ust-Kamenogorsk (Kazakhstan) titanium–magnesium plant. From 1978 to 1980 he served in the Soviet Army. In 1986 he graduated

from Leningrad Mining Institute. From 1986 to 1998 he consecutively worked as foreman, senior foreman, head of department, and deputy director for production at Sayanogorsk aluminum smelter. In 1998, he completed training in an anti-crisis management program (Academy of National Economy, Russian Federation Government). In 1998 he also held the post of Director of the Sayan aluminum plant, and in 2000/2001 he was Director of Novokuznetsk aluminum plant. In 2001, he was First Deputy of General Director of the Krasnoyarsk aluminum plant and also Managing Director of Orsk-Khalilov steel plant NOSTA. Then, up to 2005, he was General Director of JSC Krasnoyarsk metallurgical plant. He held the post of Managing Director of Bratsk aluminum smelter from 2005 to 2012.

2   Sergey Filippov began his work history as a simple worker at the Ust-Kamenogorsk titanium–magnesium plant.

References

Filippov, S., Turusov, S., Volvanskiy, V. and Erenburg, M. (2010). *Break the stereotype! Production system of Bratsk aluminum smelter.* Moscow, Russia: Institute for Complex Strategic Studies.

GT Market. (2013). The study polls: What is success and how important it is to be successful [in Russian]. Retrieved from http://gtmarket.ru/news/2013/09/19/6278 (last accessed 12 December 2016).

McCarthy, D. J., Puffer, S. M. and Vikhanski, O. S. (2005). Russian managers in the new Europe: Need for a new management style. *Organizational Dynamics, 34*(3), 231–246.

Naumov, A. and Petrovskaya, I. (2011). Business culture changes in Russia (1996–2006). Vestnik Moscovskogo Universiteta, series 24, *Management, 1,* 65–96.

Naumov, A. I. and Puffer, S. (2000). Measuring Russian culture using Hofstede's dimensions. *Applied Psychology: An International Review, 49*(4), 709–718.

Nye, J. S. (2006). Soft power, hard power and leadership. Retrieved from www.hks.harvard.edu/netgov/files/talks/docs/11_06_06_seminar_Nye_HP_SP_Leadership.pdf (last accessed 12 December 2016).

Polyakov, E. and Vinokurova, N. (2011). Russia: Father–daughter succession in a russian family business: A case study. In D. Halkias, P. W. Thurman, C. Smith and R. S. Nason (eds), *Father–daughter succession in family business: A cross-cultural perspective* (pp. 157–165). Farnham: Gower Publishing.

Vinokurova, N., Kratko, I., Raskutina V. and Nazarenko, N. (2012). Russia: Entrepreneurship and sustainability. In Halkias, D. and Thurman P. W. (eds), *Entrepreneurship and sustainability: Business solutions for poverty alleviation from around the world* (pp. 169–177). Farnham: Gower Publishing.

14 *Aye bin?*

Leading a changing 'traditional' Scottish family business

Claire Seaman

Introduction

Family business is the predominant form of business worldwide, contributing somewhere between 65 and 80 percent of businesses in developed economies (GGiS, 2015; Poutziouris, Smyrnios and Klein, 2006; Poutziouris, Wang and Chan, 2002; Sharma, 2004). While the challenges that occur during the succession process are relatively well-documented (Anderson, Jack and Drakopolou Dodd, 2007; Howorth and Ali, 2001; Miller, Steier and Le Breton-Miller, 2006; Ward, 2011), a more subtle challenge presents in the ongoing leadership of incremental change that could be perceived as 'changing tradition'. This is not solely a feature of family business – many businesses have well-established traditions – but it is perhaps a particular challenge for family businesses where the tradition is perceived to be an important part of family identity (Dixon and Hart, 2010). Indeed, within the Scots language there is a phrase, *aye bin*, which means simply that that is how things have always been, with the implicit assumption that that is how they will remain. The case study presented here from Scotland, therefore, considers a business manufacturing traditional Scottish sweets. The leadership of incremental change that acknowledges both the importance of tradition and the importance of a fresh strategic direction for the business is not simple, but it is vital to the future success of businesses in rapidly changing markets.

Case study

Background

Scotland has a long history in the manufacture of high-sugar, non-chocolate sweets, driven in part by the historic availability of relatively cheap sugar from ships docking in the major ports. This group of products – which includes fudge, tablet[1] and boiled sweets – are commonly produced by small family-owned and family-run businesses, and sold to a customer base that was historically local but is now highly influenced by the tourist market. The business considered here produces tablet and fudge for the traditional market and sells the product to local stores and via traditional Scottish events, primarily Highland Games. The business under study is currently in its third generation and faces a number of significant leadership challenges, which can be summarized in three distinct areas. Changes in the external environment include the closure of many small shops and a government-led drive to reduce dietary sugar. The closure of many small shops and indeed manufacturing firms has led to a market where many of the competitor products are produced using commercial manufacturing techniques. However, one product – tablet – is made via boiling sugar in a production process that does not scale easily to commercial manufacturing, and hence the traditional product has remained largely the preserve of small companies. While commercial alternatives exist, they vary from the traditional product in taste and especially texture, and the company sees the traditional product as one of its major strengths. However, traditional tablet is also fragile and requires careful packaging. While relatively simple packaging works well for the local market, developing the product for sale in a wider range of outlets requires change. The perception that the 'tradition' is being changed is in itself a challenge and one where leadership plays a key role.

Business structure and ownership

The business is formally in its second generation, although the transition has been a two-stage process. Started by a husband and wife team, the husband died around 7 years ago. The mother led the business alone until about 2 years ago when the son joined the business upon graduating. Their son now runs the business, which is partially owned by himself, his widowed mother, and a sister who does not work in the business. The first generation holds 50 percent of the business, with son and daughter holding 25 percent each. This creates a number of leadership challenges: while the son is tasked with the formal leadership role, the balance of power (in terms of ownership) lies with the wider family circle. Further, there is a workforce of 17 individuals, mainly employed on a part-time basis, for whom tradition and familiarity with the business play an important role. The dynamic here, therefore, is of a formal leader (son) who must lead within both the family and the workforce. The two spheres are not distinct. Both mother and sister are well known to the workforce and indeed the workforce contains many who have worked for the company for a considerable time. The network ties within and between workforce and family are strong and play a key role in the ongoing business dynamic. The leadership dynamic could therefore be expressed as two dynamics: the formal manner in which the business is constituted and led (Figure 14.1), and the informal manner in which the business operates (Figure 14.2).

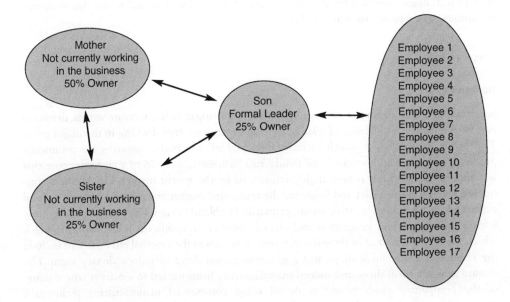

Figure 14.1 The formal business structure

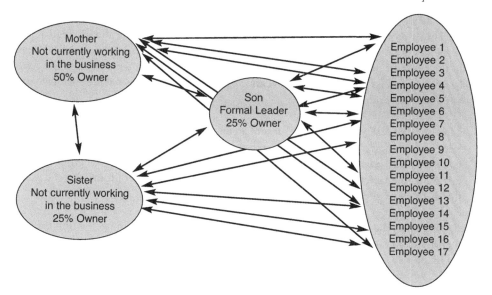

Figure 14.2 The network perspective

The purpose of the network perspective in Figure 14.2 is not to detail every network tie that exists within the company. Simply, the network mapping is included to support the idea that within a small organization with a number of long-standing family members and employees, there are numerous network ties that will influence the role of the leader and the manner in which influence – formal and informal – is generated. The idea that family, friendship, and business networks overlap and interact is becoming established in micro and small businesses (Martínez, Palacios and Seaman, in press), as is the idea of familiarity, and may indicate one important difference between smaller family businesses and their larger, more formally constituted competitors.

Next-generation leadership

The case presented here is a business theoretically in its first-to-second generation, but where significant succession activity has already occurred in the transfer of ownership of the business from a husband and wife team to a scenario where the surviving wife owns the business with her children. In terms of the leadership of change, this has important implications for the dynamic within the family. The sudden death of the leader of a family business (in this case, the father) is a sadly typical cause of unplanned succession that in this case has been initially successful. This is acknowledged by the son to have both advantages and disadvantages in terms of leading change: "That's difficult … we'd have argued about the changes, sure. Probably a lot. But then, he knew a lot about the business, too."

The perception, too, is that the history of unplanned succession has made some of the changes easier to acknowledge. As the son put it: "I think, well, from Mum's viewpoint, none of this was what she wanted. But then, we have to do what we can with where we are … and she does see that, I think."

The balance between family change and business change would appear to be an important component of the leadership process. By acknowledging the negative family change, there appears to be scope for the son to acknowledge a pragmatic worldview as the basis for business change. This is probably in part a reflection of the timeframe; the father died around 7 years before the development of this case study and while the pragmatic view appears to be strong within the family at present, acknowledging the successes of the next generation in the future will be important. The perception is that acknowledging future successes will be easier within the workforce. According to the son:

> They've been really positive; there's less of an emotional link to the past in some ways and even though the successes have been pretty small so far they like to see the work that has gone into this (i.e. developing the business) rewarded ... We've had a couple of wins; getting it (the tablet) into airports was a great move because lots of tourists see it ... but the margins are pretty small ...

In reflecting upon the major theories of leadership and their potential impact within this case, two theories stand out. One is the importance of charismatic leadership, which appears to play an important role and is reflected by the acknowledged importance of humor, as the son observed: "We can have a bit of a laugh with the team ... we all know change is hard work and we do want to respect tradition but ... we need new markets."

A strong element of path–goal leadership also appears to be present, with the leader attempting to adopt a leadership style most likely to achieve the desired results from the workforce (House, 1971). Path–goal leadership is an area that has merited some study within family business (House, 1971; Seaman, McQuaid and Pearson, 2014) in part because the proposed adaptive nature of leadership fits well with a scenario where a family member joins the business and adapts to the environment. "Well, I'm committed to the family business," the son said, "and I suppose you try to lead in a way that works. Don't always get that right."

Finally, the importance of the leader–follower dynamic should not be discounted. A family business often contains a leader–follower dynamic that sits in parallel to the formal power structures, and this case is no exception. While much of the formal power lies within the ownership structure, a next-generation leader is emerging for both the workforce and the business dimension of the family. This last distinction is important; there is no particular suggestion that the son is now the family leader. This was not really explored within the development of the current case study, although it would form an interesting additional dimension. The role of business leader does, however, appear to have been successfully transferred. Drawing on theory from the family business domain, the twin or multiple rationalities associated with family/friendship and business are clear and likely to apply also in leadership.

Conclusions

The manner in which change is led is vital, but within the perspective of the small, family owned-and-managed business two aspects appear to be key. One is the ownership structure and hence the formal power structures of the business, but a second lies in the networks within the business that may support or undermine change and the ability of the leader to move the process forward. Further, while the characteristics of the formal business leader are important, so too are the characteristics of those who follow. This importance of the leader–follower dynamic appears to hold true even where the 'follower' is both mother to the leader and the majority shareholder in the business. This raises interesting questions about the role of the leader–follower dynamic in family business succession because the role of follower here appears to have largely been adopted voluntarily, albeit in response to bereavement. This is an area that would merit further and more substantive research to combine aspects of leader–follower theory and indeed the gender dynamics of mother–son succession.

Note

1 Tablet is a brittle, sugary confection from Scotland. It is usually made from sugar, condensed milk, and butter, boiled to a soft-ball stage and allowed to crystallize. Tablet differs from fudge in that it has a brittle, grainy texture, whereas fudge is much softer. Well-made tablet is a medium-hard confection, not as soft as fudge, but not as hard as hard-boiled sweets.

References

Anderson, A., Jack, S. and Drakopolou Dodd, S. (2007). *Entrepreneurship as a nexus of change: The syncretistic production of the future.* Working Paper 2007/002. Lancaster: Lancaster University Management School. Retrieved from www.research.lancs.ac.uk/portal/en/publications/entrepreneurship-as-nexus-of-change-the-syncretistic-production-of-the-future%28ff67e6a0-358a-4ce8-831c-31c8b284dbaa%29. html (last accessed 12 December 2016).

Dixon, M. L. and Hart, L. K. (2010). The impact of path–goal leadership styles on work group effectiveness and turnover intention. *Journal of Managerial Issues, 22*(1), 52–69.

GGiS. (2015). *Sustainability: The challenge facing Scotland's SMEs and family businesses.* The Goodison Group in Scotland (GGiS). Retrieved from www.scotlandfutureforum.org/sme-succession.html (last accessed 12 December 2016).

House, R. J. (1971). A path goal theory of leader effectiveness. *Administrative Science Quarterly, 16*(3), 321–339.

Howorth, C. and Ali, Z. A. (2001). A study of succession in a family firm. *Family Business Review, 14*(3), 231–244.

Martínez, A. T., Palacios, T. M. P. and Seaman, C. (in press). Evaluating family engagement (familiarity) in the family firm (title translated from Spanish: Medicion del grado de familiaridad de una empresa). *Academia Revista Latinoamericana de Administración*, Special issue from the 11th Annual Family Enterprise Research Conference, June 4–7, 2015, University of Burlington in Vermont, USA.

Miller, D., Steier, L. and Le Breton-Miller, I. (2006). Lost in time: Intergenerational succession, change and failure in family business. In P. Z. Poutziouris, K. X. Smyrnios and S. B. Klein (eds), *Handbook of research on family businesses* (pp. 371–387). Cheltenham: Edward Elgar Publishing.

Poutziouris, P. Z., Smyrnios, K. X. and Klein, S. B. (eds). (2006). *Handbook of research on family business.* Cheltenham: Edward Elgar Publishing.

Poutziouris, P., Wang, Y. and Chan, S. (2002). Chinese entrepreneurship: The development of small family firms in China. *Journal of Small Business and Enterprise Development, 9*(4), 383–399.

Seaman, C., McQuaid, R. and Pearson, M. (2014). Networks in family business: A multi-rational approach. *International Entrepreneurship and Management Journal, 10*(3), 523–537.

Sharma, P. (2004). An overview of the field of family business studies: Current status and directions for the future. *Family Business Review, 17*(1), 1–36.

Ward, J. L. (2011). *Keeping the family business healthy: How to plan for continuing growth, profitability, and family leadership.* London: Palgrave Macmillan.

15 Transformative leadership

A Swedish case

Cecilia Bjursell

Swedish culture is characterized as feminine and non-hierarchical in the literature. In international business encounters, Swedish leadership can be perceived as odd because a masculine and hierarchical style is still the norm. This traditional style of leadership works well in times of war and crisis, but for areas characterized by complexity and collaboration, the Swedish leadership style can provide guidance towards performance. This chapter presents a case study of Swedish leadership and defines this approach as transformative leadership in which the manager's genuine interest for people is at heart.

Tom – A manager in progress

> If we are to break cultural barriers, we must have respect for each other and build trust. If you like a person, those cultural things don't matter. If you trigger irritation or defense or create uncertainty, you will get irritated and focus on the cultural differences.
>
> (Tom Söberg, 2015)[1]

Tom Söberg lives in Sweden, but he is an international manager at heart. To succeed in international research and development (R&D) companies, he has found that Swedish leadership works well. Tom was born in Canada, went to school in Norway, and moved to Sweden to study electrical engineering. He has a military background and spent one year in Lebanon. As an engineer, he has worked at Ericsson, Sony Ericsson, and Husqvarna, in Sweden and abroad. While working at Ericsson, he spent four years in Japan and then several years in India and China. When Sony Ericsson started, he was involved in the development of the basic technology and had to travel to customers all over Asia to show the platform. This meant that Tom, an introvert, was put in situations that forced him to interact with many different kinds of people: "I had an extrovert position in the company, and I am more of an introvert, so this was challenging and changed me as a person."

Tom describes life's challenges, weaknesses, and hard times – both private and professional – as sources of personal growth. His childhood values, in which respect for others was important, have continued to evolve into a mature approach characterized by responsiveness, humility, and respect for differences. Tom sees this as an ongoing inner journey where it is important to keep one's feet on the ground. In contrast to this would be a leadership in which a big ego takes over and runs the show:

> A lot of people want to project a perfect image of their life and present it all nicely packaged, but that's not how it is. In leadership, when I work with the team, I have to be

myself in order for them to trust me. As a leader, I give them feedback but I also need feedback from them … This works pretty well in all cultures.

Tom emphasizes over and over again the need to listen and learn from situations and to meet people on an equal level, human to human. In this kind of leadership, softness and hardness are not mutually exclusive characteristics: "I'm quite soft as a person. I have no problems with being tough if needed, but I don't use hardness to achieve things. That is not how I do it." This relational focus has impact on the kinds of activities that Tom prefers to engage in:

> If I sit in on all the meetings and watch all power point presentations – what value have I created for the company at the end of the day if I have not been talking to people and been visible in the organization. The more you engage people and make sure they are comfortable, the better they deliver. Then we create value for the company, and I think many managers miss out on this.

Tom talks about recognizing emotions, positive and negative, because they are important for the energy in the organization. At the same time, leadership often means controlling one's own emotions in order to be self-possessed. Working with change in an organization can often be stressful. A systematic and open approach that involves people on all levels of the organization can move things forward in a productive sense. At the same time, this can be strenuous for the leader, and Tom thinks that it is important, as a leader, to have a "safety valve" – trusted people that one can talk to about the situation.

> As a manager, you create a palette with different behavioral patterns that you can use in different situations. And then you have to realize that "I have come this far, but I still have a lot to learn." You make mistakes and you have bad days, but you have to move on.

Interacting with humans in an equal, respectful, and responsive way bridges cultural distance in leadership, according to Tom. This also means realizing that, as a leader, one has strengths and weaknesses that can be improved upon – leadership is a work in progress.

A Swedish leadership model

One of Tom's key points is that to be an initiated leader, one has to move beyond cultural stereotypes. National stereotypes can, however, be a useful starting point if regarded as an expression of a symbolic structure rather than a natural law. Stereotypes give clues to values and assumptions that guide behavior and can help us understand how people make sense of their reality. Approaching culture as expressed through language also emphasizes communication as an important part of managerial work (Bjursell, 2015).

One much-described feature of the Swedish leadership model[2] is the decision-making style. The Swedish decision making process has a strong *consensus orientation*. Achieving consensus was critical in Swedish history when different stakeholders such as employers, unions, governmental representatives, and other groups agreed on what came to be known as the Swedish welfare model. With this, consensus orientation became an integrated way of working in society and in business. Consensus in decision making means that a thorough discussion takes place before a decision is made; and when a decision is made, people are usually committed and act in accordance with the decision (Bjursell, 2007). This style is often contrasted with a style in which decisions are made quickly and then things are corrected along the way. These two approaches have been called *discussion oriented* and *action oriented* (Vaara, Risberg, Søderberg and Tienari, 2003). As discussion oriented, the Swedish leader tries to involve people in an egalitarian way by acting as a coach (Grenness, 2011). Engaging in discussion is furthermore said to be a way to anchor decisions within the work team, which motivates employees to perform well. The optimum motivation of people in the organization is a core objective of Swedish leadership (Kling and Goteman, 2003) and this work is based on trust and respect:

> To build trust and respect, you have to listen … In a cultural situation you make mistakes all the time, and then you have to be responsive and see how people react, and if you do this, you get useful feedback. And then you have to be willing to change to show respect for the person in front of you. These are not hard things, but they are hard to keep doing over and over.

Swedish leadership competencies, such as cooperation, teamwork, skill diversity, and creativity, are often described as relative strengths in business growth and adaptation (Larsson, Brousseau, Driver, Holmqvist and Tarnovskaya, 2003). Among the Swedish companies that work in the global arena, IKEA has embraced the idea of *Swedishness* on several levels. Swedishness is said to represent desirable values in the company, and while it guides leadership, it is also an important part of the company's external image. Swedishness in the IKEA sense compounds a nostalgic notion of nature and connections to the welfare state's heyday inhabited by thrifty, innovative, strong-willed, and humble people (Wigerfelt, 2013). Managers at IKEA are said to work with situational leadership, but leadership styles are ascribed different statuses depending on how well they fit with the notion of Swedishness. Directive leadership and being a manager are considered old-fashioned, dreary, and unappealing, whereas supportive and coaching styles of leadership are favored (Jönsson, Muhonen, Scholten and Wigerfelt, 2014).

IKEA's Swedishness, although built on what are perceived to be positive values, has been criticized for being ethnocentric and for excluding diversity in the organization (Wigerfelt, 2013). This illustrates how a simplistic and normative perception and application of culture, even when the culture is based on values such as cooperation and humility, can lead to exclusion and positioning. IKEA has however included diversity as a central value, and with this, the notion of Swedishness is changing as well. Another possible change in the Swedish leadership model might be triggered by the younger generation entering the workplace:

> It is becoming increasingly important to crack the [behavioral] code and to get comfortable with nuances. This is even more important with the younger generations because they have other driving forces, more in terms of 'what's in it for me?' So you have to be even better at describing the added value rather than threats, duty, and fairness. They are in a way softer and more sensitive.

Forces of change can also come from emerging industries. In addition to the major areas of Swedish export, which include machinery, motor vehicles, paper products, pulp, wood, iron, steel products, and chemicals, a new wave of IT companies has emerged, such as Spotify, Skype, King (Candy Crush Saga), Klarna, and Mojang (Minecraft). These companies are born global, and although they might be built on Swedish values and assumptions such as collaboration and openness, they may also have other characteristics that influence leadership in these organizations.

Concerning Swedish leadership, it is also useful to recognize that although an informal collaborative style may provide the basis for innovation and creativity, it does not lead to these in and of itself (Bröchner, Josephson and Kadefors, 2002). The soft leadership style in the

Swedish leadership model can be either weak or strong. Soft leadership becomes weak when leaders are vague, avoidant, or purely rhetorical. Soft leadership is strong when it supports and motivates employees to perform their best. The question is how to engage in activities that support strong leadership.

Transformative leadership

A central idea in Swedish leadership is a collaborative approach in which motivation of employees is a core activity, and this has similarities with transformational leadership. Transformational leadership is suggested as an alternative to transactional leadership. The latter is based on financial rewards in exchange for productivity, whereas the former works with inspiration and vision to create meaning and empower employees to achieve extraordinary outcomes (Bass and Riggio, 2006). Transformational leadership means acting as a role model for followers, giving personal attention to each follower, showing genuine concern, and, at the same time, intellectually challenging followers (Bass and Riggio, 2006). A misinterpretation of transformational leadership is that it is only about leaders' charisma and rhetoric, but studies have shown that rhetoric and job design in combination can maximize followers' performance (Grant, 2012). In addition, context plays a major role in determining the possibilities for transformational leadership (Wyld, 2013).

The notion of transformational leadership is a good place to start for understanding Swedish leadership – except for one thing: transformational leadership seems to be built on hierarchical assumptions involving leaders and followers. If employees are regarded as followers, the leader sets the limits for how far employees can go. Swedish leadership emphasizes equality and is thus less paternalistic. Engaging in transformative learning and focusing on change at the individual level to improve performance is one way to engage in productive soft management. Tom gives an example of transformative leadership as he recalls a situation when he chose to act according to what he thought was right, rather than what was expected.

> I have an example from when I was in China. We had developed a technical platform and there was a lot of pressure, and everything was extremely complex. We still managed to do it, and we got to present our project to a large American company. It was a prestigious meeting, but the project manager was inexperienced, insecure, and focused on the wrong things. He gave a really bad presentation. A Chinese manager sitting next to me leaned over and said that this person had to go, and people around the table heard what he said. Instead of removing him, I put a lot of effort into talking to him about the presentation, to understand why he had done it that way, and I gave him concrete feedback. He felt genuinely supported, gained confidence, and started to perform on a high level. What was even better is that it created ripples throughout the organization. People around me felt secure and started to bloom. That was not my plan but it had those positive effects.

That the team feels that their own developmental journeys and feelings of uncertainty are legitimate in the workplace can be an effect of leader humility (Owens and Hekman, 2012). Transformative leadership begins with questions of justice and democracy and creates an inclusive and socially just learning environment (Shields, 2010). Transformative learning at the individual level and transformational change with an organizational focus have been proposed as complementary approaches to effective organizational change efforts (Henderson, 2002). Seeing one's leadership as a work in progress and supporting one's fellow employees in their development places learning at center stage of a transformative leadership. Being a learning spirit works well with the values of equality, collaboration, and humility in the Swedish leadership model.

Recommendations for working as a leader in Sweden

In addition to the Swedish leadership model described above, this chapter ends with some hands-on advice for a person about to work as a leader in Sweden:

- *On equal terms.* Swedish culture is characterized by flat hierarchies and by the fact that employees in all positions in the organization have expectations of participation in decision making. A flat hierarchy is still a hierarchy, however, and people tend to have subtle ways of positioning themselves and others. For example, in Sweden, silence can mean either approval or disapproval.
- *Genuine meetings with people.* As Tom pointed out, a leader can learn much by actively listening to people in the organization. An opportunity to get to know people is by participating in "fika," the collective morning and afternoon breaks in the workplace. Having breaks at work is enforced by law and is a strong tradition in Sweden.
- *Language matters.* Although people in Sweden speak English fairly well, this is not the same as speaking effortlessly. Swedish is the preferred language at work.
- *The Swedish leadership model.* The Swedish leadership model is in line with values in the Swedish culture. It is only a model however, and Swedish people will adhere to it in different ways and to different extents. It is a good starting point for understanding what is going on, but you have to learn about the individuals and the context to be able to adapt your leadership.

Notes

1   All quotations from Tom Söberg are from an interview conducted with him by the chapter author in 2015.
2   From a global perspective, the Swedish and other Scandinavian leadership models are often grouped together based on their cultural similarity. An essential shared value is equality, referring to gender equality and equal distribution of economic goods, political influence, regional development, social life opportunities, and cultural experiences (Grenness, 2011). Sweden is usually regarded as the "softest" of the Scandinavian cultures.

References

Bass, B. M. and Riggio, R. E. (2006). *Transformational leadership* (2nd edn). London: Lawrence Erlbaum Associates.

Bjursell, C. (2007). *Integration through framing: A study of the Cloetta Fazer merger.* Doctoral dissertation. Linköping, Sweden: Linköping University Electronic Press. Retrieved from http://urn.kb.se/resolve?urn=urn:nbn:se:liu:diva-8964 (last accessed 12 December 2016).

Bjursell, C. (2015). The critical role of language in changing culture: Cross-border mergers and acquisitions. In D. D. Warrick and J. Mueller (eds), *Lessons in changing cultures: Learning from real world cases* (pp. 163–171). Oxford: Rossi Smith Academic Publishing.

Bröchner, J., Josephson, P. E. and Kadefors, A. (2002). Swedish construction culture, management and collaborative quality practice. *Building Research & Information, 30*(6), 392–400.

Grant, A. M. (2012). Leading with meaning: beneficiary contact, prosocial impact, and the performance effects of transformational leadership. *Academy of Management Journal, 55*(2), 458–476.

Grenness, T. (2011). Will the 'Scandinavian leadership model' survive the forces of globalisation? A SWOT analysis. *International Journal of Business and Globalisation, 7*(3), 332–350.

Henderson, G. M. (2002). Transformative learning as a condition for transformational change in organizations. *Human Resource Development Review, 1*, 186–214.

Jönsson, S., Muhonen, T., Scholten, C. and Wigerfelt, A. S. (2014). Illusive inclusion–construction of leaders and employees based on nationality. *Cross Cultural Management, 21*(2), 245–260.

Kling, K. and Goteman, I. (2003). IKEA CEO Anders Dahlvig on international growth and IKEA's unique corporate culture and brand identity. *The Academy of Management Executive, 17*(1), 31–37.

Larsson, R., Brousseau, K. R., Driver, M. J., Holmqvist, M. and Tarnovskaya, V. (2003). International growth through cooperation: Brand-driven strategies, leadership, and career development in Sweden. *The Academy of Management Executive, 17*(1), 7–21.

Owens, B. P. and Hekman, D. R. (2012). Modeling how to grow: An inductive examination of humble leader behaviors, contingencies, and outcomes. *Academy of Management Journal, 55*(4), 787–818.

Shields, C. M. (2010). Transformative leadership: Working for equity in diverse contexts. *Educational Administration Quarterly, 46*(4), 558–589.

Vaara, E., Risberg, A., Søderberg, A.-M. and Tienari, J. (2003). Nation talk: The construction of national stereotypes in a merging multinational. In A.-M. Søderberg and E. Vaara (eds), *Merging across borders: People, cultures and politics* (pp. 61–86). Copenhagen: Copenhagen Business School Press.

Wigerfelt, A. S. (2013). Diversity and Swedishness: A paradox within IKEA. *International Journal of Information Technology and Business Management, 20*(1), 1–14.

Wyld, D. C. (2013). Transformation leadership: When is it redundant? *Academy of Management Perspectives, 27*(2) (online only). Retrieved from http://dx.doi.org/10.5465/amp.2013.0064 (last accessed 12 December 2016).

16 The impact of early multicultural experience on later creative leadership

A case study of the influence of Barack Obama's early years

Grant Jewell Rich

Though his public life as the 44th President of the United States of America is well known, this chapter examines the early life of Barack Obama as a case study with implications for better understanding the influence of early multicultural experience on leadership and change management. Using a strengths-based positive psychology perspective, Obama's development will be explored through the use of primary sources such as his books (Obama, 2004, 2006), existing scholarly analysis of his childhood and youth (e.g., Gielen, 2013; Sharma, 2011; Sharma and Gielen, 2014), including a version of this chapter published as an article (Rich, in press), and information from various news media.

Brief biographical background

Barack Hussein Obama was born in 1961 in Honolulu, Hawai'i. His mother, Stanley Ann Dunham, was born in Kansas, in the Midwestern region of the US, while his father, Barack, Sr., was born in Kenya. Ann and Barack, Sr., met in 1960 at the University of Hawai'i where Barack, Sr., was a scholarship student. By the time Barack, Sr., graduated and left for graduate school at Harvard in 1962, the marriage was effectively over, though officially the divorce was finalized several years later. The senior Obama returned to Kenya in 1964 and died in an auto accident in 1971, when Barack was 21 years old. It is important to recall how unusual such racially mixed marriages were at the time in the US. For example, in 1961, the year of Obama's birth, almost half of the US states (22 states) had anti-miscegenation laws banning marriage and sexual relations between different races, and a 1958 Gallup poll found that 96 percent of white Americans opposed such mixed marriages (Gielen, 2013). Only in 1967, with the famous *Loving vs. Virginia* case, did the US Supreme Court decide that such laws were unconstitutional (Davis, 2001). Ann Dunham met her next husband, Lolo Soetoro, an Indonesian graduate student at the University of Hawai'i in 1963 and soon moved to Indonesia. Though she would divorce Lolo, Ann eventually began extended anthropological fieldwork in Indonesia – over almost two decades – and earned her PhD in 1992, before her death in 1995.

Though born in Honolulu, Barack went with his mother to Indonesia where he lived with her and his stepfather from 1967 to 1971, when he returned to Honolulu and lived with his maternal grandparents, until his graduation from the prestigious Punahou High School in 1979. After high school graduation, Obama attended Occidental College in California for two years before transferring to Columbia University in New York City, where he graduated in 1983. After some work in New York, Obama became a community organizer in Chicago from 1985 to 1988 and then entered Harvard Law School. After graduation from law school Obama returned to Chicago, where he became a faculty member at the University of Chicago, beginning his well-known rise in politics, from State Senator (1997–2004), to US Senator (2005–2008), to his election as US President in 2008.

Psychological theories of multicultural experience, creativity, and leadership

Psychologists typically define creativity as a novel product that has some social value; that is, to be creative one must make something new that has some utility to other people. Thus, a successful political leader is creative when she or he develops a new role or a new solution to social or political issues or problems that is recognized by at least some others. Classic theories of creativity, such as that of Graham Wallas (1926), suggest the creative process works through several stages. First is the preparation stage where the creator acquires the needed background knowledge and experience to make the breakthrough. Next comes a stage of incubation, which often includes a period of quiet reflection or seclusion, and time away from actively working on the issue. Third is a brief stage of insight or illumination, when the actual discovery or creative product is realized. Finally, in the last stage, the creator enters a period of verification, which may include extended time spent evaluating and elaborating on the original creative insight, modifying and adapting it in response to feedback from others (e.g., Sawyer, 2006; Simonton, 1994). More recently, a number of psychologists have investigated the influences that shape successful leaders, including the impact of multicultural experience on creative insight (e.g., Gardner, 1993, 1995; Leung, Maddux, Galinsky and Chiu, 2008; Rich, 2009a).

The more recent theories of creativity tend to be sociocultural theories, rather than theories focused more exclusively on the individual's neurological, cognitive, or personality characteristics. For instance, Csikszentmihalyi (1996) argues for a systems theory of creativity that asks not what is creativity, but where is creativity, answering that to understand creativity one must recognize the influences not only of the creative person, but also of the domain in which the creator works, and the environment that shapes the creator, including the field of critics, gatekeepers, and evaluators who judge the merits of the creative product (Csikszentmihalyi and Rich, 1997). Csikszentmihalyi's systems theory has been incorporated into Gardner's approach to understanding creativity and leadership through the latter's theory of multiple intelligences, with political leaders such as Gandhi and Martin Luther King scoring high on interpersonal intelligence (Gardner, 1993, 1995).

How may multicultural experience enhance creativity? Leung *et al.* (2008) argue that a broad range of practices geared to increasing multicultural experience are associated with increases in such correlates of creativity performance as insight learning, remote association, and idea generation, increases in such correlates of creativity-supporting cognitive processes as retrieval of unconventional knowledge, and recruitment of ideas from unfamiliar cultures for creative idea expansion. Additionally, the authors argue that openness to experience of foreign cultures is associated with creativity. Among the multicultural experiences described by the authors are school exchange programs, college diversity education, and diversity management in the workplace. Rich (2009a) largely agrees that multicultural experience is linked with enhanced creativity, but expands on the work of Leung *et al.* (2008) by arguing that scholars should consider both the type of creativity and the type of multicultural experience when examining this topic. Rich suggests a theoretical framework with which to evaluate multicultural experience and creativity that divides multicultural experience into "Big M" experiences (such as living abroad for an extended time as an expatriate or immigrant) and

"Little m" experiences (such as spending a week's vacation in a foreign country or taking a college course in the history of a different nation). How may these theories be applied to the childhood and youth of Barack Obama to illuminate aspects of his development associated with his later success?

Applying psychological theories to Barack Obama's childhood and youth

Hawai'i

When Barack Obama was born in Hawai'i in 1961 it had only been a state for two years. Prior to that, Hawai'i had been a US territory since 1898. Its location in Oceania in Polynesia makes it the only US state outside the Americas, and its demographics are also unique, as one of the few 'minority majority' states in the US. According to the 2010 US Census data (US Census Bureau, 2010), Hawai'i is almost 25 percent Caucasian, 38.6 percent Asian, 10 percent Native Hawai'ian/other Pacific Islander, 1.6 percent Black, 1 percent other race, and 23.6 percent two or more races. In contrast, for the US as a whole, about 63 percent are Caucasian, 4.7 percent Asian, under 1 percent Native Hawai'ian/other Pacific Islander/Native American/Alaska Native, 12 percent Black, and 2 percent two or more races. Many have argued that Hawai'i is the most diverse US state (Sharma, 2011). Notably, just as Hawai'i reflected a recent colonial legacy, so did Kenya, birthplace of Obama's father. Following Ghana's 1957 Independence, Kenya in 1963 was among the first African nations to become independent, and Obama's father was devoted to earning an education in the US in economics and then returning to build his nation.

Though Barack's father left by 1962, his mother remained a strong presence in her son's early childhood. Born in Kansas, she relocated with her family to Hawai'i and is often described as an independent and idealistic thinker who had an optimistic vision of a multicultural, post-colonial world. Many who knew her argued she was a community activist working in the guise of a development expert and anthropologist. Some have argued that she was at times naïve or overly optimistic in her positive imaginings of peoples and places, and that in some respects her social activism fit with certain parts of the Beat Generation and later hippie movement's social consciousness (e.g., Gielen, 2013; Sharma, 2011).

In terms of creativity theories, these early years from birth to age six could certainly be considered part of the preparation stage as well as a Big M, multicultural experience, in that young Barack was fully immersed in a diverse milieu each day as he experienced life as a mixed-race Black child in Hawai'i, a social category that, as a Black, made him unusual statistically on the island, but as a mixed-race person of color, also made him part of the minority majority.

Indonesia

From 1967 to 1971, when he was aged 6 to 10 years old, Barack Obama lived with his mother and Indonesian stepfather, Lolo Soetoro, in Jakarta, Indonesia. He attended a Catholic school and then a public school. Though Indonesia is the world's fourth most populous nation, and the most-populous Muslim-majority nation, it is largely unfamiliar to most Americans, many of whom would have difficulty pointing to it on a map, or naming its capital city, Jakarta. Fewer still would know that just two years before Barack's arrival, between one half million and one million people were killed after a failed coup d'état. In 1967, the year of Barack's arrival, General Suharto became acting President of Indonesia (Gielen, 2013). Soetoro offered a male role model for Barack, and also offered a different perspective on Indonesia, with his military background and involvement in American-Indonesian corporations, as opposed to his mother's developmental advocacy and peacenik anthropological approach.

During his time in Indonesia, Barack learned to speak the local language (Bahasa Indonesia) fluently by the second or third grade (Sharma, 2011), and was exposed to the great poverty that was then pervasive in Jakarta. He spent approximately two years there in a poor Catholic Franciscan school, and then about two years in an upper-class Indonesian school that immersed him in a tolerant form of Islam. While today Indonesia and its Islam are considerably more conservative, notably, Barack's mother was non-religious and his stepfather was arguably a Muslim in name only, as on census-type forms (Gielen, 2013; Sharma, 2011). His family in Indonesia also included his half-sister Maya Soetoro-Ng, who was nine years younger than Barack. Barack's time at the Besuki public school exposed him to the five principles of Pancasila, on which all such Indonesian public schools were founded after 1945 Independence. These principles covered "belief in the One and Only God, just and civilized humanity, the unity of Indonesia, democracy guided by the inner wisdom in the unanimity arising out of deliberations among representatives, [and] social justice for all the Indonesian people" (Sharma, 2011, p. 87).

Again, in terms of creativity theories, these childhood years, like his earlier years from birth to age six, could certainly be considered part of the preparation stage as well as a Big M, multicultural experience, in that young Barack was fully immersed in a diverse milieu each day. Sharma (2011) argues that such deep cultural immersion offered Barack a perspective on Islam, on international relations, and on linguistic and cultural diversity that is truly unique among US presidents. Such first-hand experiences with language and cultural barriers and with religious and political views coexisting in close quarters profoundly shaped the young Barack, especially when modified through the influence of his mother who, as some of her colleagues and friends noted, and her son understood, seemed to want Barack to grow up to be some "sort of cross between Einstein, Gandhi, and Belafonte" (Sharma, 2011, p. 197).

High school in Hawai'i

As Ann and Lolo's marriage deteriorated, in part due to disagreements about Lolo's focus on for-profit business in contrast to Ann's social justice focus, Barack returned to Hawai'i where he attended the prestigious Punahou High School in Honolulu and lived with his maternal grandparents. In keeping with research on racial and ethnic development, the high school years were especially formative for Barack as he began to explore his ethnicity. While Hawai'i has been justifiably referred to as the most multicultural state, and words for persons of mixed race and mixed ethnicity are plentiful – such as *chop suey* for persons of four or more ethnic lineages, *poi dog* for those of mixed heritage, and *hapa* for those of two/mixed races (Sharma, 2011) – persons of African or African-American descent were quite rare, representing under 2 percent of the population. Thus, though according to Obama's homeroom teacher, the Punahou school favored a philosophy that "we're all different, but it does not make a difference" (Sharma, 2011, p. 135), the lack of sociocultural and peer group support for his Black background would figure more prominently in Barack's future identity explorations.

Also while at the Punahou school, Barack was exposed to a character education-type school philosophy that aimed to educate students for future civic engagement with exposure to and discussion of leading figures in social justice from various faith traditions and nations, such as Martin Luther King, Gandhi, and Jefferson (Sharma, 2011). Barack's passionate enthusiasm for basketball, despite not being a leading player, was also a formative experience in terms of developing a sense of teamwork and engagement with a challenging but enjoyable activity, and the team won the state championship during his senior year (Rich, 2014a, 2014b). As a number of scholars have noted, co-curricular activities often are as crucial or even more crucial than academic activities for personal and career development (e.g., McCormick, Rich, Harris O'Brien and Chai, 2014; Rich, 2009b). Another powerful influence during these high school years was his grandmother. Her practical business acumen and pragmatic outlook offered Barack a model that contrasted with, and suggested the possibility of balance with, his mother's more dreamy, idealistic vision of the world.

In sum, the high school years in Hawai'i continued the preparation stage of creativity in Barack's life, providing more perspectives and encounters with diverse persons and institutions, and with various role models that offered contrasting viewpoints with what he had experienced in Indonesia. Such a rich milieu broadened Obama's understanding of social and political issues at home and internationally, and offered him further opportunities for self-discovery and insight, as several researchers who cite the benefits of international and multicultural education have argued (e.g., Leung *et al.*, 2008; Takooshian, Gielen, Plous, Rich and Velayo, in revision).

California, New York, and Chicago

Though space precludes a detailed account of Barack's time on mainland US and his rise to political power, it is valuable to sketch some critical events. On arrival in California, Obama attended Occidental College, a somewhat multiracial, upper-middle class, small liberal arts institution, for two years. His identity as an African-American becomes more salient in this mainland US environment, and he tests his political leadership skills in a student-organized anti-apartheid rally in 1981, where his public speaking oratory skills become apparent. Apartheid would not end until 1994, and the events of the 1976 Soweto Uprising in which many South African students were killed by police were probably quite raw in Obama's mind in this era (Rich and Kuriansky, 2015). Moving to New York City to attend Columbia University, Barack soon learns of the death in Africa of his father, Barack, Sr., and, not long after, also learns of the death of his half-brother in Africa. These events are deeply emotional for Barack and further intensify his exploration and engagement with his identity as a Black man (Obama, 2004; Sharma, 2011). It would be appropriate to see in terms of the creative process that he entered an incubation period (Sawyer, 2006; Simonton, 1994) during these New York years, as he has been described as reclusive and withdrawn, reading deeply, and reflecting upon his identity and values. In addition, in terms of identity theory, such as Marcia's (1980) extension of Erik Erikson's famous identity vs. confusion stage, it could be theorized that Obama was in the midst of an identity moratorium – that is, an active period or crisis of considering possible identity alternatives – and was on a path to commitment to a firm identity. One could argue as well that at the end of this incubation stage Barack experienced what creativity researchers would call illumination, as he discovered an identity that fit well and worked well for him; importantly, around this time he took on the full name of his African father, Barack, rather than the nickname Barry he was typically known by up to this point.

Around this time Barack decided to change his life direction and headed to Chicago in 1983, a city known for its strong Black identity, and was able to find his calling as a community organizer on its South Side and as an aspiring politician. By this time, identity researchers would term his identity status as achieved, in that an identity has been established after full consideration of alternatives (Marcia, 1980). In 1988, Obama first journeyed to Kenya, his father's birthplace, where he met many relatives for the first time. Within a few years he attended Harvard Law School, where he became the first African-American editor of its famous *Law Review*, and then returned to Chicago where he joined the law faculty of the prestigious University of Chicago in 1991. Importantly, it was also in Chicago where he met his wife Michelle, with her strong Black identity and local connections, and became Christian (Sharma, 2011). Of course, his subsequent political rise is well documented, from becoming Illinois State Senator in 1997, then a US Senator, and ultimately his national election in 2008 as 44th President of the United States of America.

Conclusion

A number of scholars have expressed the view that Obama's diverse upbringing and multi-cultural experiences in childhood and youth positioned him well to be the first "Global President" (Sharma and Gielen, 2014). Indeed, this chapter also supports that interpretation.

Obama's mixed-race heritage and island upbringing taught him the virtues of striving for inclusivity in leadership (Hollander, 2009), as islanders must learn to get along with each other, yet also reach out beyond the local or risk isolation. Obama's childhood and youth truly represent Big M multicultural experiences (Rich, 2009), and such immersion is linked with enhanced creativity and insight indispensable for a political leader. In addition, in terms of creativity and identity theory, his early life experiences prepared him well for illuminating insights into not only his own hybrid identity, but also the increasingly hybrid identity of the nation and the world.

Obama is not the only politician who has succeeded in part by being viewed as an outsider. Other politicians in the US also have recently achieved considerable success by locating themselves as outside the business-as-usual Washington, DC mold; for instance, Sarah Palin viewed herself as a rogue, and John McCain viewed himself as a maverick, both aiming to position themselves politically as creative, fresh, think-outside-the-box alternatives to existing politicians (Rich, accepted). Of course, Obama's position as outsider is not a popular one with all, especially in a nation such as the US where many citizens – and even politicians – do not have a passport and have not traveled internationally, and Obama has faced and continues to face many who critique him as un-American, falsely claiming he was born in Africa and not in the US and thus is ineligible to be President, or perpetuating the false belief that he is a Muslim (Sharma, 2011). At any rate, despite challenges, continuing debates, and controversies surrounding the pros and cons of globalization, it is clear that the US and the world are changing economically, politically, and demographically in the twenty-first century.

From his personal journey as a child of mixed-race parents, to his daily life experiences living in the Islamic world and on a minority majority island in the Pacific, to his multicultural encounters in college, Obama's early life positioned him well to extend his own hybrid identity to his increasingly hybrid nation and world (Gielen, 2013). During his campaign and during his first months and year in office in particular, he was especially well regarded in international polls, despite a few exceptions in nations such as Iran and Afghanistan. For instance, some in Africa and Indonesia were happy to see "one of their own" be the head of such a powerful nation as the US. Obama's familiarity with Islam and the Pacific Region, given the diplomatic, economic, and political pivot to Asia, and his deep personal immersion in successful, tolerant multicultural societies may serve him well in leading the way to the new world of the twenty-first century. The precise legacy of his terms in office on change in the US and the world remains to be seen, as does its enduring impact on the man.

References

Csikszentmihalyi, M. (1996). *Creativity.* New York: Harper Collins.

Csikszentmihalyi, M. and Rich, G. (1997). Musical improvisation: A systems view. In K. Sawyer (ed.), *Creativity in performance* (pp. 43–66). Greenwich, CT: Ablex.

Davis, F. J. (2001). *Who is black?* University Park, PA: Pennsylvania State University Press.

Gardner, H. (1993). *Creating minds.* New York: Basic Books.

Gardner, H. (1995). *Leading minds.* New York: Basic Books.

Gielen, U. (2013). Barack H. Obama, Jr.'s hybrid identity and the global 21st century. Paper presented at the annual meeting of the American Psychological Association, Honolulu, HI.

Hollander, E. P. (2009). *Inclusive leadership.* New York, NY: Routledge.

Leung, A. K., Maddux, W. W., Galinsky, A. D. and Chiu, C-y. (2008). Multicultural experience enhances creativity. *American Psychologist, 63*(3), 169–181.

McCormick, M., Rich, G., Harris O'Brien, D. and Chai, A. (2014). Co-curricular activities and student development: How positive nations encourage students to pursue careers in psychology. In H. Agueda Marujo and L. Miguel Neto (eds), *Positive nations and communities: Collective, qualitative, and cultural-sensitive processes in positive psychology* (pp. 101–118). New York: Springer.

Marcia, J. (1980). Identity in adolescence. In J. Adelson (ed.), *Handbook of adolescent psychology* (pp. 159–187). New York: Wiley.

Obama, B. (2004). *Dreams from my father* (revised edn). New York: Three Rivers Press.

Obama, B. (2006). *The audacity of hope.* New York: Vintage.

Rich, G. (2009a). Big C, little c, Big M, little m. *American Psychologist, 64*(2).

Rich, G. (2009b). Character education. In S. J. Lopez (ed.). *The encyclopedia of positive psychology* (pp. 129–135). London: Blackwell Publishing. doi:10.1002/9781444306002

Rich, G. (2014a). Finding flow: The history and future of a positive psychology concept. In J. Sinnott (ed.), *Positive psychology: Advances in understanding adult motivation* (pp. 43–60). New York: Springer.

Rich, G. (2014b). Positive institutions, communities, and nations: Methods and internationalizing positive psychology concepts. In H. Agueda Marujo and L. Miguel Neto (eds), *Positive nations and communities: Collective, qualitative, and cultural-sensitive processes in positive psychology* (pp. 17–34). New York: Springer.

Rich, G. (in press). A cross-cultural perspective on creative leadership and change management. *International Journal of Teaching and Case Studies.*

Rich, G. (accepted). Sarah Palin and Hillary Clinton: Portraits in psychological contrast. In D. Sharma (ed.), *The global Hillary: Psychological perspectives on Hillary Clinton.* New York: Routledge.

Rich, G. and Kuriansky, J. (2015). Saths Cooper: Post-apartheid psychology and leadership in South Africa and beyond. In G. Rich and U. Gielen (eds), *Pathfinders in international psychology* (pp. 241–256). Charlotte, NC: Information Age Publishing.

Sawyer, R. K. (2006). *Explaining creativity.* New York: Oxford University Press.

Sharma, D. (2011). *Barack Obama in Hawai'i and Indonesia: The making of a global president.* Santa Barbara, CA: Praeger.

Sharma, D. and Gielen, U. (eds). (2014). *The global Obama.* New York: Routledge.

Simonton, D. K. (1994). *Greatness: Who makes history and why.* New York: Guilford Press.

Takooshian, H., Gielen, U., Plous, S., Rich, G. and Velayo, R. (in revision). Internationalizing undergraduate psychology education: Trends, techniques, and technologies. *American Psychologist.*

US Census Bureau. (2010). 2010 census data. Retrieved from www.census.gov/2010census/data (last accessed 12 December 2016).

Wallas, G. (1926). *The art of thought.* New York: Harcourt Brace.

17 Special topic

Leadership and change management in military training programs

Joseph E. Hamlett

Introduction

Many of the changes in the military have been highly publicized and visible throughout the history of the United States (US) and, with the explosion of the information age, the exposure has increased tremendously, especially in recent years (Martin, 2015). Some of the changes are evident in the latest aircraft flown overhead in the blue skies without detection; they are also evident in the massive ships that are afloat in the oceans and seas around the world. Some of the changes are in the form of ground-crawling armored vehicles that smash through anything in their path, and the latest changes or developments are in the form of unmanned drones that frequent the sky more than we know (Flaherty, 2015; Rule, 2015). What may not be as visible or as widely known are the many changes that have occurred in regards to military personnel and some of the training requirements that are expected of our military members (Kem, 2007; McCue, 2012).

Although the US has proven its air superiority in the many wars fought in the past 100 years or so, the fact remains that the US Air Force was part of the Army until September 18, 1947, when it became its own separate entity (Meilinger, 2009). The Air Force we know today went through a series of designations before becoming a stand-alone organization. The original Air Force was started as the Aeronautical Section, Signal Corps in 1909, later changing to the Aviation Section, Signal Corps in 1914, the United States Army Air Service in 1918, the United States Army Air Corps in 1926, the United States Army Air Forces in 1941, and finally the United States Air Force was born in 1947.

Much like the history of the Air Force and the many changes that have occurred in a little over 100 years, having been a member of the military for nearly 30 years and serving in several branches of the armed forces, I have been part of and witnessed my fair share of changes. Not only from branch to branch, but also the constant changes that occur from within each entity (Lewis, 2011). This is compounded even further when the military branch is a National Guard unit or a Reserve Component. As a "Citizen Soldier," men and women are expected to answer their nation's call when disaster strikes, war is declared, or when there is disorder in our nation (Segal and Tiggle, 1997; Vest, 2014). Whatever the case may be, these volunteer weekend warriors are expected to respond when called to duty without hesitation. The mission of the National Guard is two-fold, meaning that there is both a state obligation as well as a federal obligation. This translates to National Guard members potentially being called to active duty to support neighboring states when national disasters strike such as Hurricane Katrina 10 years ago (Haskell, 2005), the tornado that ripped through Joplin Missouri in 2011 (Pellerin, 2011), or a recent national distress that occurred in Ferguson Missouri (Siegel, 2014). In addition to that obligation or commitment, National Guard members may also be called upon in support of a National Contingency as in recent years, such as Iraqi Freedom and Enduring Freedom.

In reference to the many changes that occur in the military, one of the most frequent changes in my career has been the number of leaders I have worked for while serving as a traditional guardsman in the Air National Guard. During my 22 years of service in the Air National Guard I have worked under 7 different Wing Commanders who all bring different leadership styles, management experience, and characteristics with them. One of the jobs they are tasked with is preparing, assisting, and providing members with coping strategies aimed at embracing the constant changes in the military, which seems to be a recurring theme for senior leaders throughout all of the branches of the armed forces. A specific example of how things change frequently and evolve in the military environment occurred at the beginning of the fiscal year, October 1, 2015: Air National Guard members who have aspirations to reach the rank of E-8 or E-9 will have to earn a two-year associate degree through the Community College of the Air Force (Murray, 2005; Savage and Smith, 2000). This requirement is in addition to continuous upgrade training, the mandatory professional military education requirement, the obligation to stay physically fit, and the need to remain proficient in their respective career fields.

The main driver for this requirement is based on the fact that the military has embraced a new approach to defending our nation in regards to utilizing all services in unison to capitalize on all of the benefits each entity has to offer. This approach is commonly referred to as Total Force Integration, which includes active duty members and reserve and National Guard members working together with one common goal (Johnson, Kniep and Conroy, 2013). The inception of this concept has been touted as the key to current and future success for the military. In recent years, many joint exercises have been conducted to further validate this Total Force Integration approach; this is evident in the joint operations that not only integrate neighboring Air National Guard units, but also include Army National Guard units.

The infusion of these three distinct entities has reaped many rewards and makes sense from a strategic point of view; however, in contrast to the benefits associated with alignment, there are clearly some drawbacks to this concept as well (Segal and Tiggle, 1997). For instance, now that these three components are blended and gelled closely together as one, some of the issues that arise are based on the different organizations' doctrines guiding their engagements. Just one example of how this impacts one group more than others is evident when members are selected to serve in different capacities and positions within the infrastructure of these blended entities. Members of the active duty Air Force are afforded many benefits that neither the National Guard nor the Reserve Components are privy to (Mueller, 2014). It goes even further, because often times the Reserve Component is afforded more benefits than the National Guard, which is the last of the three entities to be considered. Therefore, National Guard members are often far behind their counterparts by the time the dust settles and it is finally rolled out to the National Guard, so it is very difficult to compete when the playing field is not level (Segal and Tiggle, 1997). This places undue pressure on members from a National Guard unit to remain as competitive and qualified as active duty members and reservist when resources are limited.

Based on that introduction, how does a part-time military unit such as the Air National Guard and its members prepare for those changes? To gain a better understanding of how this is accomplished by leaders at the wing (base) level, I reached out to a member of our current wing-level leadership group. Colonel Edward Black is the Vice Wing Commander of the 139th Airlift Wing located in St. Joseph, Missouri. He is ultimately responsible for the well-being of nearly 1,200 Air National Guard members. The interview that follows was conducted with Colonel Black specifically for this text.

Interview with Colonel Edward Black on leadership and change management in military training programs

Q1: *Colonel Black, looking back through your many years of service including the many different assignments you have held, how have you personally managed change through-out the years, particularly when it comes to changes in training programs?*

A: I started my Air Force career as an enlisted member in 1989; first attending basic training and technical school which led to my first career as a security policeman where I served for approximately four years. From there I entered the pilot training program that consisted of officer training school, a flight training program, specialized flight training for C130 aircraft, aircraft flight commander training program, instructor pilot training, and an evaluator and checkout training program. During the time those numerous training programs were occurring I was also responsible for deploying to many locations all around the world, so in my opinion from 1989 to 2015 it has been a continuous training program.

The main objective of each training program was to induce changes in me personally; each change prepared me for the next level. Based on my perception, the environment we are in, how we operate in the military, the culture of the organization, and the constant change at the unit level, we are managing individual change through the training programs we are exposed to. So the evolution of an individual such as myself from the age of 19 years old when I first joined the Air Force until the age I am now at 45; what a heck of a change and those training programs are the catalyst that initiated those changes in me. How I managed those changes at the personal level while going through those training programs was by keeping in mind what I was trying to achieve. The training programs are set up to be the bar that measures your progress which is achieved when you graduate from the program. The outcome of that graduation determines whether you move on to the next level, whether it is another job, another level or another rank, or something tangible at the completion of the program. Individuals that do not do well in those programs are unable to adapt through that training and are unable to adapt to the next level of responsibility or maturity and probably never understood what those training programs were meant to accomplish.

Q: *So, in your opinion do you believe most military training or Air Force training is geared toward that concept or that mindset that it is preparing you for the next thing and if you succeed at that training program you are ready for that next level or that next opportunity?*

A: I would look at our military training programs as the absolute base level that you have to accomplish to be ready for that next level. In other words, if I am going to achieve the next level in rank I have to complete the professional military education or the base-level training requirements before I am considered for that next level of command or level of rank. It does not mean that I have received all of the necessary skills for that next level of responsibility from our training program; typically the remaining skills are acquired from the work that is accomplished based on the training I received.

Q: *So, would that particular training be considered a prerequisite?*

A: Absolutely, I think most of the military training programs are very well structured and organized so success in those programs is highly dependent on the individual having the confidence they will complete the course. For example, pilot training has a standard washout rate of about 20 percent, so individuals have to be equipped with the ability, drive, and focus to complete that course. One way to achieve the ability, drive, and focus is to maintain the proper balance in your life and have the ability to handle the stress from those changes. People that I have witnessed who have failed in those training programs are those people who are not able to balance their personal, emotional, or physical life to adapt to the changes those training programs dictate.

Q: *Anything else to add before we move on to the next questions?*

A: One thing I learned early on in the military is the fact that the rank structure provides you with a clearly defined path to outline your entire career so that you are not wondering what is next. For instance, if you are a second lieutenant you must first achieve the rank of first lieutenant before you can move on to captain. The same goes for the enlisted side of the house; if you are a master sergeant you must achieve the rank of senior master sergeant before you can become a chief master sergeant. The established rank structure provides each member with a natural goal-setting tool to help them map out their career.

Q: *Do we have that type of structure in the civilian sector?*

A: Having worked in the banking industry I would say there are some structured career paths, but not always at the lowest level equivalent to the military. The military does a good job of containing all of the tools within the military culture that supports you reaching the next level. One of the options available to individuals in the private sector is to actually leave an organization in order to gain additional training or knowledge, which may include a financial risk associated with having to pay for additional education or changing lifestyles to achieve those goals. The Air Force has some of those features built in like the Community College of the Air Force, Professional Military Education, and the National Defense University. For the most part, change management is mapped out for those individuals who choose to accept those opportunities and make the decision to move forward.

Q2:   *As you are aware, Colonel Black, each year there are many changes that occur in the military or in our case the Air National Guard that directly affect our organization; as a leader how do you manage personnel who have difficulty with these changes?*

A: In my opinion one of the hardest things for an individual to do is to accept change, but more importantly it is even more difficult for people to decide where they are going and what they are trying to achieve. It has been my experience that most people don't accept change mainly because they don't have a true understanding of where they are trying to go. For instance, a technical sergeant on the surface may say they would like to be chief one day, but the reality is he or she has no clue how to get there. One example is of how an increase in training requirements could potentially sideline someone who is not prepared or willing to accept those changes. Locally, training programs in the past 20 years have increased the training requirements for pilots. Pilots are now required to fly at night using night vision goggles, flying in different weather conditions, all-weather drop capability based off of radar systems and Weapons Instructor School. The individuals who have excelled in these additional training requirements are those individuals who understand the need for the changes and how those changes impact the organization. Those individuals that don't excel either don't personally understand where they are going or have not received the signal that change is needed in the organization. There are some members within the organization that don't accept the change and believe that things will go back to the way they were; they are confident this is a fad or the new flavor of the month.

One of the keys to effective leadership is to incentivize individuals to excel in the changing environment by continually talking openly and repeatedly about where the organization is going. Having open and candid communication about what they need to accomplish to get to the next level and the impact it may have if they don't achieve those requirements. Helping them understand where they fit in the organization and how that impacts the overall mission is one thing we don't do well within our organization.

The mechanism that helped me the most was actually witnessing others succeeding and talking to those individuals to see what steps they took to get there. I also chose to spend time with successful people rather than those individuals that did not succeed or those that were not willing to change. Obviously there are people who don't want to change and dig their feet in to resist the change and of course there are those individuals that are always out front and leading the change. The group that I try to focus on is the group of individuals that are still undecided about changing; I try to relay to them how the change will positively impact them as well as the organization. I also try to stress to them about how the benefits reach further than just the Air National, but rather that it will open up many opportunities in the future.

I believe providing them with that additional information lessens the amount of perceived risk; people typically resist change because they are comfortable where they are and they don't see the benefits associated with the change. What I try to get people to understand is the fact that they are taking a much greater risk by not doing anything at all. The risk of not adapting is extinction or the possibility of becoming unqualified for the next level, or being passed over for rank or being viewed as not adding value and thereby being removed from the organization. It is our responsibility as leaders to help people understand that it is just as big of a risk by not taking action or not moving forward.

Q3: *You have talked about managing change personally and assisting others who have difficulty accepting change, the third question has to do with managing change at the organizational level, so, Colonel Black, how do you manage change at the organizational level in regards to training requirements?*

A: In the past 10 years here at the 139th Airlift Wing the pace has been frantic to say the least; with the increased operational intensity, the increased amount of deployments, increased amount of inspection requirements, and the amount of additional workload that our unit is under would seem unrecognizable to someone who was a member 20 years ago. I can remember back in the 90s when we deployed one aircraft for three weeks we would spend an entire year planning this event; it would take an unbelievable Herculean effort to get that mission accomplished. We would place an in-route support team at every stop to deploy for 3 weeks to Saudi Arabia; 25 years later we just returned 4 aircraft from a 120-day deployment to Qatar and it seems like it happens every year now.

Based on the level of effort that is required at the unit level and the additional training that entails those changes be made and the expectations of the members managing the training programs has increased to manage the expected output. To help manage those changes I had to find commanders and managers who were willing to buy in to those changes and link them together, which helped to build that bridge between the command staff and supervisory staff. Those commanders and managers invest their time articulating to their members where we are going and allow them to be part of the strategy to get us there. We have created reporting mechanisms in the form of quad charts and yearly reports to allow units the opportunity to tell us what they are doing. My thought is if I control at the top level all of the decisions then the military tends to get classified as an autocratic organization where the Colonel tells everyone what to do and they salute smartly and march out to do what they are told. I don't believe that is how we manage a changing organization.

You have to be willing to decentralize and let everyone be part of the change, which creates buy-in from the very beginning from your leadership team. Building those bridges on base first with people placed in key roles and enlisting allies outside the base to increase the bridge-building activity. So far we have built great relationships with the National Guard Bureau, the test center in Tucson, Arizona, and many entities within the active duty Air Force; the goal is to extend that changing culture to external parties who also buy in, which in turn will provide credibility to the need for the organization to change. For instance, if we say we want to be the first blimp flying unit in the nation and everyone internally was on board yet nobody in the market place needed blimps you have zero credibility as a command staff. With that approach we would likely not be able to positively affect change; having that external credibility would provide us with the position we would need to be accepted as making positive changes.

Communication is one of the hardest parts of creating an environment of change; it takes telling the story over and over again until it is totally saturated in everyone's mind. For example, before we added the Weapons Instructors Course we went through great pains to ensure everyone knew what we were trying to accomplish. As a strategic leader you have to have a strategic communication plan that puts consistent influence on the intended outcome. The one thing that I would like to add is that we have to be okay with small failures and minor setbacks; we have to refrain from crushing the spirits of the people who are having small failures because they are the same individuals who are pushing the ball forward. There is a mindset in the military that we don't fail and we are going to soldier on and that we will always succeed, which will lead to ribbons for achievements and a slap on the back signifying success, and the reality is that this does not occur in a changing environment. What I tell people is that I want to see them fail while performing minor tasks because that induces learning; I also tell them that I don't want them to fail morally or legally, and I don't want them to fail in situations that people get hurt. I want them to have the ability to fail quickly, regroup, and keep trying to move the ball forward.

So, in leading organizations the change agents and senior leaders or the person managing that change has to be the cheerleader just in case someone slips and has a setback. They have to be quick to get in there and pick that person up, meanwhile letting them know that you will not crush their efforts and that you expect them to fail to some degree, at the same time informing them that you appreciate them taking the risk. That needs to be the attitude of senior leadership or you won't have any risk-taking behavior within your organization, which equates to no one moving the ball forward. That goes back to getting all the commanders and leadership team involved and helping them envision the future.

Q: *Colonel Black, I appreciate you taking time out of your business schedule to provide insight into how you have managed change throughout your extraordinary military career.*

A: You are welcome; thank you for giving me this opportunity!

Epilogue

As we are all aware, the one thing that remains a constant is that change will occur; the one thing we ultimately have control over is how we manage that change. As identified in this passage, over the years the military has changed its face numerous times and with the some-times unidentifiable threats waiting in the winds, that would be the best approach that should be embraced to help thwart our known and unknown adversaries. As the military changes so do the requirements for its personnel to change along with it; after conducting this interview I am highly confident that the men and women in today's military as well as future members will continue to answer the call and continue the legacy in developing adaptable leaders who will inspire others to lean into the unknown and face those challenges head on.

References

Flaherty, M. S. (2015). The constitution follows the drone: Targeted killings, legal constraints, and judicial safeguards. *Harvard Journal of Law and Public Policy, 38*(1), 21–42.

Haskell, B. (2005). Air guard response to Katrina's challenges. *The Officer, 81*(9), 34–35.

Johnson, B. K., Kniep, S. and Conroy, S. F. (2013). The symbiotic relationship between the Air Force's active and reserve components. *Air and Space Power Journal, 27*(1), 107–129.

Kem, J. D. (2007). Finding the target: The transformation of American military policy. *Air and Space Power Journal, 21*(4), 117–118.

Lewis, T. A. (2011). Stop the change: We've got it right. *Air Force Journal of Logistics, 35*(3/4), 30.

Martin, S. C. (2015). Air Force intelligence support to nuclear operations: Pre post-incident. *Air Power History, 62*(1), 40–49.

McCue, J. (2012). The science of war: Defense budgeting, military technology, logistics, and combat outcomes. *Air Power History, 59*(4), 50.

Meilinger, P. S. (2009). Establishing the US Air Force Academy: The early years. *Air Power History, 56*(2), 3847.

Mueller, J. R. (2014). Alternative organizational design and its impact on the future of work. *Journal of Strategic Innovation and Sustainability, 9*(1/2), 48–58.

Murray, G. R. (2005). Developing airmen: Building a world-class noncommissioned officer corps. *Air and Space Power Journal, 19*(4), 5–11.

Pellerin, C. (2011). National Guard helps storm-damaged communities. US Department of Defense. Retrieved from http://archive.defense.gov/news/newsarticle.aspx?id=64093 (last accessed 12 December 2016).

Rule, T. A. (2015). Airspace in an age of drones. *Boston University Law Review, 95*(1), 155–208.

Savage, J. S. and Smith, A. B. (2008). General and specific goal orientations as correlates of adult student degree completion: Lessons from the Community College of the Air Force. *Journal of College Student Retention, 9*(4), 461–485.

Segal, D. R. and Tiggle, R. B. (1997). Attitudes of citizen-soldiers toward military missions in the post-Cold War world. *Armed Forces and Society, 23*(3), 373–390.

Siegel, J. (2014). Can the National Guard really help calm an already militarized Ferguson? *The Daily Beast*, August 19. Retrieved from www.thedailybeast.com/articles/2014/08/19/can-the-national-guard-really-help-calm-an-already-militarized-ferguson.html (last accessed 18 January 2017).

Vest, B. M. (2014). Finding balance: Individuals, agency, and dual belonging in the United States National Guard. *Human Organization, 73*(2), 106–115.

Index

For Product Safety Concerns and Information please contact our EU
representative GPSR@taylorandfrancis.com Taylor & Francis Verlag GmbH,
Kaufingerstraße 24, 80331 München, Germany

Printed and bound by CPI Group (UK) Ltd, Croydon, CR0 4YY

01/05/2025

01858414-0013